EX-REDS REMEMBERED

50 LIVERPOOL PLAYERS OF THE 80s, 90s AND 00s

This Is Anfield
www.thisisanfield.com

First published worldwide by This Is Anfield, 2013

Text copyright © Steven Speed, 2013

ISBN 978 1492 12255 5

For Charlie.

Contents

About the author

Steven Speed was born in Liverpool, England in 1977. He was raised in the suburbs of Bootle and Aintree and graduated from Edge Hill University College in 2000, with a BA degree in English Language and Literature.

He has supported Liverpool FC since he was two years old and refused to wear a blue and white scarf that his mother had purchased for him. His first game at Anfield was a Merseyside derby on April 25, 1987 when Ian Rush scored two goals to eclipse Dixie Dean's record for derby goals.

His first Liverpool FC idol was Paul Walsh and his favourite player of all time is Robbie Fowler.

He lived in New Zealand between 2002 and 2004, when his loyalty was seriously tested by having to watch games in the early hours of the morning.

In May 2005, he moved to Vancouver, Canada, the morning after Liverpool beat Chelsea in the Champions League semi final. In 2006, he joined the executive committee of the Vancouver Liverpool Supporters Club, also known as LFC Vancouver. He helped to take the supporters club from 7 members to over 150 within 12 months. He has served as the president of LFC Vancouver since 2008.

This is Steven's first book, but he has previously contributed many articles to the website 'This is Anfield' and he has written the LFC Vancouver newsletter since 2007.

He tries to visit Liverpool at least once per year and coincides his trips for when Liverpool are playing at home. He became a Canadian citizen in 2011 and resides in the suburb of Coquitlam, just outside Vancouver, with his wife Tracy and baby son Charlie.

Preface

The idea to write about these Ex Red's came to me many years ago while reading a *Wikipedia* article about Craig Johnston. I knew nothing of his post Liverpool life and found it fascinating. So I said to my friend Keith that we should write our own features in our Vancouver Supporters Club newsletter, talking about a different player each week. The intention was to cover players that people in Canada might not know that much about, hence why the likes of Jamie Carragher, Kenny Dalglish and Ian Rush are not included. We decided to take it in turns and I wouldn't cover anyone pre 1980's, because I didn't want to write about anyone I didn't have personal memories of. I had no desire to write a simple biography that anyone could read at anytime on various different websites. They had to be more personal to make them stand out, which is the reason why so many of the biographies I have written contain personal anecdotes involving games and goals the players were involved in, and how they may have affected my life in the moment.

Keith wrote a few of his own, mostly covering players from his childhood in the 1960's and 1970's but he soon got too busy to continue writing. I kept the series going for a few years on my own and as I said, I decided not to exclusively feature just the all time greats. There are enough articles and books written about the really big names and I'm not sure I can really add to what is already out there. When I started writing the Ex Red articles, I had no idea that I would enjoy the process so much and I certainly didn't realise I would write so many of them! The idea to turn them into a book didn't enter my mind until I realised how many of them I had written. I then thought that I would love a way to compile them all together.

I have written about fifty former Liverpool players from the 1980's to the modern day and all fifty are included in this book. Some of them are true legends and others are better described as 'cult heroes'. One thing that all of these fifty players do have in common are that they all wore the Red shirt with pride, and every one of them left a mark on the history of Liverpool FC, whether their contributions were small or large.

This book has been a true labour of love for me and a lifelong dream realised. I truly hope that you will enjoy reading the anecdotes as much as I enjoyed writing them.

YNWA
Steven Speed
July, 2013

The 1980s

The 1980's were without doubt the most successful decade in Liverpool FC's history. The Reds reached three European Cup finals, winning two of them, and dominated domestically, winning five league titles, two FA Cups and four League Cups in a row.

The greatest Liverpool side I have ever seen was assembled for the 1987/88 season. The side that featured Barnes, Beardsley, Aldridge, Houghton, McMahon and others, played football that rivalled the great Brazilian teams. The 5-0 victory over Nottingham Forest in 1988 is regarded as one of the best performances ever seen by an English team.

For me personally though, the biggest highlight of the 1980's was the 1986 all Merseyside FA Cup final. This is my favourite football match of all time. It was a massive game in which Liverpool where going for their first ever league and FA Cup double and Everton were looking for revenge for blowing the league title. Anybody who lived in Liverpool at the time will know just how truly massive this game really was. I remember at my school on the day before the final, the entire day was devoted to the game and we all wore Liverpool or Everton colours. We had a special assembly were we sung 'Abide With Me' and then we had a Liverpool V Everton game of our own on the school field in the afternoon. On the day of the game, there were many areas that had street parties, including where my family lived in Bootle. Decorated tables were laid out in the middle of the road and filled with buffet food. There was bunting and flags hanging from the lampposts and people had posters and flags in their windows. It was an absolutely brilliant day and something I think could only ever of happened in Liverpool.

I still think that it was the best FA Cup Final ever and I don't even think the 2006 final can better it. Apart from the fact it was Liverpool V Everton, it came at a time when both teams were the best in England. It really was a tremendously exciting game played at a great tempo. It had plenty of goals and memorable moments such as the Bruce Grobbelaar save from Sharp's header and the little row Bruce had with Jim Beglin.

Gary Lineker put Everton into a first half lead and by half time the Blues had the game well under control. The second half was a totally different story. Liverpool scored three times, Ian Rush got two and Craig Johnston the other. Jan Molby put in a career best performance as he dominated midfield. He ran the second half setting up the first and second goals and then had an important hand in the third goal too with a sublime blind pass to Ronnie Whelan who chipped it over the defence to Ian Rush.

Liverpool took home the trophy that day but the entire city of Merseyside were winners. It still excites me when I watch that game and reminisce about the days before bitterness took over and spoilt the atmosphere of the derby.

The decade ended on a sour note with the loss of 96 lives at Hillsborough in 1989. This is the greatest tragedy in the history of the club. It continues to affect thousands of people, not just in

Merseyside but all around the world. The findings of the independent panel in 2012, was the first huge step in the ongoing fight for justice for the 96, who wii! remain in our thoughts forever.

Alan Hansen

The word legend is often thrown around far too easily, but in the case of Alan 'Jocky' Hansen, it is highly appropriate. During the 2008/09 season, on an episode of Match of the Day, the host Gary Lineker asked Alan if he was sticking with Liverpool to win the league title. The response was sincere and as follows; "through thick and thin son." This speaks volumes about the man and his unwavering loyalty to the club. When I heard those words during that broadcast my immediate response was to shout "What a legend!"

Alan Hansen was born in Clackmannanshire, Scotland in June 1955. He was a talented sportsman growing up and represented Scotland at volleyball, squash, golf, and of course football. He was actually so good at golf when he was a teenager that he had to decide whether to pursue that as a career or become a footballer. Fortunately for Liverpool fans he chose the latter and joined his brother John at Partick Thistle just after his sixteenth birthday. This was just after they had beaten Celtic 4-1 in the 1971 Scottish Cup Final. Ironically Alan had a trial with Liverpool that summer but was rejected for not reaching the required standards at the time. Alan made it into the first team at Partick Thistle in 1973 and quickly established himself a fine reputation as a cultured central defender. He was watched by many top clubs and in May 1977 he was signed by the European Champions, Liverpool.

The 'Anfield Iron' Tommy Smith had been due to retire in the summer of 1977, but decided to play another season after playing well in 1976/77 and having a marvellous game (and scoring) in the 1977 European Cup Final. Emlyn Hughes was still the club captain and Phil Thompson was just entering into his prime, so this meant that Alan wasn't a regular in the first team during his first season at Liverpool. He made sporadic appearances after making his debut on September 24th in a 1-0 win over Derby County at Anfield. He missed the League Cup final defeat to Nottingham Forest in early 1978 but an unfortunate accident in May 1978 was to prove lucky for Alan. Tommy Smith injured his foot in a DIY accident at home and was ruled out of the 1978 European Cup Final against Bruges. This meant that Alan got the nod to start the game alongside Thompson and Hughes. Liverpool won the trophy with a Kenny Dalglish goal and after just one season at Anfield, Alan had a European Cup winner's medal.

The following season Tommy Smith left for Swansea City and Emlyn Hughes moved to Wolves, so Alan and Phil Thompson became the established partnership in defence. They were a revelation as Liverpool romped to the First Division title in 1978/79. Thanks to the form of Alan and Phil during this season, Ray Clemence kept twenty eight clean sheets and Liverpool conceded just four goals at home. His performances for the Reds were rewarded with a debut cap for Scotland in May 1979, in a 3-0 defeat to Wales. His international career was to prove extremely frustrating in subsequent years as Alan was never a regular in the Scotland team despite being regarded as one of the finest defenders in Europe in the early to mid eighties. The Aberdeen partnership of Alex McLeish and Willie Miller were the preferred partnership of the manager Jock Stein.

Liverpool carried on the success from the previous season by retaining the First Division title in 1979/80. Hansen and Thompson were now without doubt the finest defensive partnership in British football with both players having the ability to play football and pass, rather than being the traditional hard man style centre backs so popular in England at the time. The league title was conceded to Aston Villa in 1981 but Liverpool still had a successful season by winning two trophies in 1980/81. The first trophy was the League Cup, which the Reds won for the first time against West Ham United after a replay. Alan scored the winning goal in a 2-1 victory, which was the first of four successive victories in the League Cup final from 1981 to 1984. The European Cup was then won for a third time after a 1-0 victory over Real Madrid in Paris.

The 1981/82 season started off badly for Liverpool when Bill Shankly passed away in September 1981. Liverpool's early season form was patchy and they were as low as tenth position on Christmas Day. Things came to a head after a home defeat to Man City on Boxing Day, which included some dreadful errors from Thompson and the new goalkeeper Bruce Grobbelaar. Thompson was stripped of the captaincy and after getting injured he lost his regular place to Mark Lawrenson who had been signed the previous summer from Brighton. Liverpool went on a surge back up the table in the new-year and by May they were back on top and reclaimed the First Division title. The title was won in a 3-1 victory over Tottenham Hotspur, a game in which Glenn Hoddle scored one of the most spectacular goals by an opposition player in front of The Kop. Liverpool also retained the League Cup over Tottenham, although Alan was to miss that game through injury.

The Lawrenson, Hansen tandem was a sensation and eventually became, in my opinion, the finest defensive partnership in Liverpool's recent history. Lawrenson complemented Hansen perfectly with his precision tackling. Blessed with speed and superb timing, Lawrenson was one of the best tacklers in British football.

Alongside him, Hansen was unbelievable at playing the ball out of defence with incredible calm and coolness. His vision was sublime and if you watch old videos from the eighties, you'll see many examples of Hansen carrying the ball forward and playing a perfect pass for Dalglish or Rush to score. There is no better example of this than the move that led to Rushie's opener in the 5-0 rout of Everton in 1982.

Alan went to the 1982 World Cup in Spain with the Scotland squad. The tournament went badly for the Scots as they failed to progress beyond the group stages. Alan was involved in an embarrassing moment when he accidentally collided with Willie Miller and allowed the Russian striker Shengelia a clean run on goal and led to a 2-2 draw.

The 1982/83 season was to be Bob Paisley's last as manager and he went out in style as Liverpool easily won the league by eleven points ahead of new boys Watford. The League Cup was also won for a third season in a row with victory over Man Utd in the final. The most memorable moment of the season came after that victory when Bob Paisley led the team up the stairs and lifted the trophy.

Under new boss Joe Fagan, Liverpool retained the First Division title and League Cup in 1983/84. The League Cup (now rechristened as The Milk Cup) was won after a replay against Everton. The first game, which ended in a 0-0 draw, was the first Wembley final between the two Merseyside rivals. Alan was involved in a controversial incident during the game when he appeared to handle a shot on the goal line, but no penalty was given. The Reds completed a magnificent treble in May 1984 when the European

Cup was won for a fourth time. This time Liverpool had to defeat Roma in their home stadium. The game ended in a 1-1 draw and went to a penalty shoot-out. Alan went hiding when penalty takers were chosen and after Grobbelaar's spaghetti legs routine, the trophy was won when Alan Kennedy scored the final penalty.

The following season 1984/85 was a poor season for Liverpool despite Alan maintaining his position as one of the finest defenders in the game. Liverpool lost the league title to Everton and they were defeated in the meaningless 1985 European Cup Final by Juventus after the terrible Heysel tragedy. Liverpool was then banned from European competitions for six years and Alan never played in a European game again.

Tragedy was to turn into triumph for Liverpool and for Alan personally in the following season 1985/86. Kenny Dalglish became player manager in the summer of 1985, and one of his first decisions was to make Alan the new club captain. He was now one of the senior players at the club and was to prove to be a fine choice as captain. The season could not have gone any better as Liverpool were to win their first ever league and FA Cup double. The league title was won in exciting fashion although it didn't start too great and it has since been revealed that Alan went to see Kenny Dalglish and told him that Liverpool would never win anything with that current team. After an injury to Paul Walsh, Kenny put himself back in the side after he had not been playing too often. Kenny picking himself for the remainder of the season has often been described as a major reason why Liverpool ended up winning the league title. With only a handful of games remaining, Everton were leading the First Division by miles. When Everton won 2–0 at Anfield the title race seemed all but over. Then Liverpool went on an amazing run of eleven wins and one draw in the last twelve games. With King Kenny back in the side Liverpool started to gain momentum as Everton started to collapse. When Everton lost away to lowly Oxford Utd destiny was in Liverpool's own hands as they just needed to beat Chelsea away in the next game to take the title. In fairytale fashion Kenny was to score the goal that clinched Liverpool's sixteenth league title. Alan then lifted the First Division championship trophy in front of a packed Anfield in what had to be the proudest moment of his career so far. He didn't have to wait very long for another great moment as he completed the full set of domestic medals. This time he was to proudly lift the FA Cup after a 3-1 victory at Wembley over Everton in what I still believe is the greatest FA Cup final of all time. Not a bad way to start his captaincy of the club!

Alan was then incredibly left out of the Scotland squad for the Mexico World Cup in 1986. This decision caused obvious controversy at the time, but Jock Stein (and later temporary manager Alex Ferguson) maintained that the reason Alan was dropped was because of his refusal to play in friendly matches during the warm up to the World Cup. It has since been rumoured that this decision caused a falling out between Kenny Dalglish and Alex Ferguson but this has been denied by both men and also Alan himself.

The title was conceded back to Everton in 1986/87 and the Reds also lost the 1987 League Cup final to Arsenal. This was just the calm before the storm though as the following year was possibly the best ever, in terms of football played. John Aldridge had joined in early 1987, to replace the departing Ian Rush. He was followed that summer by John Barnes, Peter Beardsley and Ray Houghton, who joined early into the new season. Alan, despite his advancing years, was still at the very top of his game and captained easily the most exciting football team that I have ever witnessed. Mark Lawrenson had to retire this season due to a serious Achilles injury, so Gary Gillespie stepped in to partner Alan at the back and there were never any problems there. In fact with the way Liverpool's attack and midfield played it's a surprise the opponents even got near our goal. The Reds went on a twenty nine game unbeaten streak from the start of the season, until a typical scrappy goal by Wayne Clarke in the Goodison derby ended the run. The league title was a foregone conclusion that season and Liverpool also reached the FA Cup final in 1988 as well. Incredibly Liverpool was defeated 1-0 by Wimbledon in one of the biggest upsets of all time. A great shame as Alan deserved to win a second double after the way the team had played that season.

Alan then seriously injured his knee during pre-season in 1988 and was out for the next nine months. He has since revealed that it was so bad that he considered retiring at the time as due to his age the knee took a long time to heal. Fortunately he did recover and he was set to make his comeback in an FA Cup semi final on April 15th 1989. As we all know this was to be the most important date in the history of Liverpool Football Club. After the Hillsborough tragedy, Alan led by example as he helped to carry the families of the victims and survivors of the tragedy through the following weeks and months. Kenny Dalglish along with his wife Marina was a tower of strength to everybody, which eventually led to a serious decline in his health. Alan was a great support along with the rest of the players and staff at the club, as he attended funerals, visited survivors in hospital and acted as a counsellor for those needing to talk.

After a period of mourning and reflection the decision was taken for Liverpool to finish the season, as that's what the victims would have wanted. Liverpool defeated Nottingham Forest in the rescheduled semi final, and the appropriate opponents in the final were Everton who had defeated Norwich City on the day of the Hillsborough disaster. Alan played superbly in the final, which went into extra time after a last minute equaliser by Everton's Stuart McCall. Liverpool eventually won the game 3-2 after two goals by substitute Ian Rush. Alan graciously allowed Ronnie Whelan to lift the famous trophy as Ronnie had captained the side superbly during the time that Alan had spent injured. Unfortunately for the second season in a row Liverpool was denied a league and cup double in the final game of the season. Arsenal came to Anfield needing to win by two goals to snatch the title away. Nobody gave them a chance but Liverpool seemed to have nothing left in the tank after playing so many games in such a short period and the effects after Hillsborough were bound to take a toll. In one of the most dramatic endings to a league season ever, Michael Thomas scored with the final kick of the game to give Arsenal the 2-0 victory they needed to win the title.

Alan was in the side on a more regular basis in the 1989/90 season, sharing the central defensive positions with Glen Hysen, Gary Gillsepie and Gary Ablett. Hansen and Hysen formed a fine partnership but with Hansen still struggling with his knee, Ablett would often be preferred. Liverpool went on to win the First Division title for the eighteenth time in 1990 and Alan won his eighth league championship medal, three as captain.

Alan continued to struggle in the 1990/91 season and eventually retired due to injury in February 1991. This came just one week after Kenny Dalglish had shockingly resigned as manager after the 4-4 draw with Everton. This was a terribly sad time for the club with two of its greatest heroes leaving within a week of each other. There was still time for Alan to make one final impact on the first team squad though. After Kenny's resignation, Alan walked into the first team dressing room and announced with conviction that he had accepted an offer to become the new manager. He then began to unveil a new list of strict rules and watched the player's faces turn into panic. After keeping the ruse going for a few minutes he then announced that he was just joking to great relief all around.

In reality Alan has never had any interest in becoming a football manager. He was heavily linked with the Liverpool job when Kenny resigned and again a few years later when Graeme Souness was sacked, but both times he declined having any interest in the position. Instead, Alan has enjoyed an extremely successful career in the media, mainly with the BBC. The first time I can recall him being on the TV regularly was during Liverpool's UEFA Cup run in 1991/92, which was shown live on the BBC. From the early nineties to the present day Alan has been the main man on the couch for all the BBC's big football coverage including Match of the Day, live internationals and all the big tournaments. Despite maintaining an air of professionalism Alan's dedication to Liverpool often comes to the surface with some fine examples being the big argument he had with Jimmy Hill at half time in the 1992 FA Cup final between Liverpool and Sunderland and his dancing around the studio during the 2001 UEFA Cup final against Alaves. He also maintains a career in the written media having written columns for The Daily Telegraph, the BBC Website and the official LFC Magazine. Alan also occasionally pulls on the red jersey again for cameo appearances in charity games.

A perfect example of why Alan Hansen is a true legend at Liverpool FC is that any defender since he retired who has come through with any ability on the ball (e.g.; Agger) is nearly always described as the new Hansen. Alan was voted in at number twelve in the 100 Players Who Shook the Kop and was the third highest placed defender behind Emlyn Hughes and Jamie Carragher. This is a fitting tribute to one of the coolest and most talented players ever to play for the club.

Bruce Grobbelaar

Known as the clown prince of goalkeepers, Bruce Grobbelaar is one of the most popular players ever to play for Liverpool. He is definitely my own personal favourite goalkeeper of all time, I used to love the way he could be acting the fool one minute and then making a world class save moments later.

Bruce was born in 1957, in Durban, South Africa. He was a talented sportsman as a youngster and had the chance to move to America and play baseball. However, football was his passion and he started his career in 1973 with Highlanders FC in Rhodesia. In 1977, Bruce joined Durban City, but things went poorly and Bruce barely played. He later claimed he was a victim of racism as the team was predominantly made up of black players.

He then signed up for National Service with the Rhodesian army and fought in the Rhodesian Bush War. Bruce saw a lot of awful things during his service including friends and colleagues being maimed and killed. He later explained that the reason he tried to play football with a smile and a laugh was because his time fighting in the jungle showed him that football is just a game and life is precious and should be enjoyed. He considered it his role to make the fans enjoy themselves.

Brucie is well known over here in Vancouver where I now live, thanks to his stint playing for the Vancouver Whitecaps from 1979 to 1981. Although he only played twenty four games, as he was second choice to Phil Parkes, Bruce became a cult figure in

Vancouver due to his outrageous antics and colourful personality. One of my favourite stories about him during this time was when he turned up for his first ever press conference, wearing an old man horror mask.

Bruce played four games in his first season in Vancouver, when the Whitecaps won the Soccerbowl. During his second season, Parkes moved to Portland and Bruce was first choice. In 1979, Bruce was visiting friends in England when he was offered a trial at West Bromwich Albion. The manager Ron Atkinson wanted to sign Bruce but couldn't secure a work permit and the deal fell through.

During his time in Vancouver, Bruce went on loan to Crewe Alexandra in the UK where his most famous moment was scoring a penalty in his final game. Bruce was spotted playing for Crewe by Liverpool's head scout Tom Saunders and was signed as reserve goalkeeper in March 1981. Bruce was preparing to apply for Canadian citizenship and make his home in Vancouver when the offer from Liverpool came through.

When Ray Clemence moved to Spurs in the summer of 1981, Bruce had his opportunity. He was thrown in at the deep end though because Clemence left just two weeks before the start of the season and Bruce had only played a few reserve games.

His first few months as first choice goalie were tough and he made a few howlers and let in some dodgy goals. His debut came in a 1-0 defeat to Wolves and Liverpool was very inconsistent in the early part of the season. Bruce received a lot of the blame and began to hear boo's and chants from the crowd. His antics, such as walking on his hands and swinging on the crossbar, were amusing at first, but soon grew tiresome as he seemed unable to concentrate during games and was continuously making costly mistakes. Liverpool lost 3-1 at home to Man City on Boxing Day, with Bruce having another shocker. This left Liverpool in thirteenth place in the table and seemingly out of the title race. After the game, manager Bob Paisley took Bruce aside and had words with him about his performances. Bruce was left in no doubt that if he didn't start taking things seriously he would be out of the club. These words had the desired effect and Bruce's game improved to the extent that he soon became one of the best keepers in the league. He really won the fans over by saving a Frank Stapleton penalty against Man Utd at Old Trafford. Liverpool went on an incredible run during the second half of the season, winning 43 out of a possible 50 points to clinch the league title.

Bruce also got to play at Wembley for the first time that season, when we beat Spurs 3-1 in the League Cup final. The man he replaced, Ray Clemence, was in goal for Spurs that day and, in an act of true class, wished Bruce all the best after the game. Nobody who watched the game or has seen highlights will forget the sight of Bruce walking on his hands on the pitch after the game.

Bruce continued to rack up the winners medals when Liverpool won the league and the League Cup again in 1982/83. He then played a major part in the fantastic treble winning season of 1983/84, when the Reds won the league, the League Cup (then called The Milk Cup) and the European Cup.

There are so many great moments involving Bruce during his career. Probably the most well known are his antics on the goal line during the penalty shoot out in the 1984 European Cup final. In order to put off the Roma players, Bruce began biting on the goal net and pretending to have wobbly legs. The tactic worked as Roma missed two penalties and the Reds took home the trophy for the fourth time. It is one of the most famous football moments of all time and was the inspiration for Jerzy Dudek in Istanbul.

1984/85 was a poor season for Liverpool, by previous standards, as they ended the season without any silverware. Everton won the league and Juventus beat us in the European Cup final after the tragedy in the Heysel stadium where 39 Italians died after a wall collapsed when fighting broke out among supporters.

Joe Fagan retired immediately after Heysel and Kenny Dalglish took over as player manager. Kenny's first season as boss couldn't have gone any better as Liverpool won their first ever league and FA Cup double. The Reds also got revenge over their Merseyside rivals; first by overtaking them in the league after Everton had gone into April with a big points lead. Liverpool then went on to beat them 3-1 in the classic 1986 FA Cup final.

Bruce played a big part in the FA Cup final. He famously had an on the field row with left back Jim Beglin that got physical for a few seconds. My personal favourite moment of Bruce's entire career came in this game. It was an amazing save he made from Everton's Graeme Sharp in the second half. Bruce was caught out of position outside the area to the left of his goal and a clearance from Hansen went into the air perfectly for Sharp to head it into the empty net. Somehow Bruce managed to sprint back towards the goal and in an amazing feat of agility, he leapt up high and tipped the ball over the crossbar. It was an incredible save and I remember drawing lots of pictures of it for a long time afterwards. It's still my favourite moment from that match and I look forward to it every time I watch the game on DVD.

1986/87 was another poor season by Liverpool's high standards as the league title once again went back across Stanley Park to Everton. The Reds were also defeated in the 1987 League Cup final by Arsenal.

I have written several times about how fantastic the 1987/88 season was for Liverpool as they went 29 league games unbeaten with Kenny's new look side playing incredible attacking football. Bruce didn't have an awful lot to do, but was world class whenever called upon to make a save.

During the 1988/89 season, Bruce had a long period out of the side due to injury and illness. This was unusual, as he had been an ever present for his first five seasons at the club, and rarely missed a game after that. Mike Hooper stepped in and played seventeen games, but Bruce was back for the business end of the season.

Bruce was standing just yards away from the dying at Hillsborough as the tragedy took place behind where he was playing in goal. Fans were shouting at him to help and Bruce began asking the police to tear down the fences as he heard cries of "they're killing us Bruce". The players were ordered off the pitch and didn't realize the extent of what had happened until they were on the coach back to Merseyside. Like every Liverpool player and supporter, Bruce was absolutely devastated afterwards and he even considered retiring. He was a great support to the families of victims and he attended funerals and visited fans in the hospital.

Bruce decided to carry on after several weeks of contemplation and was in goal for the 1989 FA Cup final victory over Everton. The league title was lost in the final seconds of the season when Michael Thomas won it for Arsenal at Anfield.

The league title was back at Anfield for the eighteenth time the following season. When Kenny Dalglish left and Graeme Souness took over, Bruce remained as the number one keeper and won a third FA Cup medal in 1992 against Sunderland. Bruce and Souness didn't see eye to eye over various things, especially Bruce travelling to play for Zimbabwe for international matches during the season. In the summer of 1992, David James was signed from Watford and for the first time since 1981, Bruce was no longer first choice as keeper. However James had a poor start at the club and made some high profile errors, so Bruce was given his place back. For the remainder of the 1992/93 season, the goalkeeper role was rotated between James, Bruce and Mike Hooper. Bruce only played six times during the season and spent part of it on loan at Stoke City.

Bruce was back in the side and playing well in the early part of the 1993/94 season. Sadly things turned badly for the Reds and they fell away badly in the league. During the season Bruce disgraced himself by physically manhandling his own teammate Steve McManaman during the Merseyside derby. The only real highlight during the season came when Liverpool came back from 3-0 down to draw 3-3 with Man Utd. Bruce could not have done anything about any of the goals he let in and actually made some truly world class saves to keep the team in the game. He was an ever present in the team until February 1994, after a 2-0 defeat to Leeds Utd. This turned out to be Bruce's final appearance for the club.

At the end of the season Bruce joined Southampton. It was during his time there in November 1994, that the allegations of match fixing first came out, in The Sun newspaper. Bruce, along with John Fashanu and Hans Segers of Wimbledon were accused of accepting money from a Malaysian businessman of conspiring to fix the results of matches. Bruce denied the claims and said he only took the money to gather evidence to give to the police. He was found not guilty after two trials in which the jury couldn't agree on a verdict. Bruce sued The Sun and was awarded compensation. After an appeal, his compensation was changed to just one pound and Bruce was ordered to pay all legal costs, which led to him declaring himself bankrupt.

While the trial was going on, Bruce continued to play football. He spent the 1995/96 and 1996/97 seasons at Plymouth Argyle. After leaving Plymouth he then had short spells playing for various teams including, Oxford Utd, Sheffield Wednesday, Oldham Athletic, Bury and Northwich Victoria. He also continued to play for Zimbabwe until 1998.

In 1999, Bruce retired from playing and moved back to Africa where he began a coaching career. He managed various African club sides and had two short spells as the Zimbabwe national manager. He returned to England in 2006 and over the next few years he appeared on various TV shows and played charity games for the Liverpool legends team. He also came out of retirement at the age of 49 to play one game for non league side Glasshoughton in 2007. At the time of writing Bruce now lives back in Canada, where he resides in Newfoundland.

Despite the allegations of match fixing that tainted the end of his career, Bruce is still fondly remembered by all Liverpool fans and he will forever be one of the most popular players ever, as well as a true Liverpool legend. His placing at number 17 in the feature '100 Players Who Shook The Kop' is proof of his enduring appeal to all fans young and old.

Craig Johnston

For Liverpool supporters of my age who grew up in the 1980's, curly haired Australian, Craig Johnston is a bit of an icon. He was one of the most popular players during the mid 80's for his colourful personality, his flowing locks and flamboyant dress sense. We also loved him for his 100% commitment on the pitch at all times. His nickname on the Kop was Skippy after the popular Australian kids show from the 1970's about a Bush Kangaroo.

Craig Johnston was born in South Africa to Australian parents and grew up in Sydney, Australia. As a young teenager he played for local sides, Lake Maquarie and Sydney City. Unfortunately football wasn't a popular sport in Australia and there was no way for him to develop his promising skills as a player. So when Craig was 15 he wrote letters to a long list of English teams asking for a trial. His only response came from Middlesbrough who was managed at the time by Jack Charlton. His parents were right behind Craig's ambition to become a successful footballer and actually sold their house to pay for his ticket to England.

Despite being described by Jack Charlton as "the worst footballer I have ever seen", Craig was offered a youth team contract and went on to make his first team debut in 1978. After playing sixty-four games for Middlesbrough his career in England was about to take off and all his boyhood dreams were about to come true when he was signed for Liverpool by Bob Paisley in 1981.

Craig made his debut in August 1981 coming on as a substitute in the 1-0 league defeat away to Wolverhampton Wanderers. An interesting fact is that also making their debuts in this same match were Mark Lawrenson and Bruce Grobbelaar. I believe it was a Brucie error that cost us the game. Johnston's first start came in the World Club Championships with a 3-0 defeat against Flamengo from Brazil.

He had quite an explosive start to his first season as a first team Liverpool player. He scored in his first derby and then he scored the winner against Man Utd at Old Trafford.

Despite his popularity with the fans and his pace and skills on the pitch, Craig never held down a regular starting place during his six seasons at Anfield. He made fun of this situation in the 1988 FA Cup Final song 'The Anfield Rap'. Craig not only performed the following lines in the song he also wrote the whole track too.

"Well I came to England looking for fame

So come on Kenny man, give us a game

'cause I'm sat on the bench paying my dues with the blues

I'm very big down under, but my wife disagrees"

Despite playing a lot of games as a substitute he was still an effective member of a side that dominated in the First Division. He played in the 1984 European Cup Final victory against Roma and two League Cup final victories in 1983 and 1984.

Craig's finest moment in a Liverpool shirt came in the 1986 FA Cup final against Everton. He was one of the best players on the pitch that day as we secured our first ever league and cup double in Kenny Dalglish's first season as player manager. He almost stole Ian Rush's first goal as he slid in and touched the ball at the very second it was crossing the line. I must have watched that goal a thousand times over the years and still to this day I cannot say for sure if he touched the ball before it crossed the line. I've even watched it on zoom and slow motion now I have the goal on DVD. However whether he touched it or not it doesn't matter because it was Rush's goal and that's that! Craig had a goal himself anyway just six minutes later and this time there was no doubt as he put us two - one up. Rush later added his second and Liverpool's third and the trophy was ours in what I still consider the best FA Cup final I've ever seen. Yes I know the 2006 final was terrific and a classic but as good as it was, it cannot compare emotionally with the first ever all Merseyside FA Cup final. This occasion was massive in the city and as an eight year old kid at the time it was simply amazing.

It was another FA Cup final two years later that marked another milestone in Craig's Liverpool career. Unfortunately the 1988 final against Wimbledon was his last ever game for the Reds as Craig decided in the build up to the game that he was going to retire afterwards. It was a big shock at the time as he was only 28 and still in his prime. This caused problems privately between Craig and Kenny Dalglish as he gave an interview to a newspaper discussing his intentions and the news broke before the club was able to do so. Craig wasn't getting many starts during the 1987/88 season due to the brilliance of Barnes and Houghton on the wings and Beardsley playing off Aldridge, but he still had plenty left to offer the game and he was still a young man. It was later explained that the reason for his sudden departure was because his sister had become seriously ill and needed round the clock care. So he made the decision to go back to Australia and take care of her. It was a great shame at the time and there was sadness at seeing him go because he was very popular and a cult figure at Anfield.

After the Hillsborough disaster in 1989, Craig raised a fortune in Australia for the HSG fund and returned to Merseyside to attend numerous funerals and memorial services. This is a testament to what a great bloke he is and how much Liverpool and the fans mean to him. He later dedicated his autobiography 'Walk On' to the victims of Hillsborough and Heysel.

Since retiring from playing Craig has become best known for designing the Predator football boot for Adidas. When he was coaching kids in Australia he realised that it was difficult to control the ball with the boots available at the time. He took the rubber of a table tennis bat and stuck it on his boots with super glue. He went outside and kicked a ball and immediately noticed a difference. It took him five years to get the boot off the ground and eventually landed the deal with Adidas after filming Franz Beckenbauer using the boots in snowy conditions. Over time he was able to develop and improve on the original design and the boot has gone on to become the most successful of all time and is worn by such superstars as David Beckham and our own Steven Gerrard.

Craig now lives in Florida, USA after some bad business deals unfortunately left him bankrupt in the late 1990's. He has since bounced back from that with other successful inventions such as the Pig football boot and the Traxion sole for boots. He also invented a software programme called The Butler, which is a device used to show what has been removed from hotel room minibars. He intends to move back to Sydney, Australia soon in order to live nearer to his daughters and return to his homeland.

Craig Johnston's greatest achievement may be the fact that he inspired Australian youth to become footballers and dramatically increased the profile and popularity of the sport in the 1980's. He proved to kids that if you worked hard and had the right attitude you could play for one of the biggest teams in the world and be a success in a sport that wasn't popular in Australia twenty years ago. Some great Aussie players from the Premier League era such as Harry Kewell and Mark Viduka grew up inspired by Craig to take up football. He deserves some credit for so many talented Australian players making their national side something to be proud of with their recent exploits in the last two World Cups.

Craig will always be remembered with a fondness by Liverpool fans and this affection is definitely reciprocated. Whenever he was asked about playing for other clubs after he retired, he always said that he could never return to playing because he couldn't play for any club other than Liverpool.

Thanks for the memories Skippy and good on ya mate!

Gary Gillespie

Scottish defender Gary Gillespie was one of Liverpool's key players during a great period of success in the 1980's. He was cultured on the ball, a great tackler and he popped up with his share of goals, including a hat-trick against Birmingham City in 1986.

Gary was born in Bonnybridge, Scotland in July 1960 and he started his career in 1977 with Falkirk. He was made captain at just seventeen years old, making him the world's youngest team captain. He made twenty two appearances in the Scottish Division Two and made such an impact that Coventry City paid £75,000 for him before he was even eighteen. Gary spent six seasons at Coventry helping them through relegation battles from Division One virtually every season. His performances in defence were often regarded as one of the reasons for the Sky Blues remaining in the top flight season after season. During his time at Coventry, Gary was never short of admirers and a number of teams were vying for his signature. In July 1983 Joe Fagan had replaced Bob Paisley as Liverpool boss and he won the race for Gary's signature and made him his first signing for £325,000.

Gary had a slow start to his Liverpool career due to Alan Hansen and Mark Lawrenson being settled as a perfect partnership in central defence. A succession of injuries didn't help his claims for a first team place either. Gary had to wait almost an entire season before he made his first team debut in April 1984 against Walsall in the League Cup. Liverpool finished the season with an incredible three trophies by winning the First Division, the League Cup (against Everton) and the European Cup. Unfortunately for Gary his one appearance wasn't enough for him to receive any medals, but he was happy to be a part of such a great squad and as we know he certainly made up for it in the subsequent seasons.

During the following season 1984/85, Gary started to become a regular in the side as Hansen and Lawrenson both suffered with injuries. He made twenty two appearances during his second season, which unfortunately ended without a trophy for Liverpool. Gary became a real regular during the 1985/86 season and began to really make his name as one of the best defenders around. He was an important member of the team making twenty four appearances as the Reds won the club's first league and F.A. Cup double. Unfortunately he still wasn't able to dislodge the Hansen and Lawrenson partnership and he was unlucky to miss out on playing in the 1986 F.A. Cup final against Everton. At that time only one substitute was allowed and Steve McMahon was chosen for the bench, himself unlucky to lose his place to Kevin Macdonald.

It was during the 1985/86 season when Gary was involved in possibly his most memorable moment in a red shirt. It came on 26 April 1986 at Anfield and our opponents were Birmingham City. We won the game 5 – 0 and it was the day when Gary scored a hat-trick, a fantastic feat for any player to achieve but even more spectacular when a defender manages it. The only other defender I can ever recall scoring a hat-trick was Steve Nicol against Newcastle Utd. His first two goals came in open play as he made two great runs into the Birmingham area. The third goal came when Liverpool were awarded a penalty. Usually it would be Jan Molby's responsibility to take the penalties but as Gary was on a hat-trick there was only one player to take this one. Gary placed the ball superbly in the corner of the net to put his name in the history books. As Gary later said, the only way it could have been more perfect would have been if it was scored in front of The Kop. All three goals were scored at the Anfield Road end.

The following season 1986/87 was a poor one for the club as they lost the league title to Everton and the League Cup final to Arsenal. For Gary though it was his most consistent season so far as he missed just three games in the entire season. The following season 1987/88 was absolutely amazing as Liverpool dominated everything in front of them and won the league with awesome style. Liverpool went on a run of twenty nine games unbeaten and only lost two games in total. Mark Lawrenson severely injured his knee during this season, forcing him to prematurely retire in 1988 aged just thirty. Lawrenson's misfortune led to Gillespie being installed as the regular partner to Alan Hansen and he missed just five games in the entire season. Possibly the defining visual image of Gary's Liverpool career, in my opinion, came in the amazing 5 – 0 victory over Nottingham Forest. Gary scored the fourth goal and celebrated by pointing straight into the air in an aggressive style. Liverpool were denied a second league and cup double when they were defeated in shocking fashion by Wimbledon in the 1988 F.A. Cup final. Liverpool played poorly on the day but Gary was one of the better players. He played that game wearing a bandage round his head after he had cut it open the week before during a clash of heads with team-mate Nigel Spackman, who also played sporting a bandage.

It was during this season that Gary won the first of his thirteen caps for Scotland in European Championship qualifier against Belgium. He was part of the squad at the 1990 World Cup in Italy but only played in one game, the 1 – 0 defeat to Brazil.

In 1989 Gary was part of the Liverpool side at Hillsborough during the terrible tragedy. He joined his team-mates as they rallied round the families offering comfort and support. Unfortunately due to injury he missed the F.A. Cup final against Everton and for the second time he missed out on a winners medal. Gary helped the team to win their eighteenth league title in the following season 1989/90. His appearances became less regular due to the form of Gary Ablett and the arrival of Glenn Hysen, who was brought in to eventually replace Alan Hansen who was now suffering with knee injuries. Gary was to score the winning goal in a 1 – 0 victory over Derby county to clinch the title.

When Kenny Dalglish resigned in February 1991, Gary's days at Anfield were numbered. Deemed surplus to requirements by new boss Graeme Souness, Gary was sold to Celtic that summer for £925,000. Celtic was his favourite team as a child so it was fitting that this was who he would join after leaving Liverpool. He played sixty seven games at Parkhead before rejoining Coventry in 1994. He made three appearances during the 1994/95 season before he was struck down with a serious knee injury. Despite remaining on Coventry's books for another two seasons Gary never played again and in 1997 he retired due to his persistent knee problems.

After retiring from his playing career, Gary settled back on Merseyside with his family. For the last few years Gary has enjoyed a very successful career in broadcasting with BBC Radio Merseyside and also commentating on live games for LFCTV. Gary also does work for the Liverpool website and has been involved in special retro shows. Gary also plays for the Liverpool Masters team that has been very successful in indoor tournaments.

It was at an indoor veteran's tournament in 2006 that I had the pleasure of meeting Gary. It was at the event called 'The Legends of Soccer' in Vancouver, Canada and I was able to meet two other ex Reds, Paul Walsh and John Wark at the same event. It was fantastic to shake Gary's hand and thank him for the memories. I was able to thank him for the goal against Derby County in 1990 and he was nice enough to recreate the famous celebration from his goal in the 5 – 0 demolition of Nottingham Forest.

Thanks to his performances during the glory years of the late eighties, Gary was voted number 68 in the series '100 Players Who Shook the Kop'.

Graeme Souness

When we make up a list of Liverpool's greatest ever players, Graeme Souness would be a certainty to feature highly. He was described as; "a bear of a player with the delicacy of a violinist" and while that is an apt description of him, I think that the two words that describe him best are born winner. The words fear and failure simply never entered into his vocabulary. He is a complex character who combined his burning desire to win on the pitch with a love of the high life. Bob Paisley once said of him; "If he could, he'd toss for ends using his American Express card". Regardless of what took place during his later years as manager, his achievements as a player mean that his status as a bona-fide Liverpool legend can never be in doubt.

Souey was born in May, 1953, in Edinburgh, Scotland. He started his football career south of the border as a fifteen year old apprentice at Tottenham Hotspur in 1968. While at Spurs the teenage Souness allegedly showed his confidence by informing manager Bill Nicholson that he was the best player at the club. Despite this claim, he only ever made one appearance for the first team, as a substitute in the UEFA Cup.

In 1972, he spent the summer playing in the North American Soccer League for the Montreal Olympique. He played in ten of the team's fourteen games during the season and was named in the NASL All Star team.

Upon his return to England he joined Second Division side Middlesbrough for £30,000. Souness made his debut in January 1973 in an away defeat to Fulham. In May 1973, Jack Charlton was appointed as Middlesbrough manager and led the team to promotion in his first season. They were crowned Second division champions with eight games remaining. Souness played a big part in the promotion and began to gain notice for his tenacious and skilful performances. A great season for him was capped off with a hat-trick in the final game, an 8-0 victory over Sheffield Wednesday. His performances for Middlesbrough also earned him his first cap for Scotland in October 1974. He was to earn a further six caps during his time in the North East before becoming a regular part, and future captain, of the Scotland side in later years.

Throughout his time at Middlesbrough he began to realise his potential and looked every inch a star of the future just waiting for a bigger stage to grace with his immense talents. That stage was Anfield and in January 1978 Bob Paisley paid £352,000 to make him a Liverpool player. This was at the time a record fee for a transfer between two English clubs. Graeme made his debut in central midfield at West Bromwich Albion and barely put a foot wrong. He settled instantly into the side, replacing Ian Callaghan, and his first goal came in February 1978 against Manchester United at Anfield. It was a thunderous volley just inside the area that was later voted as the fans goal of the season, it was to prove a typical Souness goal.

Graeme's first taste of silverware with Liverpool came just four months after his arrival at Anfield. This was in the 1978 European Cup Final against FC Bruges at Wembley. He played a vital part in the victory, providing the decisive through ball to Kenny Dalglish for the winning goal in a 1-0 victory. With Alan Hansen and Kenny

Dalglish now regulars in the side they helped Souness to form a formidable Scottish spine through the Liverpool side that was to dominate over the forthcoming years.

During the following season, 1978/79, Graeme dominated the midfield in virtually every game he played. He orchestrated some of the most incredible performances ever seen at Anfield. His short and long range passing was as immaculate as his ferocious tackling was immense. His luxurious skill combined by his hardness complimented perfectly the wonderful talents he had playing alongside and in front of him. His bite in the tackle along with his vision allowed other great players like Terry McDermott, Jimmy Case and Kenny Dalglish to play with superb flair. Graeme's strong will to succeed was a major factor in Liverpool winning the First Division title in his first two full seasons, 1978/79 and 1979/80.

Liverpool conceded the league championship to Aston Villa in 1980/81 but found their habit of winning silverware had not deserted them. West Ham United were defeated in the 1981 League Cup Final after a replay. This was the first time Liverpool had won the trophy and the first of four successive years of winning it. Liverpool also won the European Cup, for the third time, in 1981, defeating Real Madrid in the final held in Paris. Graeme's fabulous contributions to the European Cup campaign included scoring a superb hat-trick in the quarter final against CSKA Sofia at Anfield.

In just three full seasons that Graeme had been a Liverpool player, they had won two European Cups, two league titles and one League Cup. This was a dream start to his Anfield career and things were about to get even better. After a poor performance in a home defeat to Manchester City on Boxing Day 1981, Graeme was made captain. The man he succeeded, Phil Thompson, was obviously upset with this decision. However the success Liverpool achieved during Souness's twenty nine months as captain was proof that it was the correct decision. A natural leader on the pitch, his desire to win rubbed off on his team-mates as he constantly cajoled them into better performances. A perfect example of this is described by Ian Rush in his autobiography. Rush says that every time he scored a hat-trick, Souness would be in his ear shouting at him to get a fourth goal, rather than congratulating him.

In Graeme's first season as Liverpool captain, 1981/82, they won the First Division Championship and the League Cup. This was to be repeated for the next two seasons in a row under his powerful leadership as the most successful skipper in Liverpool's history. The mark of how dominant he was as a player was illustrated in the 1982 League Cup Final against Tottenham Hotspur. He came on as a substitute, having overcome a back injury, with the Reds two nil down and being out-muscled in midfield by Spurs hard-man Graeme Roberts. From the moment Graeme arrived onto the Wembley pitch, Liverpool became the dominant side and came back to win the trophy. After the 1983 League Cup Final victory over Manchester United, Graeme insisted that Bob Paisley, in his final season as manager, lead the side up the stairs to receive the trophy. This was a marvellous gesture and one of my favourite moments ever in football.

Graeme's final season at Liverpool, 1983/84, is arguably the clubs finest and most successful. Under new manager Joe Fagan, Liverpool won an incredible treble of the League Championship, League Cup and the European Cup. The League Cup was secured after a replay against local rivals Everton. The first game at Wembley was the first 'all Merseyside' cup final and finished in a scoreless draw. Souness was the match-winner in the replay with one of his trademark long range strikes in a 1-0 victory.

In his final performance in a Liverpool shirt, Souness led the Reds into the lion's den for the 1984 European Cup Final against Roma in their home ground The Olympic Stadium. Despite this being their fourth European Cup Final in seven seasons Liverpool were considered the underdogs as they played in a hostile environment against a tough side with home advantage. Graeme was as fierce as ever as he led the side like a warrior through the game. After finishing 1-1 after extra time the game went to a penalty shoot-out. With his final kick as a Liverpool player, Graeme calmly blasted his penalty into the net during the shoot-out. Once Bruce Grobbelaar had done his spaghetti legs routine and Alan Kennedy had scored the winning penalty, Liverpool were European champions for an amazing fourth time. In his final act as a Liverpool player, Graeme proudly lifted the trophy above his head in a fitting tribute to a man who had become an Anfield legend.

In June 1984, he moved to Italy to join Sampdoria for £650,000. Although Liverpool struggled without him the following season, nobody at the club begrudged Graeme for wanting to move abroad and earn enough money to secure the future for his family. Graeme had been a superb servant to Liverpool as a player and the haul of trophies they won while he was captain meant that he left the club with nothing but well wishes and incredible memories.

He was a great success in Italy where his no nonsense style on the pitch made him a firm favourite with the crowds. While in Italy he gained the nickname Charlie Champagne that has stuck ever since in the English derivative Champagne Charlie. In his first season at Sampdoria they won the Copa Italia trophy for the first time in the clubs history. After a second season in Italy, he moved back to Scotland to become player manager of Rangers in 1986.

Graeme's playing career at Rangers started with controversy when he was sent off in the opening game of the 1986/87 season against Hibernian. The remainder of his time as a player was a mix of disciplinary trouble, great goals and long stints with injury. He finally retired as a player in 1990. It was as manager that Souness made his real mark at Rangers and his four seasons in charge became known as 'The Souness Revolution' as the Glasgow club began to dominate Scottish football. Due to the European ban on English clubs at the time, he was able to sign a number of top quality players from England. Players such as Terry Butcher, Chris Woods, Trevor Steven, Ray Wilkins and Trevor Francis all joined Rangers lured by the opportunity to play in Europe and the financial strength the club had. This reversed the old trend in the past of Scottish players being lured by the top English sides.

Over his four seasons in charge, Rangers won three league titles and three Scottish League Cups. They also won another league title four games after Graeme left the club in April 1991. Despite all of the success on the pitch, it was the signing of former Celtic hero Mo Johnston in 1989 that Graeme is most remembered for at Ibrox. It wasn't the fact that he was a former Celtic player that caused the controversy it was the fact that Johnston is Catholic. Rangers had previously had a policy of only signing protestant players. Though they had signed a few Catholic players previously, the club had kept their religious views private. This was the clubs first public and high profile Catholic signing and caused major controversy in Scottish football when it occurred. Souness even received a number of death threats, which he calmly laughed off.

In April 1991, Graeme was back at Anfield to replace Kenny Dalglish as manager. Dalglish had enjoyed a lot of success as Liverpool manager and Graeme was seen as the perfect man to continue where Kenny had left off. Unfortunately it just didn't happen as the club slumped into their worst period for over thirty years. A series of bad signings, high profile and expensive flops, combined with the sale of good players combined to undermine Souness as manager.

Liverpool won the F.A Cup in 1992 with a victory over Sunderland in his first season in charge. Unfortunately rather than acting as a platform for further success this victory merely seemed to paper over the cracks. The rot had already begun to set in for Graeme at Liverpool just a month before the F.A Cup Final after the semi-final victory over Portsmouth in a penalty shoot-out. The controversy was caused when he gave an ill-advised interview to The Sun newspaper about his heart operation. Under the headline 'LOVERPOOL' Graeme was pictured kissing his then girlfriend in a private clinic after his heart bypass operation. The Sun has been blacklisted on Merseyside since they printed sickening lies after the Hillsborough disaster. In an incredible moment of insensitivity, due to the semi-final finishing late, the interview with Souness appeared on the third anniversary of the Hillsborough tragedy. Graeme has since admitted that he hadn't been fully aware of the feeling towards The Sun as he had been in Scotland at the time of the incident. He has also since said that he probably should have resigned after the controversy of his interview.

After a poor season during 1992/93 the talk around Merseyside was that Souness was about to be sacked. The fans had turned on him with a poll in the Liverpool Echo revealing that 70% of supporters wanted him out. Even on the last game of the season, when Liverpool thrashed Spurs 6-2, the crowd booed every mention of Graeme's name. It has since been reported that the Liverpool board had decided to sack him after that season but then made a drastic u-turn and decided he should see out the remainder of his contract. Why this decision was made has long been speculated.

After another poor season in 1993/94, Graeme was to depart Anfield after a home defeat in the F.A Cup by lower league side Bristol City. Souness knew it was all over when the night before the Bristol City game he coincidentally happened to be in a hotel room next door to where the Bristol team were being given a team talk. He overheard the team talk and heard Bristol manager Russell Osman tear apart the Liverpool side pointing out individual weaknesses. His main point was that if Liverpool were put under heavy pressure they would quickly throw in the towel and surrender, which is almost exactly what took place. Souness was terribly shocked and upset with this and under extreme pressure he had to resign before he was publicly sacked.

He then moved into a career as a journeyman manager. Over the next twelve years he managed a number of clubs in various different countries. He started with Turkish side Galatasaray in 1996. While in Turkey, Graeme was involved in a very famous and iconic incident when Galatasaray defeated the big rivals Fenerbahce in the Turkish Cup final. At the end of the game, he planted a Galatasaray flag in the centre of the pitch and was lucky to escape unharmed.

He then managed Southampton, Italian side Torino Calcio, Benfica in Portugal, Blackburn Rovers and finally Newcastle United in 2004. Graeme was sacked by Newcastle in February 2006 and has been out of management ever since.

Graeme now works in the media as a television analyst for RTE in Ireland and Sky Television in the UK. I had the honour of meeting him in 2009 whilst purchasing coffee at Manchester Airport. I can report that he remains an extremely impressive presence in person and is a really nice person to talk to.

Regardless of what happened during his time as Liverpool manager nobody can deny that few people tried harder to make Liverpool successful than Graeme Souness. He made a series of poor signings although a lot of them had looked good on paper. There is a strong argument that he was let down by players who were either not willing or unable to perform to Graeme's very high standards. Unfortunately he was paid well to get the best out of his players and at the end of the day he was sadly unable to do so.

It would be a great injustice if his time as manager is allowed to overshadow his achievements as a Liverpool player. He remains one of Liverpool's all time greatest ever players and his position at number nine in the series '100 Players Who Shook the Kop' is a testament to how highly as a player he is still thought of by Liverpool fans all around the world.

Jan Molby

"Jan was simply the best foreign player ever to come to England", Ian Rush.

"Jan was a very, very talented player, with a great knowledge and appreciation of how to play football", Kenny Dalglish.

High praise from two of Anfield greatest ever players and for a lot of us who saw Jan Molby in action it's hard to disagree with their words.

Jan started his football career in Denmark with his hometown club, Kolding in 1981. After just one season he moved to the great Dutch side Ajax where he played alongside the legendary Johan Cruyff and future greats such as Frank Rijkard and Marco Van Basten. Cruyff spent time on the training ground with Jan teaching him the art of passing and it was at this stage of his development when he started to become what he later became, the best passer of the ball in the business.

In the summer of 1984 Liverpool were still celebrating the treble from the previous season of the League Cup, First Division Title and the European Cup. Team captain Graeme Souness was lured by the Lira and moved onto Italian Serie A side Sampdoria. Liverpool manager Joe Fagan then spent £225,000 on bringing the 21 year old Jan Molby to Liverpool as Souey's replacement.

Jan became a firm favourite on Merseyside very quickly after his arrival at Liverpool. Off the pitch he shared a similar sense of humour with the Scousers and he immediately settled into life on Merseyside. He also developed a distinctive Scouse accent and has been seen as an honorary Scouser ever since.

Jan's first season at Liverpool was a rare one without winning any silverware for Liverpool as Everton swept to the First Division title. It was during his second season that he really made his name on the pitch. The double winning season of 1985/86 was undoubtedly Jan's finest in a Red shirt. He scored eighteen goals that season and many of them were classics. In November 1985 Man Utd came to Anfield for a League cup match. It was during this game that Jan scored what many of those present regard as the greatest goal they've ever seen. He took the ball from Norman Whiteside in the Liverpool half and then went on a run beating three or four players before unleashing a rocket shot from twenty yards that flew into the top corner. Gary Bailey, the Man Utd keeper at the time, still insists it's the hardest shot he ever faced. Unfortunately at the time there was a television dispute and no football games were being recorded for television. Therefore there was no video record of this amazing goal at that time. Twenty five years later in 2009, Jan released a video of the goal from his private collection that had been recorded on a camcorder in the crowd by an acquaintance of former Man Utd manager Ron Atkinson.

It was also during this season that Jan became the official penalty taker, replacing Phil Neal who moved to Bolton near the start of the season. Jan Molby scored sixty goals for Liverpool of which forty-two were penalties. In twelve years he only missed two penalties, which is an incredible record, and I doubt there has ever been a better penalty taker. He scored some very important penalties including a very late equaliser in the FA Cup quarter final against Watford on the way to the final in 1986. In November 1986 he wrote his name into the record books by scoring a hat-trick of penalties in a League Cup game against Coventry City.

Jan's finest moment for Liverpool came in the first 'all Merseyside' FA Cup Final in 1986. He ran the second half setting up the first and second goals and then having an important hand in the third goal too with a sublime blind pass to Ronnie Whelan who chipped it over the defence to Ian Rush. He almost scored himself when he went one on one with the Everton keeper Bobby Mimms, but unfortunately he hit his shot straight at Mimms.

Sadly, he was never able to hit these heights on a regular basis again and he was never able to maintain a regular place in the first team. He was beset by a number of problems and every time it seemed that Jan was about to go on a run back in the side he would be struck down by injury and somebody would come in and take his place. Jan freely admits that while he was out injured he would eat too much and not keep himself as fit as he should have done. This would cause him problems when he was free from injury as he was often overweight when he was put back in the side. Regardless of how much he weighed, Jan was still always able to completely dominate the midfield and his passing was always sublime. There is a quote from Alan Hansen that sums this up perfectly.

"Right up to the day that he left Anfield, you knew that whenever he was on the ball it was going to a red shirt, no matter what his weight was. He's probably the only player who was sixteen stone (224 lbs) but could play so well. The problem was he couldn't get up and down, so he'd stand in the middle of the park and be given the ball. Then he'd play. If he'd been playing at fourteen stone, or something, then I think we'd have been talking about the best of the best."

Jan seriously injured his foot during pre-season training and ended up missing almost the entire 1987-88 season. It was during this layoff in February 1988 that he was arrested for reckless driving after outrunning a police car chasing him from a nightclub. He had quite a record of speeding fines and when the case came to court six months later, Jan was sentenced to six weeks in prison. The headlines in the media were urging the club to sack him for bringing football and the club into disgrace. However with the backing of manager Kenny Dalglish, the club decided to forgive him and within weeks of his release from prison, Jan was back in the first team. During his spell inside Jan used the time wisely by getting himself into the best and fittest shape of his career.

In his autobiography Jan describes a hilarious story about his opening night in jail. Various inmates were shouting out questions to Jan during the night when they were all in their cells. Another bloke doing a perfect impression of Jan's Danish-Scouse accent began answering the questions while Jan laid in bed laughing.

Jan wasn't in the side for the FA Cup semi final at Hillsborough in April 1989 but he was in the stands as part of the travelling party. He witnessed the chaos in the Leppings Lane end before being taken into the dressing room with the rest of the players when the game was abandoned. Merseyside holds a special place in Jan's heart and he was deeply affected by the Hillsborough tragedy. Along with the rest of the players he attended many funerals and devoted a great many hours of his time to speaking with, and comforting, the grieving families of the ninety-six who lost their lives.

Jan was back to full fitness at the start of the 1989/90 season and was in and out of the side as we won our eighteenth league title. Jan was uncomfortable with the way Kenny Dalglish was rotating the side, this was very unusual back then in the days before continental managers began introducing this system into the English game. It was during this season that he almost joined Barcelona. The Barcelona sweeper Ronald Koeman got seriously injured and the manager, Jan's former team-mate Johann Cruyff, got in touch with Liverpool to inquire about Jan's availability. A deal was agreed for him to join the Catalan giants. Jan sold his car, gave up his house and signed release forms and was all set to sign for the Barcelona when he received a phone call from Kenny Dalglish telling him the deal was off. Apparently Liverpool wanted a fee for Jan but Barcelona wanted to take him on loan instead.

After Kenny Dalglish resigned Jan fell out of favour with new boss Graeme Souness, the man he had been bought to replace seven years earlier. Souness dropped him for the first half of the 1991/92 season and Jan came close to signing for Everton. Then just as he was about to move across Stanley Park, Souness put him back in the starting line-up and the move never happened. Molby was superb for the remainder of the season and was instrumental in the FA cup victory against Sunderland in 1992. It was a shame that he was denied the chance to score in the final when Liverpool were wrongly denied a blatant penalty in the first half for a foul on Steve McManaman.

Souness never really got along with the senior players who resented him changing things too quickly and bringing in expensive players who just weren't good enough. He also sold some fantastic players such as Beardsley, Gillespie and Saunders without buying adequate replacements. After almost three poor seasons Souness resigned in early 1994 and was replaced by long time coach Roy Evans.

It was under Evans that Jan played out his final two seasons at Liverpool. He was never a regular in the side due to more niggling injuries and he also spent loan spells at Barnsley and Norwich City. After being overlooked by Roy Evans for a European game because Roy simply forgot about him, Jan decided his future lay elsewhere and it was time to call an end to his time at Anfield.

In 1996 he moved to Swansea City where he became the player manager. At the time Swansea were struggling at the bottom of Division Two (now Division One) and despite his best efforts they were relegated. In his first full season as a player manager, Jan came within a minute of taking Swansea back into Division Two when they lost the playoff final at Wembley to Northampton Town with the last kick of the game. After a bad start to the next season, and turmoil in the boardroom Jan was sacked as manager. He then began a career in the media with various newspaper columns and his own nightly show on the Manchester based radio station Century FM. He had two more spells in management with Kidderminster Harriers and Hull City from 1999 to 2004 and now currently works back in the media. He can often be heard commentating on Liverpool games for the BBC Radio Five Live and he regularly plays for the successful Liverpool senior side along with Ian Rush and others in tournaments and charity games held around the world. Jan also does after dinner speaking telling hilarious stories from his career. I had the honour of meeting him at a function at Anfield in 2012 and found Jan to be an approachable person and a great guy.

Despite struggling with injuries, weight gain and off the field indiscretions, Molby still managed to make a massive impact in his twelve years with Liverpool. His 16th placing in the '100 Players Who Shook the Kop' series is proof of just how highly he is still regarded by Liverpool fans.

Jim Beglin

Talented Irish left back Jim Beglin has the distinction of being Bob Paisley's final signing. His career was cut short by a devastating injury, but his performances in the mid eighties for Liverpool will never be forgotten.

Jim Beglin was born in July 1963 in County Waterford, Ireland. His senior football career began with the legendary Irish side Shamrock Rovers in 1980. In his final season at Shamrock Rovers, 1982/83, Jim played in the same team as Paul Whelan, brother of Liverpool legend Ronnie.

In May 1983, Bob Paisley signed Jim for a fee of £20,000. This was to be Paisley's final transfer as Liverpool manager as he was to retire at the end of the 1982/83 season. This was a season in which Liverpool won the League Cup and the First Division championship. New manager Joe Fagan put Jim straight into the reserve squad and he spent the next eighteen months developing his abilities.

After several stints as an unused substitute, Jim finally made his first team debut in November 1984. This came in a 1-1 draw with Southampton in the league. At this time Alan Kennedy was well established at left back so Jim played on the left of midfield for his debut. He had to wait a few more months until near the end of the 1984/85 season to play in his favoured position. When Alan Kennedy got injured, Jim took his chance with aplomb and played regularly during the climax to the season. His first goal for Liverpool came in the European Cup semi final against Greek side

Panathinaikos at Anfield. Jim scored the fourth goal in a 4-0 victory. He was then chosen in the starting line-up for the 1985 European Cup Final against Juventus. Unfortunately the subsequent disaster at the Heysel Stadium destroyed what should have been the proudest moment so far in his football career.

Joe Fagan stepped down as Liverpool manager at the end of the 1984/85 season to be replaced by Kenny Dalglish, who became the clubs first player manager. Alan Kennedy regained his place in the side at the start of the 1985/86 season but this lasted a mere few weeks. In September 1985, Kennedy was sold to Sunderland and Jim Beglin was handed a permanent place at left back. He went on to make fifty three appearances that season as Liverpool won their first League and FA Cup double.

One of Jim's greatest, and most famous, performances for Liverpool came in the classic all Merseyside FA Cup Final against Everton in 1986. Jim's performance in the second half was a major factor in Liverpool's comeback from a goal down to eventually win the game 3-1. His interception from Everton's Gary Stevens and subsequent pass to Jan Molby led to the equaliser from Ian Rush. However it was in a different type of situation that Jim is most remembered for. Early in the second half he got into a pushing and shouting match with goalkeeper Bruce Grobbelaar. There was confusion in the area over who had control of the ball which led to Bruce pushing Jim in the chest and looking furious gave him a hand gesture. BBC commentator described the incident with; "Grobbelaar seems to be at sixes and sevens with Beglin". However before it could get nasty they exchanged in a quick game of pass and all was resolved. Describing the incident years later, Jim said;

"I wish I had a quid for every time someone came up and reminded me about my little head to head with Brucie in the final. But again some people reckon that kind of started everybody into the fact that unless we pull it together, we're not gonna come out with anything from this game. He called me 'something' stupid and I told him where to go and he hit me. I thought, I can't really hit him back here, there's a hundred thousand in the stadium and millions watching on telly, and we're already behind. He was that type of excitable character so I thought, just get on with it, so I ran away and thankfully we won the game and made it up afterwards."

Jim started the following season where he left off, in fine form, and his position in the side was never under any threat. He seemed to be improving with every game and looking like he would be major player for many years to come. However in January 1987 it would all go horribly wrong in a terrible accident on the pitch. Liverpool were drawn against Everton in the League Cup quarter final and it was set to be a classic game, especially as both rivals were going head to head for the First Division title for the third season in a row.

In one split second Jim's Liverpool career was over just as he was on the threshold of a long stint as the Reds' left back. He went into a fifty-fifty tackle with Everton's Gary Stevens and came out of it with one of the most horrific broken legs ever seen in football.

Jim never played in the first team again. While his leg was mending Steve Nicol took his place and then Gary Ablett came through the ranks. Steve Staunton also came into the side and by the time Jim had regained fitness he was down in the pecking order due to the form of Ablett and Staunton. Jim attempted a comeback with the reserves but ended up damaging the cartilage in his knee.

In June 1989 Jim moved to Leeds United to try and restart his playing career. He hardly made any appearances at Elland Road over the next two seasons and spent two brief loan spells at Plymouth Argyle and Blackburn Rovers. Regrettably, the terrible injuries he suffered at Liverpool had taken too much toll on Jim's leg and in 1991 he was forced to retire at the young age of just twenty seven.

Fortunately for Jim he has been able to carve out a very successful career with the broadcast media. For many years he has worked as a main presenter and commentator for RTE in Ireland and for ITV. His voice can be heard on a regular basis commentating on Champions League games for ITV.

Despite only playing one full season for Liverpool, Jim Beglin is remembered very fondly by Reds' fans. The left back position has often been a very difficult one to fill and it is a real tragedy that a player who could have been an all time great was cut down in his prime. Jim regularly appears in a prominent part on the official Liverpool DVD releases and his place in the Liverpool family is not in   any   doubt.

John Aldridge

Midway through the 1986/87 season the shocking news was announced that Ian Rush was leaving Liverpool to join Juventus for three million pounds at the end of the season. At the time this was very upsetting and devastating news for Reds fans, imagine how you would feel if you woke up tomorrow and saw the headlines that Gerrard or Carragher were leaving Liverpool. That gives you a rough idea how it felt back then with the news about Ian Rush going to Italy.

So the speculation naturally began as to who would replace Rushie. I don't think anyone genuinely believed it was possible to be honest, which just added to the pain and worry. A few names were bandied about in the press including Mark Hateley whose father Tony played for Liverpool in the 1960's. Also linked was Charlie Nicholas of Arsenal, who a few months later went on to score the winner against Liverpool in the League Cup Final. An interesting fact about that particular match is that it was the first occasion in which we lost a game when Ian Rush had scored first. In January 1987 the speculation was finally over when Kenny Dalglish signed a Scouser who was also an Ian Rush look-alike, it was our man John Aldridge. He was signed from Oxford United on January 27th 1987 for £750,000.

Aldo grew up on Merseyside as a huge Liverpool fan, spending many hours standing on the Kop cheering on his heroes. He was a great footballer at school and my dad and his brothers actually played against him in school matches. Due to lack of money for proper boots, my dad used to play footy wearing his dad's old hobnail boots that were two sizes too big. One time in a game involving Aldo playing for a rival school team, my dad went to kick the ball and his boot flew off hitting the referee in the head, knocking him unconscious. What made the incident even funnier was that the referee was also my dad's school headmaster!

John Aldridge didn't turn professional until he was almost twenty-one after plying his trade in non-league football for South Liverpool. He played for Newport County and then Oxford United with an outstanding goal scoring record at both clubs and at Oxford he had the fantastic achievement of a goal every 1.25 games.

The end of the 86/87 season was quite depressing for Liverpool fans. We finished the season without winning a trophy. Everton won the league title, we lost in the League Cup Final and Ian Rush moved to Italy. Things could only get better but I don't think even the most optimistic Kopite could have predicted just how much better things were about to become. The double signing of Peter Beardsley from Newcastle United and John Barnes from Watford was a masterstroke from King Kenny in the summer of 1987.

The opening day of the 87/88 season was a sign of things to come as we beat Arsenal at Highbury with goals from Aldo and Steve Nicol. I've said this many times before and I will say it again now, this was the best Liverpool team I have ever witnessed. It wasn't just the twenty nine game unbeaten streak; it was the way we played. It was a joy to watch the skill, especially from Barnes and Beardsley as we simply outplayed everyone we came up against. Memorable victories that season include the Barnes one man show against QPR and the famous 5-0 victory against Nottingham Forest. Aldo went on to score twenty six goals in thirty six games to help drive us to our seventeenth league championship.

The only blip on the season came right at the end with the 1988 FA Cup final against Wimbledon. Aldridge had scored both goals in the semi final win against Nottingham Forest and going into the final we were the overwhelming favourites. I remember the night before the match I was talking about it with my dad and he was so confident he predicted a 5-0 win for Liverpool. We listened to the 'Anfield Rap', which was our cup final song that year and got in the mood for the next day that would surely end in a second double for Liverpool. Unfortunately The Crazy Gang had other plans. Vinnie Jones instantly made his intentions clear when he whacked Steve McMahon hard from the kick-off and after that we never really managed to get into the game. I haven't seen it since watching it live but from memory there were only two moments in the match in which I can recall us threatening to score. The first was a disallowed goal from Peter Beardsley when the referee had already blown for a Liverpool free kick and didn't play the advantage. The second big moment is one of the most famous in football history when John Aldridge had a penalty saved by Dave Beasant. It was the first penalty ever to be missed in an FA Cup Final. A goal from Lawrie Sanchez was enough to give Wimbledon the trophy and stop us winning a second double in three years.

Heartbreak was soon turned into excitement in the summer of 1988 when Ian Rush made a surprising return from Juventus after spending only one season in Turin. Speculation soon mounted as to who would be the preferred strike partnership with Aldridge and Beardsley both assumed to be competing to partner Rush. Most people predicted it would be Aldridge who would make way for Rush as it was thought that Aldo and Rushie were too similar and wouldn't play well together. However this was proved wrong and people forgot that they had already played well together in the second half of the 86/87 season. It was actually Aldridge who had the more successful season as Rush took a long time to really get his form back after a bad season with Juventus. Starting with two goals in the Charity Shield win against Wimbledon, Aldo went on another goal scoring streak while Rush spent long periods on the bench.

On the 15th April, 1989, ninety-six Liverpool fans died at Hillsborough during the FA Cup semi final against Nottingham Forest. The tragedy deeply affected the entire city of Merseyside and the players themselves. The entire team was absolutely devastated and local born players such as Aldridge and Steve McMahon were affected in an even deeper way having been supporters themselves. After a number of weeks without play the difficult decision was made between the club and the bereaved families to continue with the season and try to win in honour of those who had died.

Aldridge scored in the replayed FA Cup semi final to set up the second 'all Merseyside' FA Cup final of the 80's. It was the perfect final for this time as supporters of both teams came together. On Merseyside lots of families, including my own, contain both Blues and Reds. It was a terrific game, Aldo opened the scoring and Rush came off the bench to score twice in extra time and win the trophy for Liverpool in a three- two victory. Liverpool may have won the cup but the real winner that day was the city of Merseyside as the fans and players truly did themselves, the ninety six and the entire city proud.

Unfortunately a second double was cruelly denied for a second successive season as Arsenal grabbed two late goals at Anfield to steal the title on goal difference. The second goal from Michael Thomas came in injury time with virtually the last kick of the season. I remember the game was on a Friday night and the most abiding memory I have of that night was my dad's extreme anger when he returned from his weekly darts match at the pub.

The following season Rush was fully settled back into the Anfield groove and early in the season Liverpool accepted an offer of one million pounds for Aldridge from Real Sociedad. In true Aldo style he bid his adoring fans a fond farewell, coming off the bench to score a penalty in front of the Kop in the 9-0 destruction of Crystal Palace in September 1989. At the final whistle an emotional Aldridge repaid the supporters for their support by throwing his boots and shirt into the crowd. The next day he became the first non-Basque player ever signed by Real Sociedad.

Aldo was a huge hit in Spain and became a big favourite with the Sociedad fans. He scored thirty three goals in sixty three games before moving back to Merseyside with Tranmere Rovers in 1991. He made an instant impression at Prenton Park and scored a club record forty goals in his first season.

It was while he was at Tranmere that Aldridge was involved in one of his most famous moments. It took place in Orlando, Florida during the 1994 World Cup in the USA. With Ireland trailing 2-0 to Mexico in the final group game, manager Jack Charlton tried to send Aldridge on as a substitute but was delayed by an official's sluggishness. Aldo and Big Jack both launched into expletive-laden tirades that were clearly heard by television viewers. When Aldo was finally on, after 6 minutes of trying, he scored a goal to give Ireland a chance to get back into the match. Despite losing the game 2-1, Aldridge's goal was crucial in securing qualification for the second round as they went through on goal difference.

In 1996 he became player-manager at Tranmere before hanging up his boots in 1998. While he was manager he led Tranmere to some memorable runs in cup competitions. In 2000 they reached the League Cup final where they put up a tremendous fight eventually losing to then Premiership side Leicester City. The following season Tranmere beat Southampton in one of the greatest comebacks and giant killing acts in FA Cup history. Down 3-0 at half time they came back to win 4-3. They were eventually knocked out in the quarter final 4-2 by Liverpool who were on the way to winning the treble. Unfortunately at the end of the season Tranmere were relegated to Division Two (now Division One) and Aldridge resigned as manager.

After leaving Tranmere he began a successful broadcasting career and he now co-commentates on Liverpool games for Merseyside radio station Radio City. His commentary during the 2005 Champions League final was brilliant entertainment as he forgot all professionalism and became a fan once again.

Although he only spent two seasons at the club, John Aldridge will always be fondly remembered for his contributions and goals. It's actually hard to believe it was only two seasons when you consider just how much impact he had. His 26th place in the '100 Players Who Shook the Kop' series is proof of this. He is one of the greatest goal scorers British football has ever produced with a record of 474 goals in 882 games. I'm incredibly proud that he is also a Scouser and a great ambassador for Merseyside.

John Barnes

John 'Digger' Barnes is one of my all time favourite Liverpool players. He joined the Reds in the summer of 1987 for £900,000 along with Peter Beardsley who was a club record of £1.9 million. As we all know they turned out to be two of the best summer signings in the history of the club. I shudder to think how much it would cost to buy two players of this quality today. They represented probably the best transfers to come into Liverpool for the next twenty years until the arrival of Fernando Torres in 2007.

Born in November 1963, John was raised in Kingston, Jamaica. He moved to England because his father was Jamaica's military attaché to London in the late 70s and early 80s.

In 1981, when he was just 17, John found himself at Watford FC via recommendation from one of the club's fans. He had been making a name for himself playing for local club Sudbury Court with his dazzling skills on the ball. Watford manager Graham Taylor described Barnsie as a jewel he had unearthed and promptly signed him for the unusual fee of a new kit for Sudbury Court.

John made his first team debut in September 1981 in a Second Division game with Oldham Athletic. This was the season in which Watford would complete their incredible journey from Fourth Division to First Division in just six years under Graham Taylor and chairman Elton John. Watford finished second to Luton Town at the end of the 1981/82 season and won promotion to Division One.

These were the days when teams didn't need to be super rich to be successful and Watford had an incredible first season in Division One by finishing runners up to Liverpool and qualifying for the UEFA Cup. The following season was another great one for Watford as they reached the F.A. Cup Final, losing 2-0 to Everton. There is some famous footage from the 1984 FA Cup Final of a giant banner in the Everton section of the crowd that reads, "Sorry Elton, I guess that's why they call us the Blues!" A brilliant allusion to Watford chairman Elton John's song and Everton's shirt colour and the sort of wit only found on Merseyside. During the 1983/84 season, Watford also had a UEFA Cup campaign in which they reached the third round, eventually losing to Sparta Prague. This was considered a huge success considering they hadn't ever been in the First Division before 1982.

John was given his England debut against Northern Ireland in May 1983 when he came on a substitute for his Watford team-mate Luther Blissett. In June 1984 he was to score possibly the most famous goal of his career against Brazil in the Maracana Stadium in Rio. It was an incredible solo goal in which Barnes beat several players before rounding the goalkeeper and slotting the ball into an empty net. It remains one of the greatest solo goals of all time and helped England to a 2-0 victory. Unfortunately this great moment was soured considerably during the plane journey home when John was subjected to horrendous racist abuse from members of the National Front. These racists considered the score of the game against Brazil 1-0 because Barnes goal didn't count.

Sadly, John never reached these heights for England again and he was regularly a target for boos from the crowd. The fans were often frustrated that he never managed to produce the performances he made regularly at club level, while wearing an England shirt. Despite this, John played at two World Cups and received seventy-nine caps and remains England's most capped black player.

In the summer of 1987 John finally reached the platform that his incredible talents deserved when Kenny Dalglish signed him. As I've stated many times before this was the greatest Liverpool side I've ever seen. Ian Rush had departed at the end of the previous season and been replaced by John Aldridge. Peter Beardsley and Ray Houghton were soon to join the side and a legendary team were born. Soon after joining Liverpool, John was nicknamed Digger after a character in the TV show 'Dallas' called Digger Barnes. Liverpool fans still affectionately refer to John by this name.

Due to a collapsed sewer under The Kop, Barnes Anfield debut was postponed until September. His efforts on the road led to great anticipation amongst the fans as word of his displays on the wing began to circulate. When he finally made his debut against Oxford Utd we weren't disappointed as he played well and scored. It was in his next home game against QPR that he scored my favourite of his many superb goals for Liverpool.

We won 4–0 that day and Barnes scored two superb goals. His first was a beautiful run into the box and a one two pass before firing past David Seaman. It was his second goal that day that I've chosen as my favourite. I still remember the first time I saw this goal on Match of the Day that night. Every time I see this goal I'm transported back to being a kid again and it continues to impress me time and again. Barnes won the ball inside his own half and then went on a fantastic run towards the goal. As he got to the edge of the box he jinked past a couple of defenders before slotting the ball home with perfection in front of The Kop. I believe that it was this performance that made him a true Kop Idol, which he remains to this day.

Liverpool went on to record twenty nine games unbeaten from the start of the 1987/88 season, equalling the record held by Leeds Utd at the time. Annoyingly they were denied the record at Goodison Park, losing 1-0 to a scruffy Wayne Clark goal. However Liverpool had the last laugh by romping to the First Division title and finishing twenty points ahead of Everton. The Reds also reached the F.A. Cup final where they were upset by Wimbledon. I still cannot believe Liverpool lost that game and as previously mentioned, I still remember my dad proudly announcing the night before that he'd placed a bet on the Reds to win 5-0. I agree with John Aldridge who said; "if any team ever deserved to win a double, this was it". The only highlight to come from this F.A. Cup Final was Liverpool's official song 'The Anfield Rap', written by Craig Johnston that contained a rap from Barnes.

I consider John to have been the best player in the world in the late eighties, simply for his performances in a Liverpool shirt. In my opinion there wasn't another player around that could touch him back then and I include Maradona. At the end of a truly outstanding debut season for Liverpool, John was correctly awarded the 1988 Player of the Year by both the PFA and the Football Writers. He was the first black player to receive these prestigious honours.

What makes John's performances even more incredible was the amount of racial abuse he received from the crowd, mostly from rival supporters but shamefully a tiny minority of Reds fans too. In the 1980's racist abuse wasn't as outlawed as it is in the modern game and black players were regularly subjected to sickening chants and monkey grunts. Everton supporters gave John a really hard time when he was playing for Liverpool, shouting "Everton are white" and the even more disgusting, "Ni**erpool". There is a very famous photograph from this period of John back-heeling a banana that had been thrown at him by Everton fans. The best way to get these idiots to shut up is to score goals against their team and John certainly did that by banging in loads of goals against Everton during his time at Anfield. John was to become a huge advocate for race relations, not just in football but also in life. He was an inspiration for young black footballers and black people everywhere as he rose above the racism to succeed. John was eventually awarded with an MBE in 1998 thanks in part to his tireless work to end racism in the game.

On the 15th April, 1989, ninety-six Liverpool fans died at Hillsborough during the FA Cup semi final against Nottingham Forest. The tragedy deeply affected the entire city of Merseyside and the players themselves. The entire team was absolutely devastated and local born players such as Aldridge and Steve McMahon were affected in an even deeper way having been supporters themselves. John joined the Liverpool squad in rallying around the bereaved families, attending many funerals and helping out whenever he was needed. After a number of weeks without play the difficult decision was made between the club and the bereaved families to continue with the season and try to win in honour of those who had died.

John scored a penalty, with Aldridge also scoring in the replayed FA Cup semi final to set up the second 'all Merseyside' FA Cup final of the 1980's. It was the perfect final for this time period as supporters of both teams came together. On Merseyside lots of families, including my own, contain both Blues and Reds. It was a terrific game, Aldo opened the scoring and Rush came off the bench to score twice in extra time and win the trophy for Liverpool in a three- two victory. John had a cracking game and he set up Rush for a wonderful headed goal. Liverpool may have won the cup but the real winner that day was the city of Merseyside as the fans and players truly did themselves, the ninety six and the entire city proud.

Unfortunately the league and cup double was cruelly denied for a second successive season as Arsenal grabbed two late goals at Anfield to steal the title on goal difference. The second goal from Michael Thomas came in injury time with virtually the last kick of the season. I remember the game was on a Friday night and the most abiding memory I have of that night was my dad's extreme anger when he returned from his weekly darts match at the pub.

The following season was another great one for Liverpool and a great one personally for John. He scored twenty-two goals on his way to another player of the year award and Liverpool's eighteenth league championship. Once again we also went on an F.A Cup run before finally succumbing 4-3 to Crystal Palace in the semi final. A game most memorable personally for my dad (not the tallest fella) jumping high into the air after a Steve McMahon thunderbolt. He jumped so high that his head actually made a small crack in the ceiling, causing plaster from the artex to land in a mess on the living room carpet!

John was part of the England squad at the 1990 World Cup in Italy. Once again he was unable to take his Liverpool form onto the international stage. The most memorable playing moment for John was when he scored a cracking volley against Belgium in the second round. Unluckily the goal was wrongly disallowed for offside and John went off injured. John's most memorable contribution to the 1990 World Cup was through his performance on the official England song 'World in Motion' by New Order. We'll never forget his rap and head bobbing dance in the accompanying music video.

John started the following season 1990/91 in incredible form as Liverpool went on a run of wins with Barnes scoring incredible goals seemingly every week. I particularly recall a phenomenal solo run and goal he scored at Old Trafford (the same game in which Ronnie Whelan hit a spectacular own goal). John scored one of his greatest ever goals in the 4-4 F.A. Cup game with Everton in February 1991. Unfortunately this amazing game was overshadowed by the resignation of Kenny Dalglish almost immediately afterwards. Ronnie Moran took over as caretaker boss and was soon replaced by Graeme Souness. In the aftermath, Liverpool lost their momentum and conceded the league title to Arsenal.

The following season was a poor one by previous standards as Souness began dismantling the side, selling off great players (Beardsley) and purchasing bad ones (Paul Stewart). The saving grace of the season was a fifth F.A. Cup Final victory, with a 2-0 win over Sunderland who were then in the Second Division. Barnes missed the final due to an Achilles injury.

John spent a lot of the 1992/93 season suffering with injuries and unfortunately it was at this stage that he lost his incredible pace. It was also this season when I realised that he had a very individual dress sense. All of Liverpool's European Cup Winners Cup games were shown live on the BBC and as Barnes was often injured he regularly used to get interviewed at half time. More often than not he would be wearing an outrageous suit in a ridiculously loud colour!

It is widely known that Barnes and Souness didn't see eye to eye and it's to John's credit that he stayed at the club during these poor seasons when he could easily have signed for a lot of other teams. From what I understand Souness thought John was a trouble maker trying to take over in training sessions and not doing as he was told. After Souness was sacked, the new boss Roy Evans was quick to realise John's great motivational skills. John publicly stated that he would remain at the club and help nurture the young players coming through at the time such as, Robbie Fowler, Steve McManaman and Jamie Redknapp.

Due to his pace no longer being what it was, Roy Evans converted John to a holding midfielder. He relished this new role and although he was no longer able to beat players as easily as before. His control of the ball remained and he was a big factor in Robbie Fowler and Ian Rush scoring so many goals. Barnes and Redknapp formed a great partnership in central midfield passing through the opposition defences with flair. John could still weigh in with classic goals too, such as the spectacular overhead kick he scored against Blackburn. In 1995 John helped Liverpool to win the League Cup with a 2-0 win over Bolton Wanderers. Both goals that day came from John's replacement on the left wing, Steve McManaman.

By this stage John was entering into the twilight of his football career but he was still able to contribute during the 1995/96 and 1996/97 seasons. He helped Liverpool to reach the 1996 F.A Cup Final where they lost 1-0 to Man Utd in what was a terrible game. He also played in the fantastic 4-3 victory over Newcastle Utd, setting up Stan Collymore for the last minute winner that nearly brought the roof off the Kop.

There have been comments over the years in the media that Roy was at fault for sticking by an aged John Barnes for so long. This has been used as an excuse for Liverpool failing to win the league title during the mid nineties. This is a completely unfair criticism and untrue. Anybody who watched Liverpool regularly during this period will tell you that John was still a class act and his assistance to the younger players can not be under-estimated. John Barnes never used to give the ball away and his presence on the field would give the rest of the team a huge lift. Stan Collymore has claimed that

John ran the show behind the scenes and not Roy Evans, but enough people have refuted these claims so I don't believe that at all.

In August 1997, after ten years at Liverpool, John finally decided to leave as he was no longer a first team regular. According to Robbie Fowler in his autobiography, Barnes and Roy Evans had a blazing row after a 3-1 defeat to Man Utd and that was the last time he played for Liverpool.

John decided to rejoin Kenny Dalglish and Ian Rush with a free transfer to Newcastle Utd. John only played one season at St. James Park and it was a disappointing one despite a few highlights such as a victory over Barcelona in the Champions League and reaching the F.A. Cup Final against Arsenal. The Magpies lost the final 2-0 and this was John's last game for the club.

For the 1998/99 season, John joined Charlton Athletic, who had just been promoted to the Premier League. Defeat on the final day of the season relegated them back to Division One, and John announced his retirement as a player after 20 years and 754 appearances with four clubs.

In 1999 John was appointed manager of Celtic, with Kenny Dalglish working as director of football. Despite the 'dream ticket' hype, John's tenure was pretty awful as Celtic had a poor start to the season. After a shock exit in the Scottish Cup to lowly Inverness Caledonian, John was sacked and Dalglish took over until the end of the season.

In September 2008, John became the manager of the Jamaican national side. He guided them to a first place finish in the 2008 Caribbean Championships and qualification to the 2009 CONCACAF Gold Cup.

He returned to club management with Tranmere Rovers in June 2009, with another Ex Red Jason McAteer as his assistant. Their time at Tranmere was a disaster and they were both sacked in October 2009 after a run of absolutely horrendous results.

Since his retirement from football John has turned his attentions to working in the media. His first TV presenting job was fronting coverage of the 'African Cup of Nations' and he was then given his own show on UK's Channel Five. He regularly appears as a pundit on TV giving his opinions on games. He is also famous in the UK for his appearance on the BBC TV show 'Strictly Come Dancing'.

John continues to so a lot of charity work including being an ambassador for 'Save the Children'. He also fronted a campaign called 'Score Ethiopia' which provides football based amenities in Ethiopia, as well as improving living conditions for the people there.

In 2006 John was voted in at number 5 in the series '100 Players Who Shook the Kop'. Anybody who ever saw John Barnes at the height of his career will tell you he was one of the finest players ever to pull on the red shirt. I very much doubt there are many Liverpool fans anywhere in the world that could leave him out of their all time eleven. I am proud to have been able to witness him playing many times in person and he is definitely one of my all time heroes.

John Wark

Scottish midfielder John Wark is most famous for his three spells at Ipswich Town, but he also had a successful period with Liverpool in the mid eighties. At Liverpool he had an extremely impressive ratio of a goal every 2.6 games. He was a terrific attacking midfielder who combined skill with toughness in a similar style to Graeme Souness.

John was born in Glasgow, Scotland but actually started his career as a seventeen year old with Ipswich Town in 1975. He was part of the most successful period ever for The Tractor Boys who were managed at the time by Bobby Robson. John played in the 1978 FA Cup final against Arsenal, when Ipswich won 1–0, in what was a huge upset at the time. John came close to scoring in the game when he twice hit the post in the second half. Ipswich Town then experienced a period of tremendous success. In 1980 and 1981, Ipswich came within one game of winning the First Division Championship, won by Liverpool and Aston Villa respectively.

The 1980/81 season was probably John's best as an Ipswich player as they finished second in the league and won the UEFA Cup. John scored fourteen goals during the UEFA Cup run, including one in the final against the Dutch side AZ 67 Alkmaar. His performances that season led to John being voted as the player of the year by his fellow professionals.

His superb form and high profile also led to John being chosen to play a footballer in the Hollywood film 'Escape to Victory' in 1981. The film starred Michael Caine and Sylvester Stallone and was about a football match between prisoners of war and Nazi soldiers. John joined some of the greatest players of all time including, Pele, Ossie

Ardiles, Bobby Moore, to play in the P.O.W team alongside Caine and Stallone.

In 1982 John was part of the Scotland side that went to the World Cup in Spain. Despite John scoring two goals in the tournament, Scotland did not make it past the group stages. Between 1979 and 1984 John played twenty nine games for Scotland and scored seven goals.

Bobby Robson left Ipswich to become the England manager just two days after they were knocked out of the 1982 World Cup. The great Ipswich side he had built gradually started to break up with key players moving onto other clubs over a couple of seasons. In March 1984 John was signed by Liverpool for £450,000, with the intention being to eventually step into the position Graeme Souness was about to vacate at the end of the season.

John made an immediate impact for Liverpool by scoring against Watford on his debut in a 2–0 victory. Liverpool finished the season with a unique treble of League Champions, European Champions and League Cup winners. Sadly for John he did not qualify for any medals, but I'm sure he was still happy to be part of such a fantastic side.

The following season 1984/85 was a poor one for Liverpool but a personal best for John. Liverpool lost the league title to Everton and they were defeated in the meaningless 1985 European Cup final by Juventus after the terrible Heysel tragedy. On a personal level it was a very successful season for John, as he was Liverpool's top scorer with twenty seven goals. This was even more of an achievement when you realise that Ian Rush was in his prime at the time and John was a midfielder. Just as he had done with Ipswich, John also proved his worth in European games by scoring five goals in ten games on the way to the final.

In 1985/86 John wasn't as regular in the side after the new boss Kenny Dalglish had purchased Steve McMahon. Kenny used the rotation system and would alternate his midfield between John, Steve McMahon and Kevin McDonald. John was very useful as a substitute during this season and scored a number of valuable goals when coming off the bench. Unfortunately his season ended prematurely when he broke his leg in early 1986. John missed the remainder of the season in which Liverpool went on to win the double of the First Division Championship and the FA Cup, beating Everton in the final. Despite missing the run in to the campaign, John had played enough games to be awarded with a title medal. His disappointment at missing the FA Cup final was made worse, when he also missed out on Scotland's squad for the 1986 World Cup in Mexico.

John was back to full fitness in time for the following season but he struggled to regain his place in the side. He played most of his games as a substitute but was unable to get any regular starts. His situation got worse in 1987/88 when he hardly figured in the squad at all and in January 1988 he was sold back to Ipswich for £100,000.

By this time Ipswich had been relegated to the Second Division. John only missed two games in the next two seasons, scoring twenty goals, before he was sold to Middlesbrough in 1990. After just one season he was back for his third, and final, spell with at Ipswich. John was a regular in the Ipswich side over the next six seasons before retiring in 1997 just before his fortieth birthday. He had been able to prolong his career as a player due to his superb fitness and a successful move from midfield into central defence.

Since retiring from playing John has worked for Ipswich Town behind the scenes in the corporate hospitality department. He has never forgotten his time at Liverpool and he combines his time working for Ipswich by also representing Liverpool as an ambassador for the club. John also still plays regularly for the Liverpool veteran's side. I was fortunate to be able to meet John at a veteran's tournament held in Vancouver, Canada in March 2006 called 'The Legends of Soccer'. I also met two other former Reds, Paul Walsh and Gary Gillespie, at the same event. John and Gary were both playing for a side made up of Scottish legends.

Despite hardly playing any games for Liverpool after breaking his leg, John's final goal tally for the Reds was 42 goals in 108 games. This is an outstanding figure and one that I think should be mentioned more often when we discuss the great Liverpool players of the eighties. It is unfortunate for John that his best season for Liverpool in 1984/85 is a season a lot of people like to forget due to the Heysel disaster, and the fact that Liverpool did not win any trophies. Had the season been more successful perhaps John Wark would be more revered than he possibly is? However, John is still thought of highly by Liverpool fans and was voted into the '100 Players Who Shook the Kop' at number 100.

Kevin Macdonald

Scottish midfielder Kevin Macdonald was a bit of an unsung hero of the Liverpool side that won the league and FA Cup double in 1986. I've often wondered to myself whatever happened to him after he left Liverpool as he seemed to just disappear from the public side of football after his retirement. So when I was watching Aston Villa's opening game of the 2010/11 season and heard the commentator say "Villa's caretaker manager Kevin Macdonald" I thought to myself that surely it couldn't be the same guy that once played for Liverpool. As soon as I saw him on the television though, I recognized him straight away. He now looks older, has grey hair and has shaved off his moustache, but there was no mistaking it was the very same I guy I remember from the 1980's.

Kevin was born in December 1960 in Inverness, Scotland. He began his football career playing part time for the Highland League side Caledonian FC, while working as a civil servant. In 1980 he was spotted by then Leicester City manager Jock Wallace and offered the chance to move to Filbert Street and become a full time pro. Leicester had quite a decent side at the time with young strikers Gary Lineker and Alan Smith banging in the goals after good service from Kevin. He was a really important player at Leicester and eventually became the captain. In 1984 Joe Fagan offered Kevin the opportunity to join a Liverpool side that was the reigning First Division and European champions. Kevin was bought along with Jan Molby to help fill the void left by Souness who had moved to Italy.

Kevin was never a regular in the Liverpool side in his first season, he has described himself as a 'journeyman professional', but he did get games in the second half of the 1984/85 season and played well. He was not included in the squad for the 1985 European Cup final at Heysel which ended in tragedy. The following season was a great one for Liverpool and Kevin. Under player manager Kenny Dalglish, Kevin got more games in the first team and hit decent form that kept Steve McMahon out of the side. During the latter part of the season, in which Liverpool overtook Everton at the top of the league, Kevin was in magnificent form and started the last five games. He was playing so well that he booked himself a spot in the starting eleven for the FA Cup final against Everton. He had a fine game helping the Reds to win 3-1 and complete the famous double.

Sadly for Kevin, just months after his heroics at Wembley, he was struck down with a tragedy that was to eventually end his time as a Liverpool player. Just as he was beginning to really establish himself in the squad, he broke his leg in September 1986 after coming on as a substitute at Southampton. The injury was so severe that it took Kevin almost two years to recover from it and start playing again. He returned as a substitute during the end of the 1987/88 championship wining season. Kevin has admitted that he was never the same player after the injury and by the time he was fit to play again his time had passed at Liverpool with other players such as Steve McMahon and Ronnie Whelan playing superbly every week in midfield. He started the 1988/89 season in the frame to play for the first team again but spent parts of the season out on loan at his old club Leicester City and then back in Scotland with Rangers.

In 1989 he was transferred to Coventry City where he played forty-four games in two seasons, with a loan spell at Cardiff City in 1990/91. Kevin finished his playing career with two seasons at Walsall where he was a regular, before retiring in 1993.

After retiring from playing, Kevin went back to Leicester City and joined the coaching staff, running their school of excellence. He had a brief time as caretaker manager in November and December 1994 after the manager Brian Little moved to Aston Villa. When Mark McGhee took over at Leicester it wasn't long before Kevin was joining up with his old boss at Aston Villa and became part of their backroom coaching staff. Kevin spent over seventeen years at Aston Villa, where he held a variety of positions including coaching the first team and running the youth academy. His most successful period at Villa came as reserve team manager where he coached the side to three consecutive league titles. When Martin O'Neill resigned just four days before the start of the 2010/11 season, Kevin was asked to become caretaker manager. He began in style with a 3-0 victory over West Ham. Shortly afterward he stepped aside when Gerard Houllier was hired as the manager. Shortly after Houllier left the club, Kevin also left the club. In February 2013, he became the manager of Swindon Town in the First Division. He led them into the playoff soon afterward, were they lost on penalties to Brentford in the semi finals.

Kevin Macdonald is not one of the most famous players ever to play for Liverpool. However he was an important part of a successful squad and played his part in winning two major trophies in 1985/86. For that reason alone any Reds who watched him play for us will always remember him fondly.

Mark Lawrenson

Mark Lawrenson may be more familiar to younger Red's fans through his television work for the BBC but anyone who saw him play will tell you that he was one of the most cultured defenders ever to play for Liverpool. He really was an incredible player who could play left back, right back, centre back and even midfield.

Lawro started his career with his hometown club Preston North End (managed by Bobby Charlton) in 1974 when he was just seventeen. Over the next 3 years his reputation grew and in 1976/77 he was voted as Preston's 'Player of the Season'. That same year he was also capped for the first time by Ireland after he qualified through his grandfather.

In the summer of 1977 he moved to Brighton and Hove Albion, who ironically outbid Liverpool for his services. In 1981 after four years at Brighton, the club had a cash crisis and their most talented players needed to be sold to bring funds in to the club. Liverpool finally got their man in the summer of 1981 for £900,000, which at the time was a club record by far. As part of the deal Jimmy Case moved to Brighton were he went on to become a cult figure in the early 1980's, inspiring them to an FA Cup Final replay against Man Utd in 1983.

Not long after Lawrenson joined the club, Liverpool's captain Phil Thompson suffered a long term injury, giving Lawro his chance to partner Alan Hansen in central defence. Unfortunately for Thommo he never really got his place back after he returned because the double team of Lawrenson and Hansen was pretty invincible. If anybody out there can tell me a better central defence partnership in the 1980's I'd love to hear it. Hansen was terrific playing the ball out of defence and his vision was sublime. Just check out old videos of goals in the 1980's, particularly those from Ian Rush. You'll see Hansen play the ball to Dalglish and then a through ball to the onrushing Rushie.

Lawrenson complemented 'Jocky' Hansen perfectly with his incredible tackling. Blessed with speed and superb timing, Lawro was one of the finest tacklers the game has seen. Just when an opponent seemed to have run clear his foot would whip the ball from his path cleanly and it was as if he had come from nowhere. I remember a tremendous photo of Lawro making a sliding tackle on Graeme Sharp of Everton in the 1984 League Cup Final. When I was a kid I used to always admire that picture and wish I could tackle like that myself. I was recently watching the 1984 European Cup Final and some of the tackles Lawro made that night were truly awesome. It was watching this game that really showcased for me just how special he really was. He also had another memorable game in the 1986 FA Cup Final against Everton. I still have the newspaper clippings from after that game and in the Daily Mirror he was rated as our second best player with a nine out of ten rating.

During the 1980's we had the best of the best in every position throughout the team, but the solid defence in that time must take a lot of credit for all the success we achieved. We hardly conceded goals and at the other end we had the best goal scorer in the business, it's hard to believe we ever lost a game when I think about it. It's actually frightening just how good a side we were back then.

Lawro scored seventeen goals during his Anfield career and several of them came in famous victories. The goal that springs to mind instantly is the one he scored in the 5-0 at Goodison Park (when Rush got four). His fist clenched salute after scoring is an image that will be etched in my mind forever. His first goal for Liverpool came in the 7-0 win against Oulun Palloseura in the European Cup. Interestingly a certain Ian Rush also scored his first Liverpool goal in that very same match.

The partnership he enjoyed with Hansen in 1985/86 was a vital part of the double winning team. He was absolutely fantastic in the 1986 FA Cup final victory over Everton.

Sadly his career was ended prematurely in 1988 with a serious Achilles injury, Lawro was only thirty at the time. He moved into management almost immediately with Oxford United. However his time there was short lived when he was sacked after seven months. In his defence, he wasn't sacked because he wasn't a good manager it was because he had a famous and public bust up with the chairman over the sale of Dean Saunders (another ex Red) to Derby County. What made the situation more interesting at the time was that the Oxford chairman was Kevin Maxwell and the Derby chairman was his father, the infamous media tycoon Robert Maxwell.

He also had a spell as manager of Peterborough United from September 1989 to November 1990, but unfortunately he was sacked from this job as well. This time it was for the team's performances on the field rather than anything more controversial.

This was his final dalliance in the world of football management, although he did work as Newcastle United's defensive coach in the mid 90's under Kevin Keegan (another ex Red!) Also on Newcastle's coaching staff at that time was yet another ex Red, Terry McDermott. Looking back it's hard to believe Newcastle had a defensive coach under Kevin Keegan. Anyone who remembers the swashbuckling attacking play and virtually zero defending will agree with me there!

I remember during the time he was with Newcastle he seemed to be interviewed every week on the BBC Saturday lunchtime programme 'Football Focus'. Rather than Keegan or one of the players it was always Lawro getting interviewed and I used to really enjoy his witty banter with the host, former Tranmere Rovers goalie, Ray Stubbs. I wasn't surprised when the BBC offered him a job when he left Newcastle.

It's funny how our players seem to end up linking up again after leaving Anfield, and Lawro did it again when he was teamed up once more with Alan Hansen. They became the main analysts for 'Match of the Day' and at least one of them has been on TV, Lawro usually on co-commentary and Hansen in the studio, for almost every game screened by the BBC ever since.

One of his most memorable moments as a TV pundit was when he shaved off his trademark moustache. He made a bet on 'Football Focus' that Bolton Wanderers would be relegated from the Premiership in the 2001/02 season. Bolton survived the drop that season and Lawro kept his word by shaving off the moustache and he hasn't grown it back since.

My favourite personal story involving Lawro doesn't have anything to do with his playing career. It concerns an incident at Royal Birkdale golf course a few years ago. He actually lives near there in the same community as Dalglish and Hansen. My mate's brother was at the course with a few mates to watch the British Open when they spotted Lawro walking a few yards away from them. The lads began to shout the words "thatched roof" over and over again at him. This is in reference to how his haircut was famously described by Nick Hancock on the comedy sports quiz show 'They Think It's All Over'. Fortunately Lawro took the joke well and didn't get upset with the shouting. Whenever I see my mate's brother I usually ask him to recount the story because it never fails to make me laugh.

Mark Lawrenson is one of the finest players in Liverpool history. He was a versatile defender of amazing quality and he was a pivotal figure in some of the club's greatest successes. His partnership in central defence with Alan Hansen is regarded by many to be among the best ever in British football.

Mike Hooper

Goalkeeper Mike Hooper was affectionately referred to by Liverpool fans as Hooper Man. He was possibly the best reserve goalkeeper Liverpool will ever have and he was always a really popular player despite not playing too often. My own personal example of his legacy at Liverpool is the fact that at my school, in the late 1980's and early 1990's, any lad with red hair was usually referred to as Hooper, whether he played football or not.

Mike Hooper was born in February 1964 in Bristol, England. He started his football career with local side Bristol City in 1983. He only played one game in two years before moving to Wrexham in 1985. He received a degree in English Literature at Swansea University and received many plaudits for his performances in goal during 1985. After thirty four games for Wrexham he was signed by Kenny Dalglish for £50,000 to act as deputy to Bruce Grobbelaar.

Mike made his Liverpool debut at Wembley during the 1986 Charity Shield against Everton. Bruce Grobbelaar got injured during the game and Mike came on as substitute. The game finished 1-1 and back then there was no penalty shoot-out so both clubs shared the Charity Shield.

Due to Brucie's injury, Mike started the 1986/87 campaign in an away game at Newcastle Utd. He played the first eight games of the season before Grobbelaar was fit again. One of his finest performances for Liverpool came during an FA Cup 3rd round game away to Stoke City in January 1988. He prevented an upset by making a string of superb saves including one world class stop near the end of the game.

During the 1988/89 season, Mike had an extended run of four months and twenty four games in the starting line-up. Bruce Grobbelaar was struck down with meningitis and Mike took his chance to play regularly. He proved to be a superb deputy and became one of the most popular players with the Anfield crowd. Mike did so well at this time that even when Bruce was fit, Kenny Dalglish kept him in the team. It was starting to look like he might genuinely have a chance to become the reds regular keeper but Grobbelaar was looking over his shoulder. The veteran keeper was starting to put the pressure on for a return to the team and with Mike looking nervous at times he lost his place to Bruce in early 1989.

With his opportunities become increasingly limited at Liverpool, Mike was loaned out to Leicester City in late 1990. He was brought back by new manager Graeme Souness in 1991 and was given a starting place against Manchester Utd in October 1991. He produced a man of the match performance in a 0-0 draw and it looked like he was going to be given a run in the team. However he was injured soon after and lost his place once again to Grobbelaar.

In 1992 David James was brought to Anfield from Watford and it appeared that Mike's days were numbered. However Mike was given another extended run in the team during the 1992/93 season. David James had a poor start to his Liverpool career and was suffering from a loss of confidence. Grobbelaar had fallen out with Souness over his constant travelling to Zimbabwe to play for the national side and for two months Mike was the starting keeper. Mike didn't play badly during this period but unfortunately he was playing behind a constantly rotating defence and Liverpool were playing poorly and shipping goals. Mike was unfairly used as a bit of a scapegoat for the poor results. After a 2-0 loss to then Division One side Bolton Wanderers in the FA Cup, he was dropped and never played for Liverpool again.

In August 1993, Mike signed for Kevin Keegan at Newcastle Utd for a fee of £550,000. Nobody could blame Mike for taking this terrific opportunity and he left with nothing but good wishes from Liverpool fans. He started his Newcastle career in great style with a victory over Everton. In this game he almost scored a spectacular goal when he hit the crossbar from a goal kick. His great start at Newcastle continued when they thrashed Liverpool 3-0 in a game televised live on Sky. Unfortunately things began to go sour for Mike at St. James Park and he began a run of erratic and often poor displays. The final straw came when he was blamed for an FA Cup defeat to Luton Town and a 4-2 loss to Wimbledon. He became a target for boos from the crowd and even received sickening hate mail. The abuse got so bad at one stage that Kevin Keegan actually threatened to resign unless it stopped. Keegan himself eventually lost patience with Mike and in February 1994 he did him a favour and dropped him from the side to be replaced by Pavel Srnicek.

During the following season Mike was back to being a deputy keeper as Srnicek was preferred to play in goal. Mike played one more game for Newcastle when he came off the bench during a 3-3 draw with Tottenham Hotspur. He signed off in memorable style by saving a penalty from Jurgen Klinsmann in what proved to be his last ever appearance in a football match. Mike spent a loan spell at Sunderland but never played a single game for them. In the autumn of 1995 Newcastle signed another keeper, Shaka Hislop to deputise for Srnicek and Mike's opportunities became even more limited. He remained at the club during the 1995/96 season until his contract expired at the end of the campaign.

Newcastle Utd released Mike in the summer of 1996 and with his confidence well and truly shattered he decided to retire from football. He was only thirty two, which is really young for a keeper to retire, a sad end to what was once a very promising career. The last time I heard anything about Mike since his retirement is that he was working as a doorman in a Durham nightclub.

Mike Hooper takes his place in the history of Liverpool FC for his reliable displays as a deputy keeper over eight years. With his red hair and giant frame, Mike remains a memorable Liverpool player from the late1980's. This is quite an achievement considering he spent the majority of his Liverpool career on the substitute bench.

Paul Walsh

Paul Walsh was a popular and talented striker for Liverpool in the mid eighties and one of my favourite players when I was a kid. His Liverpool career was often spoilt by injuries that always seemed to strike when he was hitting top form, most notably during the double season in 1985/86. Despite him being injury prone he was always extremely popular with Reds fans due to his positive attitude and his obvious joy whenever he was playing. His boyish good looks and long blonde hair made him popular with the female fans too.

Paul was born in Plumstead, London, in October 1962. He began his football career for Charlton Athletic in the Second Division making nine appearances in the 1979/80 season. He made his first team debut at just sixteen years old against Shrewsbury Town. Charlton were relegated at the end of Paul's first season but were promoted back up the following year. Paul played well in his third season, scoring thirteen goals and helping Charlton to finish in mid table.

In 1982 he signed for First Division new boys Luton Town for £400,000. In his first season for The Hatters, they barely survived relegation by winning away at Man City on the final day of the season. The finish to the game remains one of the most famous and parodied moments in English football when Luton manager David Pleat ran onto the pitch waving his arms and dancing with joy. During the 1982/83 season Paul played for the England Under 21 side, scoring four goals in four games. Walsh was absolutely sensational in the following season. His pace, goals and an ability to create something out of nothing led to him being awarded the 'PFA Young Player of the Year' for 1983/1984.

His performances that season also earned him the first of five full England caps. Bobby Robson picked him in his squad for a three match tour in Australia in June 1984. Paul made his debut in a 0 - 0 draw in Sydney and in the following game, played in Brisbane, he scored his first and only England goal in a 1 - 0 victory.

At the end of his second season at Luton Town, the 'young player of the year' had attracted the advances of two big teams, Liverpool and Man Utd. With Liverpool coming off an amazing treble, the lure of playing for the Reds proved too much to resist. In May 1984, Liverpool manager Joe Fagan pulled off a great coup by signing Paul Walsh for £700,000.

Ian Rush was injured for the first ten games of the 1984/85 season so Paul was thrown straight into the side alongside Kenny Dalglish. In his third game, his Anfield debut, Paul took just fourteen seconds to win the hearts of all Liverpool supporters with his first goal for the Reds in a 3–0 win over West Ham Utd. Ironically, in his tenth game, Paul was injured just as Rushie was returning to the side. However, his performances had already won over everybody at Anfield and he would remain an important part of the first team squad for the remainder of the season. He would often play as a third striker just behind Dalglish and Rush and he finished the season with thirteen goals.

Paul scored some important goals during the latter stages of the European Cup competition as Liverpool were seeking to retain the trophy. He had an incredible game in the second leg of the quarter final against Austria Vienna. He scored two quality goals and almost bagged hat-trick when he had a penalty saved. Paul was rewarded for a terrific first season with Liverpool with a place in the starting line-up for the 1985 European Cup Final against Juventus at the Heysel Stadium. Sadly we all know what happened next and what should have been the greatest night of his life turned into complete disaster with the loss of 39 people's lives.

Kenny Dalglish was installed as player manager after the Heysel disaster. His first season in charge, 1985/86, was a momentous success as Liverpool won their first League and F.A. Cup double. This season also contained Paul Walsh's best run in the Liverpool side when he scored an amazing eighteen goals in twenty five games. He was absolutely sensational during this run, not only did he score plenty of goals he also created loads too. During this run Liverpool went on a fourteen game unbeaten streak with Paul scoring eleven goals in eleven games. What makes these statistics even more impressive is that Paul was often a victim of Kenny Dalglish's rotation system as he chopped and changed the side on a regular basis.

In one of those cruel moments of fate, Paul severely damaged his ankle ligaments against Man Utd in early February 1986 and he missed the majority of the rest of the season, playing in only three more games. He had played enough games to be awarded his first league championship medal but missed out on the classic F.A. Cup Final against Everton. The injury to Paul indirectly led to Kenny Dalglish putting himself back in the side after he had not been playing too often. Kenny picking himself for the remainder of the season has often been described as a major reason why Liverpool ended up winning the league title. With only a handful of games remaining, Everton were leading the First Division by miles. When Everton won 2–0 at Anfield the title race seemed all but over. Then Liverpool went on an amazing run of eleven wins and one draw in the last twelve games. With King Kenny back in the side Liverpool started to gain momentum as Everton started to collapse. When Everton lost away to lowly Oxford Utd destiny was in Liverpool's own hands as they just needed to beat Chelsea away in the final game to take the title. In fairytale fashion Kenny Dalglish was to score the goal that clinched Liverpool's sixteenth league title.

During pre-season in 1986/87 Paul damaged his ankle again and missed the first twelve games of the season. When he returned from injury he was given an extended run in the side as Dalglish began to finally wind down his playing career. I'll never forget the superb hat-trick Paul scored against Norwich City just a week after he returned to the side. By Liverpool's standards this was a poor season that finished with the Reds winning no silverware. We did reach the League Cup Final in 1987 but lost 2–1 to Arsenal in the first game we ever lost when Ian Rush had scored first. Paul played in the final but was dropped afterwards when John Aldridge was signed. This proved to be the beginning of the end for Paul's Liverpool career.

In the summer of 1987, Ian Rush moved to Juventus and Kenny Dalglish spent big money bringing in John Barnes and Peter Beardsley. Aldridge and Beardsley formed an unstoppable partnership as Liverpool went unbeaten in the opening 29 games of the 1987/88 season, playing sensational football. Paul was confined to the bench for the majority of the season and was sold to Tottenham Hotspur in February 1988 for £500,000. He later revealed that he turned down a place as an attacking midfielder, preferring to stay as a striker; this was a decision he regretted. Had he stayed in this new position I think he would have been sensational. Paul returned to Anfield for the first time on the day that Liverpool clinched the league title. He was given an emotional standing ovation from the crowd that sang; "There's only one Paul Walsh".

He spent four years at Spurs, at first forming a decent partnership with Paul Stewart in his first season. In his second year he lost his place to Gary Lineker and spent most of the season on the bench.

After missing out in 1986 he finally added an F.A. Cup winners medal to his collection as Spurs defeated Nottingham Forest in the 1991 final.

In 1992 he moved to Portsmouth for £400,000, where he became a cult hero. His scoring exploits on the South Coast took Pompey to third place in the newly named First Division and they only missed out on promotion to the Premiership on goal difference in 1992/93. Paul was so popular with Portsmouth fans that he was voted the fans player of the year despite Guy Whittingham breaking the clubs goal scoring record. His finest game for Portsmouth came in a League Cup game away at Manchester Utd in January 1994. Portsmouth were massive underdogs and Paul scored both goals in a thrilling 2–2 draw.

In March 1994 he was sold to Manchester City for £750,000. Portsmouth fans were extremely upset but at the time this was too much money to turn down for a player nearing the end of his career. He scored six times in the last ten games of the season to help Man City escape the relegation zone and finish in sixteenth place. During the 1994/95 season Paul was a big hit with the City fans thanks to his all action displays and some memorable goals. Unfortunately for Man City they ended the season in seventeenth place and new manager Alan Ball swapped Paul for Portsmouth striker Gerry Creaney in the summer of 1995. He was made the club captain for his second spell at Portsmouth and he managed twenty one appearances before a serious knee injury forced him to retire in 1996.

Since retiring Paul has carved out a decent career for himself in the media. He regularly works as a pundit and can be heard most weeks around the world providing colour commentary on English Premier

League matches. He also often plays for the Liverpool Legends team.

It was at one of these veterans indoor tournaments that I had the pleasure of meeting Paul Walsh. It was in Vancouver, Canada in March 2006 at an event called 'The Legends of Soccer'. It was an indoor competition made up of four teams of former professionals representing, England, Scotland and Canadian cities Vancouver and Calgary. Two other ex Liverpool legends were playing that night as part of the Scotland side. They were Gary Gillespie and John Wark, both of whom I also got to meet afterwards. The ex players were all nice guys and as the other 'fans' lining up for autographs were all kids, I think they enjoyed having some banter with someone who remembered them from their playing days. I was so pleased to have been given the chance to shake the hands of Walsh, Wark and Gillespie and thank them for giving me many great memories. Paul Walsh was always one of my dad's favourite players and I was really happy to have been able to get Paul to write a personal note to him.

Despite only playing at Anfield for three seasons, most of which was spent injured or on the bench, Paul Walsh remains one of Liverpool's most popular ex players. This was displayed when he was voted number 71 in the '100 Players Who Shook the Kop'.

Peter Beardsley

Peter Beardsley is a player who will always be extremely popular here where I live in Vancouver. I really love the guy and he's definitely one of my top five favourite players of all time. He's a top bloke too, I know this because I've met him, but more on that later.

Peter was born in January 1961, in Newcastle. He started his football career with Carlisle United in 1979 after being spotted playing for Wallsend Boys' Club. After making over 100 appearances he decided to accept an offer to move to Canada and joined the Vancouver Whitecaps who bought him for £275,000 in 1981.

He made enough of an impact in Vancouver for word to get back to Manchester United who paid £250,000 for him in 1982. Beardsley made just one appearance for them, in the League Cup, before rejoining the Whitecaps on a free transfer.

In his autobiography there is an entire chapter dedicated to his time spent in Vancouver. He speaks very fondly of his time with the Whitecaps and says he was tempted on a number of occasions to move there on a permanent basis, but there was no way he could eventually resist signing for his hometown club, Newcastle United. He had some memorable performances for the Whitecaps and scored some great goals and is affectionately remembered by all those who saw him play at the time. Whitecaps fans still talk about him to this day with immense pride and often bring up the great goal he scored in the first game at BC Place against their nearest rivals Seattle Sounders. Whenever I bring up his name over here, you can see how fondly he is still thought of by the smile on people's faces.

In 1983 he joined his boyhood club Newcastle United for £150,000. He had four years with the Magpies that included memorable partnerships with another Ex Red, Kevin Keegan, and also Chris Waddle. Not only did he score great goals but he also set up some spectacular ones too. Peter helped Newcastle gain promotion to Division One in 1983/84 that was Kevin Keegan's final season as a player. It was at this point that he began to attract widespread attention for his incredible ability as he scored twenty goals in that promotion season.

In the 1985/86 season Peter famously ended a game against West Ham as the stand in goalkeeper. The game ended in an 8-1 defeat for Newcastle with Peter conceding three goals. I recall watching Newcastle play on Match of the Day sometime around 1986and my dad speaking at length about how much he wanted Liverpool to sign Peter.

His stock rose even higher after impressing during the 1986 World Cup in Mexico. He partnered Gary Lineker and helped him to win the golden boot for the tournament. Peter also managed to get on the score sheet himself in the second round victory over Paraguay. In a recent interview Gary Lineker was asked who his favourite striking partner of all time was and he chose Peter.

During the summer of 1987 Kenny Dalglish smashed the British transfer record and brought him to Liverpool for £1.9 million. The season before had ended badly for us as Everton had won the league title by nine points and Ian Rush had departed for Juventus. Kenny had already brought in John Aldridge from Oxford United to replace Rushie and in the summer of 1987 he added our man Peter and John Barnes from Watford. They were followed soon after by Ray

Houghton also from Oxford United who had played a blinder for them at Anfield at the start of the season.

This side is regarded by a lot of people, including myself, as the most skilful Liverpool side ever. We went twenty nine games unbeaten at the start of the season equalling the record set previously by Leeds United. Annoyingly the chance to achieve the record was denied to us at Goodison Park against Everton with a Wayne Clark goal.

It wasn't just the amount of wins we put in that season it was the way in which we went about it. The standard of ability on show that season was truly breathtaking with memorable victories against QPR, Everton and most famously the 5 – 0 versus Nottingham Forest, which was later, voted as the 'performance of the century'. At that time Barnes was probably the best player in the world and to be honest although he didn't get as many headlines Beardsley wasn't too far behind him. It took Peter a few games to score his first goal, which came in an away victory at Coventry City. From that moment on he was flying and was involved in some really memorable moments that season. Possibly his finest goal came in the televised Merseyside derby when he smashed in a blinder off the crossbar. In the FA Cup Final defeat to Wimbledon Peter scored a fine goal, only to have it disallowed because the referee had already blown for a free kick to Liverpool in the build up and didn't play the advantage.

He had four fantastic seasons at Anfield during which he won two league titles, an FA Cup and three Charity Shields. He also won the hearts of all Liverpool supporters and the people of Merseyside when he helped to look after the families after the Hillsborough disaster. He was so upset by the disaster that he was only able to attend one funeral but his efforts are still very much appreciated and will never be forgotten.

There were rumours that Peter didn't get along with Kenny Dalglish because he was often the victim of a rotation system but this was very much untrue. In fact they were next door neighbours for six years on Merseyside and Kenny helped Peter with the sale of his house when he left the area.

In his final season at Anfield, 1990/91 Peter was in and out of the side but still managed to score eleven goals, including a memorable hat-trick against Man United in September 1990. Sadly Peter's time at Liverpool came to an abrupt end soon after Kenny Dalglish resigned as manager in February 1991.

Peter was criminally fazed out of the team, often in favour of Ronny Rosenthal, by Kenny's replacement, Graeme Souness. My dislike of Souey's management reign could have its own separate article and one of the worst things he ever did was to sell Peter to Everton for one million pounds in 1991, to help raise funds to buy Dean Saunders. This decision still leaves me scratching my head all these years later as Saunders was never ever in the same league as Peter. The stupidity of that decision was made clear at the time by the fact that Liverpool supporters were not angry with Peter for moving across Stanley Park but instead vented their anger and frustrations towards Souness and the Liverpool board. In my opinion it is not a coincidence that the sale of Peter Beardsley coincided with glory years coming to an end and us not winning a league title since 1990. Peter was just one of many great players sold far too soon during that period.

I was fortunate enough to meet Peter in early 1992 while he was an Everton player. My uncle Graham used to be a registered FA referee and officiated non league games for many years. One time he was chosen to be the fourth official at a cup game between Everton and Watford at Goodison Park and he invited me and my dad to be his guests for the evening. We got to sit in the referees changing room before and after the game and then sit in the director's box during the game. The referees changing room was in the same corridor as the two teams and I was able to meet and get the autographs of lots of players including all the Everton team and from Watford the great Luther Blissett and a young David James just months before he signed for Liverpool. My favourite memory of that night was meeting Peter Beardsley, and out of all the players I met that evening, he was the nicest. He stopped and chatted with me for a good five minutes even though he was busy. I remember him rubbing my hair and making jokes and just being absolutely brilliant with me before signing my match programme that coincidentally had a picture of him on the cover. I was already a big fan of him already but after that moment he became a real hero to me and I always followed his career wherever he played.

During his two seasons at Everton Peter joined David Johnson as one of only two players to score for both sides in Merseyside derbies. I remember being present in the ground when he scored the winner for Everton in 1992.

In July 1993 he returned to Newcastle (again along with Kevin Keegan, this time as manager) who had just gained promotion to the top division. In his first season at Newcastle, the 32 year old Peter rolled back the years with some vintage performances. He scored 25 goals and helped them to third in the Premier League. He had four glorious years back at Newcastle and almost captained them to the Premiership title in 1996. He was the team captain for that famous 4-3 game at Anfield that was later called 'The Game of the Decade'.

Peter left St James's Park in 1997 and spent the final two years of his career drifting to various teams including Bolton, Fulham, Man City and Hartlepool Utd where he won his final medal as a player in 1999 when they won the second division (now

Division One) title. His loan spell at Man City makes him the answer to a great trivia question as the only player to play for both top clubs in Liverpool and Manchester. He ended his career at the age of 38 with two games in Australia for the Melbourne Knights.

After retirement he returned to Newcastle where he worked as part of the coaching staff until 2006. In March 2009 he returned to the club as an academy coach before becoming the reserve team manager in July 2010. When Chris Hughton was sacked as first team manager in December 2010, Peter was put in charge as caretaker manager for a few days. Had he actually been manager for a first game the first one would have amazingly been at home against Liverpool.

Peter Beardsley played 175 games for Liverpool and scored 59 goals. Even though he was only with us for a short time he is regarded as an Anfield legend and one of the most talented players ever to play for the club. He was a key player in the great side of the late 1980's and formed amazing partnerships with John Aldridge, John Barnes and Ian Rush. He was voted in at number 19 in the series '100 Players Who Shook the Kop'. Peter Beardsley we salute you!

Ray Houghton

Ray Houghton is often overlooked when we discuss the greatest Liverpool sides but I would definitely include him in my best ever squad. He was a vital member of the last Liverpool side to win the league title and was the final piece of the jigsaw in the great 1987/88 team.

Ray was born and raised in Glasgow, Scotland but started his football career north of the border with West Ham Utd. He came up through the ranks and signed professional forms as a seventeen year old in 1979. After just one appearance in three years, Ray was given a free transfer to Fulham in 1982. Fulham were managed by Malcolm Macdonald at the time and had just been promoted to Division Two and it was over the next three seasons that Ray began to make a name for himself in midfield. During his time at Fulham, Ray was involved in a memorable sequence of games with Liverpool in the third round of the League Cup. The first game finished 1 – 1 at Craven Cottage as did the replay at Anfield. The tie was finally settled in the second replay after a Graeme Souness scorcher from 25 yards.

After 145 games and 21 goals for Fulham, Ray moved on to First Division new boys Oxford Utd in 1985 for £147,000. He made his debut in a 2 – 2 draw with Liverpool. Ray linked up with another future Liverpool player, John Aldridge, and had some great performances that season. He helped Oxford stay clear of the relegation zone with a win on the last day of the season. His finest moment as an Oxford player came in the 1986 League Cup Final against Queens Park Rangers at Wembley. Oxford Utd won the trophy with a 3 – 0 victory. He played well and scored the second goal in what was the biggest game in his career so far and the biggest game ever for Oxford Utd.

In the summer of 1987 Liverpool manager Kenny Dalglish added John Barnes and Peter Beardsley to the side. Ian Rush had gone to Italy and joined Juventus but John Aldridge was already there to replace him. Dalglish needed another player to complete his near perfect side and after Liverpool played an away game at Oxford Utd at the start of the season he had found his man. Ray had played superbly in the game and almost straight afterwards Kenny paid £825,000 to bring him to Anfield. Ray replaced Craig Johnston on the right of midfield and was part of possibly the greatest forward line ever seen at Liverpool.

The Reds went twenty nine games unbeaten in the league from the start of the 1987/88 season. Some of the football being played was absolutely breathtaking and Ray was an integral part of this. He also scored some important goals too, including the winner against Everton in the fifth round of the F.A. Cup and a cracker in the famous 5 – 0 win over Nottingham Forest. By the end of the season Ray had won his first league championship medal. Ray was also important in Liverpool's run to the F.A. Cup final as he also scored a superb goal in the quarter final against Man City. Unfortunately he was denied a winners medal when Wimbledon caused one of footballs greatest ever upsets.

His great year was to continue in the summer of 1988 when he was chosen by Republic of Ireland manager Jack Charlton for the European Championships in West Germany. Ray qualified to play for the Ireland side through his father. In the opening game Ray joined his fellow Liverpool team-mates John Aldridge and Ronnie Whelan to line up against England, a team that also included Reds players Barnes and Beardsley. Ray scored the only goal of the game with a looping header in what was considered a huge shock at the time. Unfortunately for them, Ireland were eliminated from the tournament after a 1 – 1 draw with Russia (Whelan scored a stunner in that game) and a defeat to the eventual tournament winners Holland.

The 1988/89 season was one of tragedy with the Hillsborough disaster claiming the lives of 96 Liverpool supporters. He played in the 1989 F.A. Cup win over Everton at Wembley only for the Reds to be denied a double again, this time by Arsenal in a dramatic last game at Anfield. In his diary of that season, speaking about the disaster Houghton said: "I am not a Scouser but I felt I belonged. I always will now."

The following season saw the league title return to Anfield for the eighteenth time in May 1990. Ray's role was restricted to just sixteen league appearances due to a back injury but he was still an important member of the squad that won the title by nine points clear of Aston Villa. He was chosen for the Ireland squad at the World Cup in Italy that summer. He helped them to qualify for the second round and scored the second in the penalty shoot-out victory over Romania. Unfortunately Ireland were defeated by Italy in the quarter finals but returned home as heroes.

The 1990/91 season saw Liverpool playing well and seemingly headed for another league title win. Out of the blue in February 1991 came Kenny Dalglish's shock resignation after the 4 – 4 draw with Everton in the F.A. Cup and Liverpool ended up finishing as runners up to Arsenal. New manager Graeme Souness immediately incurred the wrath of the fans when he sold Peter Beardsley to Everton and replaced him with Dean Saunders for almost three times the price.

In 1991/92 Liverpool had a poor season in the league but finished with a 2 – 0 win in the F.A. Cup Final over second division side Sunderland. Ray was voted the fans player of the season and had played well in the F.A. Cup Final. He scored twelve goals and finished as second top scorer behind Dean Saunders. The cup final ended up being Ray's final game in a Liverpool shirt. Souness signed the woeful Paul Stewart from Spurs in the summer of 1992 and Ray was informed he would be fighting for his place with him. After a row over pay Ray was sold to Aston Villa for £825,000 and was soon joined by Dean Saunders who had only played at Anfield for one season. The replacing of the superb Ray Houghton with the awful Paul Stewart is a perfect example of just how bad things were for Liverpool under Graeme Souness.

Ray played three seasons for Aston Villa, helping them to a victory over Man Utd in the League Cup Final in 1994. This was the only trophy he won with Aston Villa and his time at Villa Park was mostly regarded as disappointing. It was during his time at Aston Villa that his most famous moment (to the worldwide football audience) occurred. It came during Irelands opening game of the 1994 World Cup in the USA. Ireland were playing Italy who were a pre-tournament favourite to lift the trophy. The game was played at Giants Stadium, New Jersey, which is an area largely populated by Italian Americans. In the eleventh minute Ray scored a cracker from outside the area. This was to be the only goal of the game as Ireland created a huge stir with an unexpected victory. Once again Ray had scored a vital goal in a huge game that created a massive upset. The image of him doing a forward roll before being dived on by his Irish team-mates is one of the most famous from the tournament (along with Aldridge's touchline row against Mexico).

In March 1995 Ray left Aston Villa to join Crystal Palace who where relegated from the Premier League at the end of the season. After two seasons he moved to Reading in July 1997. He finished his career at the age of thirty eight in May 2000 after three appearances for Stevenage Borough in the Nationwide Conference. Ray is now in demand as a television pundit working for RTE in Ireland, as well as LFCTV.

Throughout his career Ray Houghton was always popular for whichever team he played for. Liverpool fans continue to hold him in high regard for his superb performances and vital goals which helped us win two league titles and two F.A. Cups. His continued popularity among Reds fans was reflected in his 52nd place finish in the series '100 Players Who Shook the Kop'.

Ronny Rosenthal

'Rocket' Ronny Rosenthal is one of three players from Israel to have played for Liverpool, along with Avi Cohen and Yossi Benayoun. One of the most popular players in the early nineties, he was a goal-scoring sensation when he first joined on loan. Unfortunately he will probably be best remembered for missing an open goal against Aston Villa in the 1992/93 season.

Ronny was born in October, 1963 in Haifa, Israel. When he was eleven years old, he joined the youth team for the famous Israeli side Maccabi Haifa. He made his first team debut when he was sixteen and scored twice on his debut after coming on as a substitute. Ronny spent seven years with Maccabi Haifa, despite their coach Jack Mansell trying to release him on a free transfer in 1982. The Club president Yochanan Vollach, was a big fan of Ronny and refused to allow him to leave the club for any price. He was rewarded in 1983/84 when they won their first ever League Title, with Ronny a major part of a three man strike-force. Ronny was again an integral part of the side in the following season as Maccabi retained the league title.

In 1986 he moved to Belgium, signing for Club Brugge. During the 1987/88 season he was part of the team that won the Belgian League title and reached the semi finals of the UEFA Cup. In 1988 Ronny moved to rival side Standard Liege but he never really managed to become a regular in the team. During his first season, 1988/89 he was loaned out to Italian side, Udinese. In the following season he was loaned out again, this time on a trial basis with the English side Luton Town. Ronny played a number of games for Luton's reserves but they were unable to secure a permanent transfer from Standard Liege.

It was at this point that Liverpool stepped in after being impressed with Ronny's performances in the Luton Town reserves. Kenny Dalglish offered Ronny a trial at Anfield in March 1990 and he made his debut in a reserve game against Man Utd. Ronny couldn't have made a better start by playing superbly and scoring in a 2-1 victory for Liverpool. He scored two more goals in his second reserve game against Huddersfield and followed that with another goal against Tranmere Rovers. Kenny had seen enough quality in Ronny to sign him on loan until the end of the season.

He made his debut for the first team as a substitute against Southampton at Anfield. Ronny was brought on with the Reds losing 2-1 and he changed the game. With his first touch he made an incredible run that led to a Liverpool corner. The Reds equalised from the resulting corner and led by the exciting Ronny, they went on to win the game 3-2. In the next league game against Charlton Athletic, Ronny was named in the starting line-up. Liverpool won 4-0 and Ronny scored the perfect hat-trick, one with his left foot, another with his right and the other with his head.

Peter Beardsley had fallen out of favour with Kenny Dalglish and Ronny was chosen to partner Ian Rush up front during the remainder of the season. He went on to score more goals against Nottingham Forest and Chelsea in his next two games and was an absolute sensation. Ronny scored seven goals in the last eight games of the season as Liverpool went on to win their eighteenth league championship. Unfairly, Ronny was denied a championship medal as he hadn't played enough games to be eligible. I've always thought that he should have been given one anyway because without his goals in the title run-in, Liverpool may not have won the league. I will never forget just how exciting it was watching Ronny Rosenthal during this loan period. I remember thinking something amazing was about to happen every time he got the ball. He was the type of explosive player that comes about rarely.

During the summer of 1990, Kenny Dalglish had one of the easiest decisions to make as a manager when he decided to sign Ronny permanently. Liverpool paid £1.1 million to Standard Liege to make him a full time part of the squad. At the start of the 1990/91 season, Peter Beardsley was back in the side and playing incredibly as Liverpool won their opening six games. Ronny was a substitute during this period and didn't make his first start until December when Beardsley was injured. Ronny took his chance with aplomb by scoring two great goals in a 3-2 victory over Southampton. He followed this up with a man of the match performance against Leeds Utd. Ronny scored one goal and set up the other two including one for Ian Rush in a 3-0 win.

The second half of the 1990/91 season was a total disaster for Liverpool and Ronny personally. For reasons I don't quite understand, Kenny Dalglish brought in two more strikers, David Speedie and Jimmy Carter. Neither of these players lasted very long at Anfield and they were both sold after only a handful of games each. Speedie had an explosive start, scoring against Man Utd and Everton in his first two games but was sold to Blackburn Rovers after twelve appearances. Ronny hardly played at all for the remainder of the season and only scored one more goal, against Chelsea. Despite not playing much for the first team, Ronny proved how good he was by scoring eighteen goals in twenty five games for the reserves.

The 1990/91 season was overshadowed by the resignation of Kenny Dalglish following a 4-4 draw with Everton in the F.A Cup in February 1991. Ronnie Moran took over as caretaker boss and was soon replaced by Graeme Souness. Following his appointment,` Liverpool lost their momentum and had to concede the league title to Arsenal.

The following season was a poor one by previous standards as Souness began dismantling the side, selling off great players (Beardsley) and purchasing bad ones (Paul Stewart). With the signing of Dean Saunders, Paul Stewart and Mark Walters, as well as Ian Rush still being a regular, Ronny was used mostly as a substitute during the 1991/92 season. Liverpool finished in sixth place (eighteen points behind champions Leeds Utd) during the final season before the First Division became the Premiership. This was pretty embarrassing for a side that had dominated the previous twenty years. The saving grace of the season for Liverpool was a fifth F.A. Cup Final victory, with a 2-0 win over Sunderland who were then in the Second Division. Ronny was included in the squad but wasn't named in the starting team or as a substitute.

The 1992/93 season was simply more of the same for Ronny as he was in and out of the side on a regular basis. He started in the Charity Shield against Leeds Utd, but finished on the losing side as Leeds won 4-3 with a hat-trick from Cantona. It was during this season that Ronny was involved in his most infamous moment as a Liverpool player. It was in an away game at Aston Villa, which was also Dean Saunders first game against Liverpool since he was sold after just one season. Aston Villa won 4-2 and Saunders scored two goals one of which was an absolute stunner, one of the greatest I've ever seen. The most infamous moment of the game (and probably the season) came when Ronny rounded the goalkeeper and had an empty net in front of him with no defenders pressuring him. Amazingly he somehow hit the crossbar from a mere ten yards away. I have no clue why he didn't just roll the ball into the net instead of lifting it off the ground. To this day it remains one of the funniest misses ever.

Ronny actually went through some great form in the latter part of 1992. He was part of the team that went 3-0 down to Chesterfield in the League Cup at Anfield. He scored a diving header to kick-start a Liverpool comeback and the game eventually finished 4-4. He then scored two goals in a 4-1 win over Middlesbrough and scored a late winner away at QPR. In March 1993 Ronny scored one of his most memorable goals in the Merseyside derby at Anfield. In the last minute with the game heading for a 0-0 draw, Ronny was put through on goal by Ian Rush. He cracked the ball into the corner of the net in front of The Kop and sent the crowd into absolute delirium. This had been another poor season and Liverpool had nothing to play for going into the game, so Ronny's winner had given the fans something to really get excited about. After the game Ronny revealed in a TV interview that when he finally left the pitch, after a standing ovation, the rest of the players were in the bath singing his name.

Nigel Clough was signed at the start of the following season and it was clear that Ronny didn't feature in Souness's long term plans. So after three substitute appearances at the start of the 1993/94 season, Ronny took a pay cut and joined Tottenham Hotspur for £300,000. He scored on his league debut for Spurs with an amazing twenty yard header against Sheffield Wednesday. He was one of their most important players that season as they only just avoided relegation. His most famous moment for Spurs came in an F.A Cup game against Southampton in 1995. Southampton led 2-0 at half time and Ronny came off the bench to score a hat-trick and Spurs won the game 6-2. In the following round Spurs played Liverpool at Anfield and Ronny received a thunderous ovation from the crowd before helping his new side to a 2-1 victory.

In August 1997 Ronny joined Watford on a free transfer. Graeme Taylor was in his second spell as manager and during the 1997/98 season Watford went on to win the Second Division title. Ronny scored the goal of the season against Blackpool and was a really important member of the side. Injuries ruined the following season and Ronny managed five more games for Watford before retiring at the end of the 1998/99 season. Ronny now works as a football agent and continues to live in England. His son is also a talented footballer and plays in the Watford Academy.

Ronny Rosenthal never managed to cement a regular place in the side during his three seasons as a Liverpool player despite being extremely talented. Anybody who was watching Liverpool in 1990 will tell you what an incredible impact Ronny made during his initial loan spell. His performances drove Liverpool to the 1990 First Division championship and were at times simply breathtaking. He remains to this day one of the most popular players in recent history and is regarded as a 'cult icon'. His enduring popularity amongst Liverpool supporters was reflected in his placing of 76 in the series '100 Players Who Shook the Kop'.

Ronnie Whelan

Skilful Irishman Ronnie Whelan was one of Liverpool's most important players during the 1980's. He started the decade as a teenager in the reserves and finished it as first team captain lifting the F.A. Cup.

Ronnie was born in 1961 in Dublin, Ireland. His father Ronnie Senior was also a professional footballer who played in Ireland for St Patrick's Athletic and also the national side. His brother Paul was a decent player and turned out for the famous teams Shamrock Rovers and Bohemian FC.

Ronnie was signed by Bob Paisley in 1979 for £35,000 from Dublin side Home Farm FC. After two years in the reserves he made his first team debut in April 1981 against Stoke City. Ronnie made an instant impression by scoring in the 27th minute. This was to be his only appearance in the first team for the remainder of the season.

During the 1981/82 season Ronnie became a regular on the left flank signalling the end of Ray Kennedy's Anfield career. It was a great season for him as he helped Liverpool to the League Championship. He scored a great goal against Tottenham Hotspur in the game that clinched the championship as we won 3-1 at Anfield.

A personal highlight for Ronnie came in the 1982 League Cup final against Spurs. He scored twice in a 3 – 1 victory to help the Reds lift the trophy. One year later Ronnie scored again in the League Cup final, this time in a 2 – 1 victory against Man Utd. Ronnie curled in the winner late in extra time with a long range classic.

By this time Ronnie was well and truly settled in the side on the left wing. Despite suffering with injury, he played a major part in the 1983/84 season as Liverpool won the treble of League Championship, League Cup and European Cup. The following season was a downer for the Reds as the season ended without silverware and the Heysel disaster.

With Kenny Dalglish as player manager, Ronnie had a great season as we won the clubs first League and FA Cup double in 1985/86. He had a marvellous game in the all Merseyside FA Cup final against Everton in 1986. He set up two goals in the game including a great ball to Ian Rush for the third after Jan Molby's superb blind pass. The following season ended trophy less with Everton winning the League Championship. The awesome season of 1987/88 saw Ronnie switching to central midfield when John Barnes took over on the left wing. Unfortunately he ended up losing his place through injury to Nigel Spackman early in the campaign. He was able to win back his place later in the season but sadly he wasn't picked for the 1988 F.A. Cup final defeat against Wimbledon. It's a shame Ronnie suffered the injury that season as his skill in midfield would have been a perfect compliment to the hard tackling Steve McMahon in the centre.

At the end of that season Ronnie was picked by Jack Charlton for the Ireland squad at the 1988 European Championships in West Germany. He was chosen alongside fellow Reds John Aldridge and Ray Houghton. He played in the opening game in which they defeated England 1 – 0, in what was a major upset, with a goal by Houghton. The second match of the tournament was against Russia and contained, what I consider, Ronnie's finest moment for Ireland He scored an absolutely spectacular long range volley in a 1 - 1 draw. I remember seeing the goal live at the time and thinking it was amazing and I watched it again recently for the first time in nineteen years. Past experience has taught me that memorable goals from my childhood haven't been as good when I've seen replays of them years later. However this goal by Ronnie is actually better than I remember it, and it's one I could watch over and over again. Ireland was defeated in the final group game by the eventual winners, Holland. However their performance in this tournament was a platform they used to gain further success at the following two World Cups in 1990 and 1994.

In the 1988/89 season Ronnie was given the captains armband when Alan Hansen suffered a long term injury. He took on the role with great pride and played superbly as Liverpool began to chase another double. Once Hansen returned to the side, Ronnie was allowed to remain as captain in order to maintain continuity. After the tragedy at Hillsborough Ronnie was a shining light as the players rallied around looking after the families of the victims. A very proud moment for him as a Liverpool player came when he captained the club in the emotional F.A. Cup Final against Everton. He went on to lift the famous trophy after a 3 – 2 victory in extra time with two Ian Rush goals. Regrettably he was denied the chance to lift the League Championship trophy in that season. We lost the title on a Friday night at Anfield in the final game of the season, when an exhausted Liverpool side had their hearts broken in the dying seconds by Michael Thomas and Arsenal.

Ronnie helped the side to win the League again in 1989/1990. He was involved in a very famous moment in early 1990 when he scored an amazing own goal at Old Trafford. There wasn't a Man Utd player anywhere near him and he somehow over hit a backpass from thirty yards that flew over Bruce Grobbelaar's head and into the net. He hit it so sweetly and I still can't believe it to this day. It remains one of the most bizarre own goals ever scored. Ronnie now likes to joke that it was a dream come true to score for Man Utd at the Stretford end, because he grew up supporting them. Fortunately we still managed to win the game 2 – 1 thanks to John Barnes who scored a different kind of wonder goal after a solo run through most of Man Utd's half of the pitch.

During the following four seasons he was struck down with a lot of injuries which restricted his appearances. His final major contribution for us came when he struck the equaliser in the 1992 F.A. Cup semi final against Portsmouth. Liverpool went on to win in a penalty shoot out to reach the final against second division Sunderland. In a cruel twist he was injured again shortly after the semi final and was forced to miss the final which we won 2 – 0.

After two more seasons of suffering through injuries Ronnie left Liverpool and joined Southend Utd in 1994. He became the manager in 1995 and spent two seasons there before managing clubs in Greece and Cyprus. He managed Apollon Limasoll and Olympiakos Nicosia in Cyprus and then went on to his greatest success in management with the Greek side Panionios. In 1999 he led Panionios to the quarter finals of the UEFA Cup where they were defeated by the Italian side Lazio. Ronnie is still involved with Liverpool F.C making regular appearances on the official club website and representing the club as an ex player. He combines his work for Liverpool with TV punditry and his regular gigs on the after dinner speaking circuit.

I had the honour of spending a weekend with Ronnie in my capacity as president of the Vancouver Supporters Club. We brought him over to Canada to tell stories at our summer event and he also played golf with some of our members. I can confirm that he really is a great guy.

Ronnie Whelan remains one of the most popular Liverpool players from the 1980's and is almost always remembered with great fondness. This was reflected in his respectable placing of number 30 in the series '100 Players Who Shook the Kop'.

Roy Evans

Roy Evans served Liverpool for almost 35 years in a number of different roles, starting as a youth team player in the sixties and finally becoming first team manager in the nineties.

Roy was signed by Bill Shankly in January 1964 when he was fifteen years old, on a 'B Form', which was the precursor to apprentice forms. This was a great year to be a Scouser as Liverpool led the way in the world of football and entertainment. 'Merseybeat' was topping the charts around the world led by The Beatles and Gerry and the Pacemakers and in the mid sixties they had two great football teams too. Roy's first season at Liverpool culminated with a first F.A Cup victory and was followed the next season by the First Division championship.

Roy was an accomplished player at left back and he was a regular in the England schoolboy teams. What a lot of people don't know is that as a teenager, Roy was also an excellent cricketer. He was a bit of an all rounder and played regularly at local level for Bootle and at county level for Lancashire in their schoolboy sides. Roy was selected for a Lancashire summer cricket tour in 1965 but as it would have coincided with pre-season training, Shankly told Roy that he had to stop playing cricket if he wanted to make it in football. As much as he loved cricket there was no doubt in his mind what to do and that was the end of his career on the crease. As Roy later said, "If Shankly said something, you listened."

Roy spent the vast majority of his playing career at Liverpool in the B team and the reserves. He made his first team debut in 1969 but his time in the first team was restricted to only eleven appearances in five seasons. The superb Alec Lindsay made the left back spot virtually his own which kept Roy out of the side. During this period he was a valued member of the reserve side helping them to five Central League titles between 1968 and 1974.

In 1973 Roy went over to America to spend the summer season playing for the Philadelphia Atoms in the NASL. Roy played nineteen games and scored two goals, helping Philadelphia to win the NASL championship. He was a popular player in America and even made the all star team. Roy was asked to go back for a second season in 1974 but he had to turn it down when Shankly named him in the squad for the F.A Cup Final against Newcastle.

When Bill Shankly retired in July 1974, the new manager Bob Paisley asked Roy to become the reserve team manager. He pondered the request for six weeks as he wasn't sure if he was ready to hang up his boots at the age of 25. However Ronnie Moran and Tommy Smith worked on him and convinced him that he was still young enough to go back to playing if it didn't work out. It's strange to think what may have happened if Roy had been able to accept the offer to go to Philadelphia that summer because if he had he may not have been asked to join the coaching staff and join the 'boot room boys'. John Smith, the Chairman at the time, predicted: "We have not made an appointment for the present but for the future. One day Roy Evans will be our manager."

Roy was a revelation as reserve team manager, leading them to seven Central League titles in nine seasons. In the sixteen seasons running from 1967/68 to 1982/83, Roy won twelve Central League titles, five as a player and seven as manager. At that time new players would be placed in the reserves until they were deemed ready for the first team and some of the players he nurtured as youngsters were amongst the greatest of all time. Players such as Ian Rush and Alan Hansen were helped by Roy as well as some other great players who went on to good careers at other clubs, such as Kevin Sheedy (Everton) and Steve Orgrizovic (Coventry City).

When Bob Paisley retired in 1983, Joe Fagan was promoted to become the new manager. In turn Roy was also promoted to join Ronnie Moran as a first team coach. His first season with the first team coincided with one of Liverpool's greatest ever as they romped to the treble of First Division champions, European Cup winners and the Milk Cup, beating Everton in replay. The following season was not as successful unfortunately, as it was a rare trophy-less season for the reds with Everton taking the league title and the Heysel disaster sealing a tragic end to Joe's time in charge.

When King Kenny took over as player manager he kept Roy and Ronnie as coaches and Bob Paisley was brought back to the boot room in an advisory role to help out. The glory days continued for another five seasons as we won three league titles, two F.A Cups and a few lesser trophies like the Screen Sport Super Cup. This latter trophy was created by the F.A as a mini competition for teams who had finished the previous season in a European qualification place but were unable to play in European competitions due to the ban on English sides in place at the time.

When Kenny shockingly resigned in February 1991 there was a lot of speculation as to who the new manager would be. Ex players John Toshack, Alan Hansen and Graeme Souness were the bookies favourites with Roy and Ronnie Moran also in the frame after Ronnie took over as interim caretaker manager. It was soon announced that the new boss would be Souey who had been a huge success north of the border with Rangers. I've written a number of times in these pages about what a disaster Souness's reign was (1992 F.A Cup aside) so I don't need to explain how bad the next few years were for Liverpool F.C.

In 1994 Souness left the club after a home defeat in the F.A Cup by lower league side Bristol City. Souness was terribly shocked and upset with this and under extreme pressure he had to resign before he was sacked.

Pretty quickly a new manager was announced and it was now time for our man Roy to make good on the prediction that Peter Robinson made twenty years earlier. Roy brought in former Reds midfielder Doug Livermore as his assistant and a new era had begun. This was the era of exciting young players like Robbie Fowler, Steve McManaman and Jamie Redknapp playing some of the most creative and exciting attacking football I have ever seen. Unfortunately it was also the era of terrible defending and dodgy goals conceded costing us the league title on more than one occasion. Two players most often blamed were David James and Phil Babb, both of whom were absolutely awful on a number of occasions. Although to be fair to Roy, Babb did look like a real bargain when we first bought him after he'd just had a fantastic World Cup for Ireland in USA 94.

I will always wonder how well Roy would have done if he'd been given the chance when Kenny resigned. I think he would have carried on where Dalglish had left off and not made some of the mistakes that Souness made, especially with getting rid of the senior players far too quickly and replacing them with garbage. Roy's first full season was 1994/95, which finished with a respectable 4th place in the league (considering the finish in 8th the year before) and a victory in the Coca Cola Cup Final (League Cup) against Bolton Wanderers. Steve McManaman scored two fantastic goals to win Roy his first (and only) trophy as manager. Unfortunately the League Cup victory probably built up too much anticipation from the fans and we were expecting big things the following season, especially when Roy smashed the Liverpool transfer record to sign

Stan Collymore for 8.5 million pounds. Whilst Roy's transfers weren't always successful there is no denying that he certainly knows how to mould youngsters into world class talents. Fowler, McManaman, Jamie Carragher and Michael Owen are all standout examples of this. Although to be fair Roy was also denied cash in his quest to sign certain players that definitely would have helped us move to the next level. Jari Litmanen in his prime, Teddy Sheringham and Marcus Dessailly are three players that Roy wanted to sign but was denied the funds by the board. Litmanen eventually joined a few years later when injuries had spoilt him, I shudder to think how good it would have been to have him playing with Fowler with both in their prime before injuries. Roy says that Sheringham was the one player he most regrets not being able to sign and he feels that he would have definitely taken us to the next level.

The one word that I would use to describe Roy's time in charge is inconsistent. We would be absolutely brilliant one week then bloody awful the next. For example; there was the amazing 'game of the decade' in 1996 when we beat title rivals Newcastle United 4–3 and then followed it up by losing to lowly Coventry City 1 - 0 just days later. We should have won the league that season, but there were too many losses in games we should have won and the defeat to Man Utd after two horrendous clangers from David James basically cost us the title.

However, even as inconsistent as we were in the league, we did reach Wembley for the second cup final in two years to meet Man Utd in the F.A Cup Final. The game was completely unmemorable and is only remembered for two things, the winning goal from Cantona (another James error) and those white Armani suits. The latter contributed to the media dubbing the young and handsome players 'the Spice Boys'. A victory in the F.A Cup final could have been a platform to take the club onto great things but unfortunately it just wasn't to be. Another two inconsistent seasons led to us finishing fourth and third respectively.

Roy's record in terms of end of season success was pretty consistent, winning one trophy, reaching another final and never finishing below fourth place in the league. For many clubs other than Liverpool this record would probably have been deemed a huge success. In fact if the top four had been enough for Champions League qualification as it is now, Roy may have been given more money to spend and he may have been able to take us onto the next level. Sadly, back then it was only the top two teams that qualified for the Champions League so we were never able to see how we could have done.

After the 1998 World Cup in France the French F.A's technical director Gerard Houllier was brought into the club to form a bizarre joint manager role with Roy. Houllier was a bit of a Liverpool fan after having spent time in the city teaching French and attending some big games in the early seventies. Roy now says that at the time when he was asked about it, he'd just returned from a holiday and wasn't thinking straight. If he had been thinking straight he would never have agreed to the partnership with Houllier. The joint manager role didn't go well and it seemed like Roy's nose was being pushed out. Whenever the team did badly Roy would be blamed and when we won Houllier would take the credit. The image being portrayed at the time was that Roy's ideas and boot room methods were outdated while Houllier was bringing fresh new ideas from the continent. One of the big problems with the joint managers was that the players never knew who the actual boss was. Houllier is well known for avoiding confrontation so Roy (as was Phil Thompson later on) was often made to look the bad guy delivering bad news to players on his own. Houllier and Roy would agree to give players being dropped the bad news together but when the time came

Houllier was often nowhere to be found leaving Roy to be the bad guy.

Things came to a head after an away game at Valencia in the UEFA Cup. McManaman, Paul Ince and Valencia's Carboni were all sent off after a brawl on the touchline. Roy was furious with his players and the officials and was steaming mad at full time after we'd managed to scrape through on away goals. Houllier refused to close ranks with Roy in the dressing room and instead seemed more interested in handing out shirts as gifts to the officials. On the flight home Roy realised fully that the partnership would never work and one of them had to go. Realising that Houllier wasn't going anywhere, Roy made the ultimate sacrifice for the club he loves so much and resigned a week later in November 1998.

I was never a big fan of Houllier (although the treble season had me fooled briefly) and a lot of the reason for this stems from the way he behaved in the aftermath of Roy's departure. Houllier showed a great deal of disrespect to Roy and he was very vocal in describing Liverpool as a shambles when he took over and continually spoke about the huge job he had on his hands making Liverpool successful. Liverpool were in third place in the Premiership when Houllier took over sole charge, hardly a team in crisis and the side was in a far healthier position when Roy left than they were when he replaced Souness four years earlier. Roy himself says that while he remains a die hard Liverpool supporter, it took him a number of years to get over the snub he felt from the club after 34 years of loyal service.

After he left Liverpool Roy took a break from the game, with the exception of a brief stint helping out Karl-Heinze Riedle, one of his former signings, at Fulham. In 2001 Roy became the director of football at Swindon Town although for all extents and purposes he was the manager of the team. After the team became a complete mess behind the scenes with the directors, Roy decided to leave the club when money he was promised for players was not made available. In May 2013 I met Roy at a dinner at Anfield and I asked him if he regretted not getting back into full time management. He told me that he feels he retired too young and has been itching to get back into the game for the last couple of years and regrets being out of it for so long.

When we talk about Liverpool's greatest ever servants, Roy Evans belongs right up there with all the great names like Bill Shankly and Bob Paisley. His record as a coach is up there with the best of all time and his managerial record is more than respectable. In the nineties he was easily the most successful English born manager in the Premiership and his legacy as a Liverpool legend will never be in doubt.

Steve McMahon

Scouse hard-man Steve McMahon was one of those rare players who combined toughness with superior skill. He was a very hard tackler but at the same time he had amazing grace on the ball, he could beat players and he also had one of the best shots from distance too. Steve also holds the distinction of being one of only two players to captain both Liverpool and Everton. The other player to do this was Andrew Hannah in the 1890's.

Macca grew up in Halewood, Merseyside as a massive Everton fan and as a kid he was a ball boy at Goodison Park. He came up through the ranks at Everton and made his first team debut in a blue shirt in August 1980 just four days before his nineteenth birthday. His command of the midfield led to him being voted the supporters player of the year at the end of his first season and he was awarded the captaincy. After four seasons with Everton he decided to move on because his thirst for success wasn't being met. Liverpool had been trying to sign him for a while but in May 1983 he decided to join Aston Villa so as not to upset the Bluenoses. Ironically Everton became successful almost immediately after McMahon left the club and went on to win a succession of trophies while he languished in mid table with Aston Villa.

After two seasons in the Midlands where he failed to settle, Steve finally joined Liverpool for £350,000 in September 1985 and in the process became Kenny Dalglish's first signing. A tough tackler in midfield was something the team had sorely missed since Graeme Souness left in 1984 and he immediately settled into the heart of the midfield as a major part of the team that went on to win Liverpool's first league and F.A Cup double. Steve says that when he joined Liverpool he received a torrent of abuse from Everton fans, including having damage done to his car.

Steve's first goal in a red shirt came in a famous 3 – 2 win in the derby at Goodison Park just a week after he signed. This was the game in which Kenny Dalglish scored an absolute cracker after just 20 seconds. In his first season Steve battled with Kevin Macdonald for his place and he was unfortunate not to be picked for the first 'all Merseyside' F.A. Cup Final in 1986 when he was left on the substitute bench in favour of Macdonald.

During the following season he made the number eleven shirt his own as Liverpool had a rare trophy-less season. However McMahon did have two personal highlights that season both occurring in the League Cup. He scored four goals in a 10–0 thrashing of Fulham and he made up for missing the FA Cup final by starting in the League Cup final against Arsenal. We lost that game but Steve had a good game and set up Ian Rush for the opening goal. Interestingly, this was the first game that Liverpool lost when Ian Rush had scored, and strangely lightning struck twice when it happened again against Norwich City the following week.

The 1987/88 season is regarded by many, including myself, as one of the best ever for Liverpool with some unbelievable performances. McMahon had possibly his best season in the red shirt scoring some stunning long range goals against Man Utd and Everton. He was also involved in one of my all time favourite moments, which occurred against Arsenal at Anfield. During a goal scoring chance in front of the Kop the ball was cleared way by an Arsenal defender. Macca and Tony Adams both gave chase and McMahon got there first with his electric pace and trapped the ball on the touchline before running into the advertising boards. Before you could even finish blinking he managed to turn around and get the ball past the oncoming Adams and get into the box passing to Peter Beardsley who crossed for John Aldridge to slide in and tap it into the back of the net.

We also reached the F.A. Cup Final when we met Wimbledon who were only in their second ever season in the top division. A testament to how respected Steve was came from Wimbledon tough guy Vinnie Jones, who said in his autobiography that before the final he decided that if they "stopped McMahon, then Wimbledon would stop Liverpool from playing". Jones absolutely belted McMahon in the opening minute of the game with a bone-crunching tackle to let him know the score. While Steve later said that this had nothing to do with the shocking result of the match, it has to be noted that he did have a poor game that day, as did the rest of the team.

In the build up to the final, McMahon sang/rapped the lead in his distinctive Scouse accent (with John Aldridge) on the cup final song 'The Anfield Rap' written by Craig Johnston. Also contained in the song was a line in which commentator Brian Moore suggested that England manager Bobby Robson should be playing McMahon as a regular.

"Well Steve McMahon sure can rap, it's about time he had an England cap; so come on Bobby Robson, he's your man; 'cause if anyone can, Macca can!"

After a great season for Liverpool there was widespread clamour in the press for him to play for England, which he finally did, making his debut against Israel in February 1988. He went on to play a part in the squad at the 1990 World Cup in Italy, helping England reach the semi-final stage.

The Hillsborough tragedy in 1989 affected us all deeply and Steve was personally affected due to him being a local lad. Along with the rest of the players he attended many funerals and offered comfort to the relatives of those who died. He was later criticised by Nottingham Forest manager Brian Clough, because of his hard tackling in the replayed FA Cup semi final. Clough accused McMahon of insulting the memories of the victims. What Clough failed to understand was that because Steve is a Scouser it meant so much to him for Liverpool to reach the final that year as a tribute to the victims and was even more important as the opponents were to be Everton. Liverpool went on to win the FA Cup 3–2 in extra time in a thrilling game with McMahon setting up John Aldridge for the opening goal.

Steve was once again a regular in the side that won Liverpool's most recent league championship in 1990. He also played a big part in the FA Cup semi final when we lost 4–3 to Crystal Palace. He scored an absolute cracker to put us into the lead at 3–2 and I still remember after that goal my dad (not the tallest fella) jumping so high into the air that his head actually made a small crack in the ceiling, causing plaster from the artex to land in a mess on the living room carpet! It was a very memorable moment and a very memorable game. What made the result so hard to understand was that earlier in the season we had demolished Crystal Palace in a league game 9 -0, in what was Aldridge's farewell appearance.

When Graeme Souness became manager in 1991, McMahon was one of the senior players who were wrongly and prematurely moved on from the club. He was sold to Man City for £900,000 on Christmas Eve 1991 and never properly replaced by Souness. He played 87 games over three seasons for Man City before accepting the player manager job at Swindon Town in 1994. Unfortunately when he took on the role Swindon were at the bottom of Division One (now The Championship) and he was unable to help them survive relegation. He was successful in his first full season in his first managerial role. In 1996 he guided Swindon to become Second Division (now First

Division) champions and reaching the semi final of the League Cup. He was sacked in 1998 after losing a number of games early in the 1998/99 season.

His next job was as manager of Blackpool in 2000 and just like at Swindon, Blackpool were about to be relegated. In another parallel with his job at Swindon, Steve got Blackpool promoted back to Division Two via the play-offs in his first season. I remember watching that play-off final live when I was on holiday in Greece. I was really happy to see an Ex Red doing well and I remember the great scenes after the final whistle as Macca excitedly ran onto the pitch at the Millennium Stadium. Possibly his most famous moment when he was Blackpool manager came away from football when he allegedly punched his neighbour in the face during an argument at a barbecue. The resulting court case was all over the tabloids briefly.

He left Blackpool just before the end of the 2003/04 season after an argument over funds with the legendary chairman Owen Oysten. After a short spell as a pundit for the BBC and Sky, Steve was back in management again in early 2005. This time he was about as far away from a Northern seaside town as you can get when he became manager of Perth Glory FC in Australia. He was there less than twelve months after he fell out with the board and left the club in December 2005. He currently works as a pundit for ESPN Star Sports that broadcasts football all over Asia.

Steve McMahon remains a big favourite amongst Liverpool fans for his guts and desire as well as his fabulous skills and memorable goals. This was reflected in his placing of number 42 in the '100 Players Who Shook the Kop' series on the official Liverpool website.

Steve Nicol

Steve Nicol was a very talented utility player who was able to play brilliantly in a variety of positions. He played mostly at either right or left back, but he was also able to play at centre back, in midfield and he even played as a striker on a few occasions too. Apart from being a great player he was also a great character off the field and was one of the most popular members of the squad during his fourteen years at Liverpool.

Nicol was born in 1961 in Irvine, Scotland. He started his career with Ayr United in 1979. After two seasons and seventy appearances, Bob Paisley paid £300,000 to bring him to Anfield in October 1981. He appeared in only the occasional first team game after his debut in a 0-0 draw with Birmingham City and spent most of his first two years playing in the reserves. This was the way it was in that era, when new players would be thrown into the reserves to learn 'The Liverpool Way' and to find out if they had what it takes to pull on the red shirt. It wasn't until Joe Fagan took over as manager in 1983 that Nicol was given a sustained run in the first team. By the end of the 1983/84 season he had won the first of four league championship medals.

He wasn't picked for the League Cup final against Everton at Wembley in the first ever all Merseyside final in February 1984. Although this was a big blow to the young Scotsman, bigger glory was soon to follow as he was picked in the squad for the 1984 European Cup Final against Roma, in Rome. Steve had a fine game when he came on as a substitute. The game went to a penalty shoot-out and this was where Nicol had the first of many famous moments in his Liverpool career. Phil Neal discusses this moment on the DVD – 'Liverpool FC Champions of Europe', in the episode 'There's No Place Like Rome'.

"Joe Fagan said, "Phil you take the first, Stevie Nic second, Souey third, then Rushie". Then for the fifth he pointed to Kenny Dalglish and of course Kenny had been subbed. So he's looking around and by this time Hansen and Lawrenson are fifty yards away because they don't want to be included. So he's looking between Bruce Grobbelaar and Alan Kennedy and he's gone for Alan as the last one. So when it's ready for our first kick Stevie Nicol has grabbed the ball and gone. So Souey says "just let him, he obviously wants to go. You know it's a big occasion for him in his mind, if you take him back you might disturb him in that way, let him go".

As we all know, he blasted the ball over the crossbar. Fortunately we still went on to win the European cup after Roma missed two penalties, thanks in part to the Grobbelaar wobbly legs routine, so Steve's miss didn't affect the outcome.

Steve helped Liverpool to win their first League and FA Cup double in 1986 and his fine form was rewarded with a place in the Scotland squad for the World Cup in Mexico.

Over the next several years he was practically an ever present in the side, making a total of 466 appearances and he went on to win two more league titles and two FA Cups. He also scored 46 goals and many of them were memorable including a hat-trick at Newcastle and an amazing long range header at Arsenal on the opening day of the 1987/88 season. The hat-trick against Newcastle was a great example of how incredibly fit Steve was. This is even more remarkable considering he was a smoker, a big beer drinker and would often eat seven or eight bags of crisps in one sitting. Other defenders at the club in the 1980's have remarked upon how Steve's fitness helped them to feel more relaxed on the pitch because he could cover so much ground.

Possibly his best season for Liverpool came in 1988/89, when he was named as the 'Footballer of the Year'. He was immense in defence and could be relied on to pop up with goals too as he helped us to achieve an FA Cup final victory and finish runners up in the league during what was an extremely emotional time for Merseyside after Hillsborough. After Kenny Dalglish resigned as manager, Steve was kept in the side by Graeme Souness and he helped the team win the FA Cup again in 1992 against Sunderland. This was to be the last trophy he won at Liverpool and in January 1995 after fourteen great years at Anfield he decided to move on, taking a player coach position at Notts. County under manager Howard Kendall.

His time at Notts County went from a great high to a huge low within months. In March 1995 he helped them to win the Anglo-Italian Cup at Wembley against Ascoli. The Anglo-Italian Cup no longer exists and it took place from 1970 to 1996 between teams in the English second division and Italy's Serie B. The tournament was scrapped in 1996 after increasing violence amongst the fans. Steve became the player manager in April 1995, when Kendall was sacked. At the end of his first season at Notts County, they were relegated to the third tier. After a bad start to the next season, Steve was sacked in November 1995.

He moved on to Sheffield Wednesday and made his debut at Goodison Park against his former rivals Everton. His best game for Sheffield Wednesday came a year later at Anfield in December 1996. A man of the match performance from Steve in that game helped Sheffield Wednesday to a shock 1-0 victory over Liverpool.

After short spells at West Bromwich Albion and Doncaster Rovers, Steve moved over to America to take a player coach role with the A-League side Boston Bulldogs in 1999. Between 1999 and 2002 he switched back and forth between the Boston Bulldogs and the New England Revolution in the MLS. In 2002 he returned to the New England Revolution as head coach. He was named MLS Coach of the Year in his first season and he took them to the MLS Cup final in 2002, 2005 and 2006, unfortunately they lost on all three occasions. Steve has been a tremendous success in the MLS and has been tipped to someday be the head coach for the USA national side. He parted ways with the Revolution in October 2011, after ten years and continues to live in Massachusetts, working as a pundit on American television.

Ronnie Whelan told me some absolutely hilarious stories about Nico, from his time at Liverpool. I'm, now going to share two of my favourites.

He once went on a cruise to Norway and on one trip ashore he spotted this weighing machine. He climbed on and was shocked to find that he was nearly a stone overweight. His wife was roaring with laughter and pointed out that he was holding two large bags full of bottles of lemonade and crisps!

Another story about Nico was when the players went to Israel for an end-of-season tour and every night they went out on the ale. One night Kenny Dalglish decided to stay in his room. When Steve asked where Kenny was, Alan Hansen said: "What do you mean? Don't you know?" He said: "Know what?" and the lads said: "Come on, you do know. Kenny's found out that he has got an incurable illness." Steve replied: "You're taking the piss?" and so Alan said: "Ask Graeme."

As he turned towards Souness, Hansen said: "Tell him. Kenny's got leukaemia." Souness confirmed that everyone knew about it. Steve turned to Ronnie and other players for confirmation and repeated: "What's wrong with Kenny?" It was confirmed that Hansen and Souness were telling the truth. Nico said: "I need to see him," and decided to go to see Kenny.

The lads immediately grabbed the phone on the bar and contacted Kenny, saying: "He's on his way to your room. You've got to ham it up." He apparently kept saying: "I can't believe it." Steve asked the players who had followed him, to leave him alone to talk to Kenny on his own and asked when it had happened. He was told that Kenny got a bang on his arm in the game against Spurs at the end of the season, and the reaction started from there.

Ronnie told me that he and some of the other players were standing at the door listening to their exchange. Steve said to Kenny: "I thought something was wrong with you because you have been playing so badly." Kenny said: 'I think it's best if you get off.' Ronnie said that Hansen was in the room next door and in agony from laughing so much.

Steve Nicol can definitely be considered amongst one of Liverpool's best ever players and he will remain a big favourite amongst those who watched him in action. This was reflected with his ranking of 39th in the '100 Players Who Shook the Kop'.

The 1990s

When compared to the previous decade, the 1990's can only be seen as a huge disappointment. After the league title was won in 1990, Liverpool only won one more trophy for the rest of the decade, the League Cup in 1995.

I often reflect on Kenny Dalglish's resignation in February 1991 and wonder what might have been. Would he have built another fantastic side and stopped Man Utd from dominating, or would we have still fallen away from being regular title contenders regardless of whether he had stayed as manager?

Despite the lack of silverware, the decade still had plenty of other successes and exciting moments. The emergence of Robbie Fowler and Steve McManaman was an undoubted highlight. Both of these players lit up Anfield during the 1990's and Fowler remains my favourite player of all time.

Liverpool came close to winning the league in 1995/96. This was a season that contained one of the greatest ever seen at Anfield and was later voted as the Premier League's 'Match of the Decade'. This was the incredible 4-3 victory over Newcastle. I will never forget the moment when Stan Collymore banged in the winner. Newcastle manager Kevin Keegan was slumped over on the bench and the TV camera was literally shaking due to the enormous celebrating going on inside the ground. I still get butterflies in my stomach when I remember my own reaction to that moment, as I sat on a wicker chair in the spare room at my parent's house watching it on a portable TV.

The decade came to a close with our first ever foreign manager, Gerard Houllier in charge. Gerard had transformed the club by bringing in new dietary rules and training regimes from the continent. He also started transforming Melwood from a standard training ground to a state of the art facility, which rivalled any in Europe.

The 1990's began where the previous decade left off, with a league title and the same old-fashioned method's that had provided so many years of success in the past. The 1990's ended with the club moving into the modern era, to once again start challenging for major honours over the course of the next decade.

Brad Friedel

American goalkeeper Brad Friedel only played twenty five games for Liverpool in three seasons. A lot of Liverpool fans, including myself, feel that he should have been more of a regular in the first team. Considering how much hassle the club went through to gain him a work permit, I always felt the club wasted his outstanding abilities. This opinion has since been justified by his performances for Blackburn Rovers, Aston Villa, Spurs and the US national team.

Brad was born in Bay Village, Ohio in May 1971. During his teenage years Brad was regarded as a natural athlete, excelling in several sports including football, basketball and tennis. In 1989 he received the Bay High Outstanding Athlete of the Year award.

Brad studied at UCLA where he was a member of the men's football team. Over his three seasons at UCLA (1990-1992), he established himself as one of the greatest ever American collegiate goalkeepers. In 1990, he helped the Bruins to win the NCAA Championship. In 1992 'Soccer America' magazine named Brad to its College Team of the Century.

He left UCLA early to start a professional football career in 1992. As there was no professional league in America at the time, Brad was forced to look overseas for a team. He moved over to England and tried to sign for Nottingham Forest. Unfortunately he was denied an English work permit, due to the fact he hadn't played the minimum 75% of the US national sides games in the previous two years. Problems getting a British work permit were to become a regular occurrence for Brad over the next six years. After he was unable to sign for Nottingham Forest he decided to move back to America and sign an exclusive two year contract with the US Soccer Federation to play for the national team.

The MLS (Major League Soccer) league was formed in December 1993. It was established to fulfil a promise to FIFA by the US Soccer Federation to set up a professional league, in exchange for staging the 1994 World Cup. Brad was in the squad for the World Cup but he was unable to displace team captain Tony Meola as the number one. After the World Cup ended, Brad decided to once again search for a professional club to join. He was signed on loan for Newcastle United by Kevin Keegan. He was denied a work permit so he practised with Newcastle while he looked for another club overseas. He eventually signed a loan deal with Brondby IF in the Danish Superliga. Brad played ten games in Denmark before rejoining the national squad for the 1995 US Cup and Copa America tournaments.

Brad then tried to join Sunderland and was denied a British work permit for the third time. He ended up signing for Turkish side Galatasary in 1995, managed by Graeme Souness. Galatasaray signed Brad to a full time contract and paid the U.S Soccer Federation $1.1 million. Brad played thirty games during the 1995/96 season and was involved in one of the most controversial endings to a game in European football history.

Galatasaray had won the Turkish Super League in the previous two seasons but failed to repeat that success in the 1995/96 season. However, they won the Turkish Cup in 1996 by beating their big rivals in Istanbul, Fenerbahce. This is one of the bitterest rivalries in world football and this particular game is possibly the most famous in Turkish football history. Fenerbahce were competing for the title with Trabzonspor while Galatasaray were struggling in the league. When Galatasaray reached the cup final against Fenerbahce, which was played over two legs, everybody thought it would be an easy win for Fenerbahce. The Fenerbahce chairman made some comments about Souness as a coach and didn't consider Galatasaray to be worthy opponents. Galatasaray surprisingly beat Fenerbahce in the first leg by a Dean Saunders penalty. The second leg was played in the hellish atmosphere of the Fenerbahce stadium. After 90 minutes Fenerbahce were leading 1-0, but in extra time Dean Saunders equalised, winning the cup for Galatasaray. Souness got carried away with this great victory and took a giant Galatasaray flag and planted it in the centre of the pitch. This wasn't appreciated by the opposition fans of course but he was the hero for all Galatasaray fans. Souness was lucky to leave the stadium with his life that night and departed Istanbul soon afterwards, due to Galatasaray's poor league finish.

Brad also departed Turkey at the end of the season and returned to Ohio, America, joining Columbus Crew in the MLS. He arrived mid-season and was initially the reserve goalkeeper. However, he soon became a first team starter and in 1997 he was named the MLS Goalkeeper of the Year. It was at this stage that Liverpool became interested in signing him.

David James was the number one for Liverpool in 1997 but his erratic form was one of the reasons that Liverpool lost the league title to Manchester Utd. James was nicknamed 'Calamity James' by the Liverpool fans but manager Roy Evans kept a public faith in him, despite his regular mistakes. During the first few months of the 1997/98 season, Roy decided to bring in another quality goalkeeper as a backup for James and he decided to purchase Brad from the MLS for $1.7 million in October 1997. Once again Brad had problems gaining a British work permit and he was denied at first. However Liverpool appealed the decision because Brad was only fractionally short of the minimum 75% appearance record for the US national side. In December 1997 Brad was finally approved by the

Department of Employment to start his career in the English League.

Despite David James inconsistencies between the sticks, Brad was unable to break into the first team on a regular basis during the 1997/98 season and only played eleven games. In the summer of 1998 Brad played his first ever game in the World Cup Finals for the USA. Unfortunately for Brad, they subsequently lost every single game in the group stages, including a shock defeat to Iran, and finished last overall in the tournament.

After the World Cup, Gerard Houllier joined Liverpool in a joint manager partnership with Roy Evans. Brad was again unable to break into the first team on a regular basis and only played twelve games during a poor season for the Reds. The problems between Evans and Houllier that led to Roy's departure had a bad effect on the club and they finished in a disappointing seventh place, only two points ahead of Derby County. At the end of the season David James was sold to Aston Villa and Brad was hopeful that this would be his chance to be a regular starter for Liverpool. However Sander Westerweld was signed from Vitesse Arnhem in Holland and Brad's first team opportunities became even scarcer. In the 1999/2000 season he only managed two appearances for the first team and he once again had problems with his work permit. Due to his limited appearances it would be a problem for him to extend his work permit as his legal status in Britain required him to play a certain number of games. Brad did not want to lose his work status and in November 2000 he joined Blackburn Rovers on a free transfer where he was reunited with Graeme Souness and a new work permit was secured.

His career at Blackburn was a great success and he spent eight seasons and barely missed a game in that time. In his first season he assisted Blackburn in gaining promotion to the Premiership and he went on to establish himself as one of the most consistent goalkeepers in the league. In his second season at Blackburn, he played an absolute blinder in the 2002 League Cup final as Blackburn defeated Tottenham Hotspur 2-1. Brad followed this with some tremendous performances during the 2002 World Cup in Japan and Korea. The U.S team made it through to the quarter finals where they were defeated by eventual finalists Germany. It was during the 2002 World Cup that Brad gained his reputation for saving penalties, with two stopped in open play during the group stages. This was the first time a goalkeeper had saved two penalties in the group stages since 1974.

At the end of the 2002/03 season Brad was named as goalkeeper in the Premiership Starting Eleven after fifteen clean sheets. This also earned him the award for Blackburn's player of the season. In 2004 Brad scored a goal in open play for Blackburn in the ninetieth minute against Charlton Athletic. Another memorable performance came in September 2006 when he saved two penalties in a 0-0 draw against Sheffield United. In February 2008, he signed a contract extension with Blackburn stating that; "Blackburn Rovers is home to me. This is my club and I have a special affinity with it". However at the end of the season, Aston Villa made an offer for Brad and he moved to Villa Park in July 2008.

In November 2008, Brad broke the record for the most consecutive games in the Premier League playing his 167th straight game against Fulham. His streak almost came to an end in March 2009 when he was sent off at Anfield. However the red card was overturned a few days later and his streak continued.

In June 2011, Brad signed for Tottenham Hotspur and was given the chance to play in the Champions League for the first time. At the age of forty, Brad was fantastic and was the first choice for Spurs throughout the 2011/12 season. In October 2012, his streak of consecutive games came to an end at number 310 when he was a substitute against Aston Villa. In December 2012, he signed a new contract that keeps him at the club in 2014, when he will be 43 years old.

Brad Friedel was never given a proper chance to establish himself at Liverpool and with hindsight this is a terrible shame. At the time I was a big fan of his and I was constantly frustrated that David James and Sander Westerweld were chosen ahead of him. His career since leaving Anfield has proven that he is an outstanding goalkeeper and further proof of this is that he has the record for the most consecutive Premiership appearances. He deserves the respect of all Liverpool supporters whenever he returns to Merseyside, despite the fact that he only played twenty five times for Liverpool.

Dean Saunders

Welshman Dean Saunders biggest claim to fame, from his time at Anfield, might be the fact that he's the only Liverpool player ever to have a shirt named after him! For a number of years I've always referred to the 1992 shirt (the one with the big Adidas stripes on the shoulder) as the 'Dean Saunders Kit'. I was discussing this particular shirt with a friend recently and when I was trying to describe it to him, he responded: "you mean the Dean Saunders kit?" I was surprised to find I wasn't the only person to refer to the shirt in this way, so I asked a few friends about it and I discovered, to my amusement, that I'm definitely not the only person to refer to that particular shirt in this way.

Dean Saunders football career has been interestingly linked with a number of Ex Red's. He was managed by and has worked with a number of former Liverpool players from his playing days to his coaching and management career.

Dean Saunders was born in 1964, in Swansea, Wales. He started his football career in 1980, signing as an apprentice for his hometown club Swansea City when he was sixteen years old. The Saunders father and son connection is strong at Swansea City and Liverpool as Dean's father Roy had also been a player at both clubs in the 1940's and 1950's. Dean made his full debut for Swansea City in 1982 and went on to make almost fifty appearances over the following three years. In the early 1980's, Swansea were managed by former Liverpool striker John Toshack, who was in the process of taking the club from the old fourth division to the first division. Dean's first season at the club followed what had been a great one for Swansea, who had just finished sixth in the first division. They had actually been top of the league at various times during the season too and famously defeated Liverpool in what was a big upset at the time.

Unfortunately it was downhill from there on as they were then subsequently relegated two seasons in a row and Toshack was sacked.

By 1985 the club was close to going bankrupt, due to mounting debts, and Dean moved on to Brighton and Hove Albion, where he spent two seasons. In February 1987 he moved to Oxford United, who where struggling near the bottom of the first division. He was the replacement for John Aldridge who joined Liverpool. He scored a number of vital goals in the next few months, which helped them to narrowly avoid relegation at the end of the season. During the following season 1987/88, Oxford United got a new manager, ex Liverpool defender Mark Lawrenson. Unfortunately they were relegated at the end of the season, finishing in bottom place. Dean had made a bit of a name for himself with some great goals and performances and in August 1988 he was sold to Derby County for £1 million. This was a very controversial transfer at the time, because Derby County's chairman was the infamous media tycoon Robert Maxwell and Oxford United's chairman was his son Kevin. Mark Lawrenson complained bitterly about the transfer as he was losing his best player and this eventually led to Lawro being sacked.

Dean had two seasons at Derby County and his goal scoring record there was very impressive. In his second season he scored twenty four goals despite Derby being relegated in bottom place of the first division. After Derby County were relegated, Dean became a fixture on the back pages of the newspapers as almost every top club were linked with buying him. Liverpool eventually won the race to sign him in August 1991, paying a British record (at the time) of £2.9 million.

Graeme Souness had just returned to Liverpool as manager near the end of the previous season, replacing Kenny Dalglish. Souey was a firm favourite with the fans from his playing days at Anfield and he had tasted success at Rangers in Scotland. So we all had high hopes that he would just continue where Kenny had left off and take us to more glory and league title wins. Dean Saunders was his first major signing for Liverpool and at the time it appeared to be a phenomenal move. This transfer that at first seemed exciting soon turned sour on Souness as, in a move to partly finance the transfer, Peter Beardsley was sold to Everton for £1 million. A lot of Liverpool fans never forgave Souness for this and Saunders was often left as the scapegoat for this anger as the team had an inconsistent season in the league.

He had a poor start to his Liverpool career when he failed to score in his opening three games. In his second game at Man City he missed a penalty and then in his third game at Luton Town he missed an open goal from three yards out. Things soon improved however, and he formed a decent striking partnership with his Wales team-mate Ian Rush. Saunders and Rush had a good partnership at Liverpool as well as with Wales. During his time at Liverpool, Dean scored the winning goal for Wales in a 1–0 victory against Brazil.

Dean is often wrongly thought of as being a bit of a failure for Liverpool. This stems partly by the fact that he only played one full season for us and also because we didn't have a great season in the league. However when we look back at what Saunders achieved in the 1991/92 season, it's clear that he was actually far from a failure. He scored 23 goals that season in all competitions and he became the first Liverpool player to score four goals in a single European game, against Kuusysi Lahti from Finland. He also broke Roger Hunt's record of total goals in Europe in a single season, with nine in the UEFA Cup. This was a record that had stood for over twenty five years. He also helped the club to finish the season with an FA Cup final win over Sunderland with a good performance and assisting in the second goal for Ian Rush.

Sadly for Dean, after just one season he was transferred to Aston Villa for £2.5 million. Souness appeared to prefer Ronny Rosenthal up front with Rush. I never understood this decision at the time and I still think it was a massive mistake to sell him so quickly. This decision came back to haunt Souey as quickly as Saunders home debut for Villa, which was against Liverpool. He scored two amazing goals and Rosenthal missed an open goal in one of the all time great football bloopers. He had a good couple of seasons at Villa in which he scored the goals to help them finish second in the first Premier League season in 1992/93. He later scored two goals in the League Cup final victory against Man Utd in 1994.

After his time at Aston Villa ended in 1995, Dean spent the final six years of his career as a bit of a journeyman. He rejoined Souness in Turkey at Galatasaray. During his time at Galatasaray they won the Turkish Cup against Fenerbahce, in the game where Souness planted the flag in the centre of the pitch. Dean then had disappointing spells with Nottingham Forest and Sheffield Utd before rejoining Souness in Portugal with Benfica. His final club was Bradford City where played for three years before retiring in 2002.

He then moved into a coaching career at Blackburn Rovers, where he worked with Souness for a fourth time. In 2004 he joined Souness at Newcastle Utd, where he worked alongside another Ex Red, Terry McDermott. Souness and all of his staff were sacked by Newcastle in 2006. In 2007 Dean joined his old boss John Toshack as his assistant for the Welsh national side. He held this position until Toshack was sacked in 2010.

In 2008, Dean combined his role with Wales with his first management job, at Wrexham. He spent three years at Wrexham leading them to mid table finishes in the Conference. In September 2011, he moved to Doncaster Rovers in The Championship. Sadly they were relegated at the end of his first season. In the summer of 2012, Dean came out of retirement at the age of 48, in a pre season friendly against Cleethorpes Town. He came off the bench and scored in a 4-2 win. During his second season at Doncaster, Dean led them on a promotion challenge and led them to the top of Division one by January 2013. He then left the club in the same month to join Wolverhampton Wanderers, who were struggling in The Championship. After Dean became manger, it took ten games for them to record their first win, and at the end of the season they were relegated and he was sacked after just four months in the job.

Despite the bad feeling a lot of Reds fans have for the Graeme Souness managerial reign at Anfield, there are still fans who respect Dean Saunders for his efforts at Liverpool. He always gave 100% effort during his time at the club and he scored some very important goals too.

Jamie Redknapp

Jamie Redknapp has to be the most unfortunate Liverpool player of recent times. He was blessed with fabulous abilities but was struck down by serious long-term injuries on a fairly regular basis. 19 operations during his career eventually forced his premature retirement at just thirty two years old.

Jamie was born in Hampshire, England in June 1973. He was born into a football family, his father is manager Harry Redknapp, his cousin is Frank Lampard and his uncle is Frank Lampard senior. Jamie started his football career as a youth team player at Tottenham Hotspur. He rejected the offer of a senior contract to sign with Bournemouth in 1989 when he was just sixteen. At the time Bournemouth were managed by his father, Harry, and they were in the old Second Division. At the end of the 1989/90 season they were relegated back to Division Three.

Jamie had played just thirteen times for Bournemouth when he attracted the attentions of Liverpool. In January 1991, Kenny Dalglish paid £350,000 to bring the seventeen-year-old Jamie to Anfield. This was to be Kenny's final signing as Liverpool manager because he resigned just a few weeks later after the 4-4 draw with Everton in the FA Cup.

Jamie made his first team debut in October 1991 under new boss Graeme Souness. It came in the UEFA Cup game against Auxerre. He was at the time the youngest Liverpool player ever to play in European competition as he was just eighteen years old. His league debut came in an away game with Southampton. He came on as a second half substitute for Jan Molby and scored Liverpool's goal in a 1-1 draw. After this great start to his first team career at Liverpool,

Jamie then entered into a transitional phase. He spent the majority of the next season on the fringe of the action as a substitute and playing mostly in the reserves.

During the 1993/94 season, Jamie became a first team regular, replacing Mark Walters in the centre of midfield. When Souness was sacked and replaced by Roy Evans, Jamie's Liverpool career really took off. During the mid nineties he was one of the most important players in a terrific Liverpool side. He enjoyed a phenomenal partnership in midfield with John Barnes in the 1994/95 season that culminated with a victory in the League Cup Final against Bolton Wanderers.

Jamie's main attributes were fabulous control of the ball combined with great stamina and determination. His eye for a pass was outstanding and he was a master of playing killer long passes. He was also adept at shooting from long range and scored some unbelievable goals. Two of the most crowd pleasing examples of his spectacular shooting are the last minute free kick against Blackburn Rovers in May 1995 and a thirty yard blockbuster against Spartak Vladikavkaz in September 1995.

In the mid nineties a group of Liverpool players became dubbed as the Spice Boys by the Daily Mail. This was referring to the fact that Liverpool had a group of good looking young players who enjoyed a night out and hung out with celebrities. It is a derogatory term that was picked up by a large section of the media and unfortunately the team of the 1995 to 1997 era is often referred to with the name. However what that nickname doesn't refer to is the fact that Liverpool played some of the best and most exciting football I've ever seen. The players linked with the nickname included Jamie, Robbie Fowler and Steve McManaman who were three of the finest players to grace English football in the last twenty years. One of the things that gets brought up in jest is the cream suits that the team wore before the 1996 FA Cup Final against Man Utd. While nobody is denying the suits looked a bit silly, it is a shame that this image has been used to define a team criticised as having more style than substance. While it is true that Liverpool possibly under achieved during the Roy Evans era, we did come close to winning the Premier League and reached two cup finals, winning one.

Jamie is a handsome lad who dated, and later married, the pop star Louise. He was picked up by the media and focused on heavily for his looks and lifestyle rather than his football abilities. However, unlike the image portrayed at this time Jamie and Louise are actually very down to earth people who don't go out of their way to court publicity. I doubt that Harry Redknapp would be the kind of bloke to tolerate such behaviour either.

In 1995 Jamie made his England debut against Columbia at Wembley. This game is most memorable for the scorpion kick save from the outrageous Rene Higuita, after a cross from Jamie. Sadly, Jamie was severely injured on three occasions playing for England. In the game against Scotland at Euro 96, Jamie came off the bench and turned the game with one of the best individual performances I've ever seen. He received a broken ankle in this game and entered the downward spiral of injuries that curtailed the remainder of his career. He also broke his leg playing for England against South Africa in 1997. In an interview with the Daily Mail in 2007, Jamie commented on his injuries suffered while playing for England.

"I am convinced that playing for England cost me three years of my career. Three times I left on a stretcher during games for them, two broken ankles and a torn hamstring. And Liverpool were paying my wages.

Fans would come up to me in the street and say: "This should be what matters to you, not England". And they had a point. I loved playing for England, but it did make me question my loyalties."

When he returned from the broken leg, Jamie played excellently alongside Paul Ince in the 1997/98 season. He was making up for lost time and things were going superbly until recurring knee trouble halted his momentum in early 1998. These injuries caused Jamie to miss out on the 1998 World Cup but England's loss was Liverpool's gain as he regained fitness on time for the 1998/99 season. Liverpool now had a new management regime in place with the experimental joint partnership between Roy Evans and Gerard Houllier. Once Evans was squeezed out of the club, Houllier took full control of the side and began slowly dismantling the side Roy Evans had built. During the summer of 1999, Ince acrimoniously exited the club to join Middlesbrough. Jamie was given the club captaincy and began the 1999/2000 season in glorious form. Now entering the prime of his career, Jamie looked to have put his injuries behind him. Unfortunately he was injured again in the winter of 1999 and didn't return until the last few weeks of the season.

The 2000/01 season was an incredible one for Liverpool as they won the glorious treble of League Cup, FA Cup and UEFA Cup. Unfortunately Jamie missed the entire campaign. He had knee surgery in America to try and curtail his injury problems and didn't manage to play a single game during the season. After the FA Cup Final victory over Arsenal in 2001, vice captain's Robbie Fowler and Sami Hyypia pushed Jamie forward and invited him to lift the trophy as club captain. This gesture showed just how highly Jamie was thought of by his teammates and the Liverpool supporters.

He made a comeback during the 2001/02 pre-season tour in the Far East and received rapturous receptions from the supporters. He started the season and then got injured again. He fought his way back into the side and played a few more games before his Liverpool career was brought to an end after eleven years. In October 2001, Jamie scored in the 2-0 victory over Charlton Athletic and he never played for the club again. After plenty of speculation in the press Jamie joined Tottenham Hotspur on a free transfer in April 2002, thirteen years after refusing a contract when he was a youth team player. Jamie left Liverpool with nothing but best wishes from the supporters and his popularity has remained high.

Jamie spent two seasons at Spurs and then rejoined his father at Southampton in January 2005. Despite giving his all, Jamie struggled with his fitness and was unable to prevent Southampton from relegation at the end of the season. In June 2005 Jamie announced his retirement from his playing career due to too many successive injuries. He later revealed that the complications suffered in the broken ankle at Euro 96 were a major factor in the amount of injuries he went on to suffer for the remainder of his career.

Since his retirement Jamie has begun a successful broadcasting career with Sky Sports, usually sat in the studio for the Sunday afternoon live matches.

Despite his Liverpool career being hampered by injuries, Jamie Redknapp remains one of the most popular players ever to play for the club. He was voted at number 40 in the series '100 Players Who Shook the Kop'.

Jason McAteer

Scouse midfielder Jason McAteer is probably best remembered for his unintentionally hilarious moments off the field. There are many great stories about him that have gone into football folklore such as the time he ordered a pizza and asked for it to be cut into four slices because he wasn't hungry enough to eat eight. Another funny story is about the time he was in a Dublin nightclub and bumped into the world famous snooker player Jimmy White. When he came across White apparently Jason's reaction was to shout 'one hundred and eighty'! Another good one is about the time he was injured and called a teammate to ask what the final score in a game was. Upon being told nil-nil, Jason responded by asking what the score was at half time. No wonder he was nicknamed either Trigger or Dave by both the Ireland and Liverpool squads. This is in reference to the famous character in the classic comedy show 'Only Fools and Horses' who is known for not being very bright.

Jason was born in June 1971 in Birkenhead, Merseyside. He was a well known amateur player around Merseyside in his teens and began attracting the notice of professional clubs during his stint at the legendary non-league side Marine. In 1992, when he was twenty, Jason was signed by Bolton Wanderers who were in the old second division at the time, having just been promoted from Division Three. One highlight of his first season at Bolton came when they knocked Liverpool out of the FA Cup in the third round in 1993. At the end of the season they gained promotion to Division One. Jason was highly rated during his time at Bolton and he was rewarded in 1994 by getting called up to play for Ireland. He was part of the squad for the 1994 World Cup in the USA. Jason played in all of Ireland's four matches during the World Cup until they were eliminated in the second round by Holland.

In 1995 Bolton reached the League Cup final where they lost 2-1 to Liverpool. Jason played well during the game and within a few months the Reds boss Roy Evans signed him for £4.5 million. This was a dream come true for him as he has been a mad Liverpool fan his entire life. Up until this moment Jason had played in central midfield, which was probably his best position, but Roy Evans decided to convert him to a right back. Liverpool had John Barnes, Jamie Redknapp and Michael Thomas in central midfield at the time and Roy didn't want to break that up. The change in position actually worked out quite well at first and he made his debut in a 3-0 home win over the reigning premier league champions Blackburn Rovers in September 1995. His debut season went well for him as Jason forged a fine partnership on the right flank with Steve McManaman. At the end of the 1995/96 season Jason was playing at Wembley again as Liverpool was defeated by Man Utd in the most boring FA Cup final ever.

In the mid nineties a group of Liverpool players became dubbed as the Spice Boys by the Daily Mail. This was referring to the fact that Liverpool had a group of good looking young players who enjoyed a night out and had too many of those with celebrities. It is a derogatory term that was picked up by a large section of the media and it is frustrating that the team of the 1995 to 1997 era is often referred to with the name. However what the nickname doesn't refer to is the fact that Liverpool played some of the most exciting football I've ever seen, during that period. The players linked with the nickname included Jason, Jamie Redknapp, David James, Robbie Fowler and Steve McManaman who were among the finest players to grace English football in the nineties. One of the things that gets brought up in jest is the cream Armani suits that the team wore before the 1996 FA Cup final against Man Utd. While nobody is denying the suits looked a bit silly, it is a shame that this image has been used to define a team criticised as having more style than substance. Jason's image at this time wasn't helped when he appeared in Irish TV adverts for Head and Shoulders.

Jason was an important member of the Liverpool team under Roy Evans and was a great utility player as he would play at right back as well as in his favoured central midfield position. Unfortunately his performances and those of his teammates were not good enough to win any trophies during his Liverpool career. We came close to winning the league in 1997 but had a poor run in after losing at Old Trafford and then to Coventry City after some bad mistakes by David James in goal. In 1997, Paul Ince was signed to add some steel to the flair of Liverpool's midfield and Jason found himself isolated from his favourite position in the centre of the park. In 1998 Gerard Houllier joined as co-manager in one of the most ridiculous decisions ever made by Liverpool FC and Jason found himself out of the side on a regular basis. He made his final appearance for the Reds in midfield during the 2-1 defeat to Man Utd in the FA Cup in 1999.

Jason was sold to Blackburn Rovers for £4 million and he was immediately thrust into a relegation battle. Incredibly just four years after winning the Premier League, Blackburn was relegated at the end of 1998/99 after a scoreless draw against treble winners Man Utd. Blackburn had an up and down season in Division One in 1999/2000 and missed out on the playoffs. They had three managers during that season as Brian Kidd was sacked, then Tony Parkes took over, before being replaced by Graeme Souness in March 2000. The following season was a much better one as Jason became an integral member of the team that gained promotion back to the Premier League in 2001.

Jason then became a national hero in Ireland in September 2001. On the very same day that England beat Germany 5-1, Jason scored the winning goal for Ireland against Holland in a crucial World Cup qualifier. This was the goal that guaranteed Ireland at least second place in the qualifying group and a playoff place for the finals. Incredibly this goal also eliminated Holland from the forthcoming World Cup. Jason then helped Ireland to guarantee their place at the 2002 World Cup with a two-legged victory over Iran.

After the goal against Holland, Jason left Blackburn and joined Sunderland for £1 million. Despite playing well for the Black Cats he was unable to prevent them being relegated at the end of the 2002/03 season. The most notorious incident in this season came when Roy Keane was sent off in September 2002 for elbowing Jason in the face and breaking his nose. At the time there was speculation that it was in retaliation for comments Jason had made after Keane walked out on the Ireland squad at the 2002 World Cup. Jason played one more year with Sunderland helping them to reach the playoffs in 2004. He played in both legs of their semi final defeat on penalties to Crystal Palace and was then released by the club.

In the summer of 2004, Jason returned to Birkenhead to finish his career at his hometown club Tranmere Rovers. He was immediately made captain by manager Brian Little and helped Tranmere to finish third in Division One in 2004/05. Unfortunately they entered the playoffs in a poor run of form and they were defeated in the semi-final by Hartlepool. Jason was taken off during the game with a concussion and despite Tranmere coming back from 2-0 down, they went out on penalties. This was the second time in consecutive years that Jason had lost a playoff semi-final in a penalty shoot-out.

In March 2005, Jason was a main organizer of the Tsunami Aid game at Anfield to benefit survivors of the disaster in Asia in December 2004. He captained the Liverpool Legends team to a 6-2 victory over a team of celebrities. Jason remained at Tranmere for another two seasons, during which time he started taking his coaching badges and became a player coach at Prenton Park. In the summer of 2007 he announced his retirement after being released by the club.

After he retired from football, Jason spent his time doing occasional media work on television and playing in the Liverpool Legends team in Masters Tournaments around the world. In June 2009 he returned to Tranmere as assistant manager to his former Liverpool teammate John Barnes. Sadly for Jason and John they were both sacked after just 4 months. Jason can currently be seen regularly as a pundit for LFCTV before and after the Liverpool matches.

Jason McAteer remains a popular figure on Merseyside amongst both Liverpool and Tranmere supporters. His never say die attitude on the pitch and his hilarious antics off it, have ensured that he is impossible to dislike. He was an integral part of a great attacking side under Roy Evans and his positive attitude will ensure that he will never be forgotten at Anfield.

Mark Walters

Mark Walters is the answer to a good trivia question for Reds fans, due to his middle name being Everton. When asked if he would ever consider changing his middle name, Mark said: "No, well unfortunately my mother told me that if I change any part of my name she'll disown me, so that one's for life." He was an excellent player but in my opinion, his time at Liverpool was disappointing.

Mark was born in 1964, in Birmingham. He joined the team he supported, Aston Villa, as an apprentice in 1980, when he was sixteen. He became a professional a year later shortly after Villa had won the First Division. He made his debut in April 1982, but was not included in the squad for their victory over Bayern Munich in the European Cup final. Mark began to make regular appearances in the side during the 1982/83 season when he was still only eighteen. He played 22 league games that season and impressed as Villa finished in sixth place. He became a permanent fixture in the side during the 1983/84 season and was one of the best young players in the league with his dazzling skills and great pace. Villa was relegated in bottom place in 1986/87 and Graham Taylor joined as manager. Mark played 24 games in the second division for Villa, but it was only a matter of time before a bigger club called for his services.

He was heavily linked with his namesake, Everton, but on New Year's Eve 1987, Mark joined Rangers in Scotland. Due to English teams still being banned from Europe, the Rangers manager Graeme Souness, had been able to attract some of the best talent from England to join him and play European football at Ibrox. He made his debut in the old firm game on January 2, 1988, and received a torrent of racial abuse from some Celtic fans throwing bananas at him and making monkey noises. Some of the Celtic fans even went as far as to disgracefully turn up wearing monkey costumes. At one point the game had to be stopped so that the fruit could be removed from the pitch. Celtic condemned their supporters but the Scottish FA stayed silent. Black players were quite rare in Scottish football at the time but this behaviour was outrageous and shocking even in 1988, when racist abuse was still fairly prevalent, especially by today's standards. He received abuse at other away games in Scotland, with Mark saying that the worst came at Hearts.

Despite the abuse he received, Mark was a big success at Rangers. During his time at Ibrox, he won three consecutive league titles in 1989, 1990 and 1991, as well as two Scottish League Cups. He was one of the best players in Scotland at the time and unlucky not to be part of the England squad. He made just one appearance for the national side in June 1991, against New Zealand in Auckland.

When Graeme Souness became Liverpool manager in 1991, Mark was one of his first signings. Souness anticipated the same sort of performances in England that Mark had been displaying in Scotland for the previous three years. Sadly it didn't turn out quite that way, but he did have some highlights with Liverpool, especially in his first season 1991/92. His first goal for the Reds came in the 88th minute from the penalty spot in a 2-1 win away to Notts County. His greatest and most famous performance for Liverpool came in the second leg of the UEFA Cup second round against Auxerre. Liverpool had lost 2-0 in the first leg and needed a 3-0 win to go through. It was one of those famous European nights at Anfield and Mark was unbelievable, terrorizing the Auxerre defence all night. Liverpool scored two goals and the game was heading for extra time when Mark latched onto a beautiful through ball from Jan Molby in the 84th minute. Mark raced through and slotted the ball inside the near post in front of The Kop, and the stadium erupted in absolute chaos. Mark scored the winner against Man Utd in April 1992, but his season was to end in a personal disappointment, when he was an unused substitute in the FA Cup final victory over Sunderland.

The 1992/93 season was his most prolific as he scored thirteen goals and Liverpool finished sixth in the league. Mark scored Liverpool's first ever Premier League goal, against Sheffield Utd. He also bagged the first Premier League hat-trick for Liverpool in a 4-0 win over Coventry City. Another fine performance came against Blackburn at Anfield in December 1992, when he scored two brilliant late goals. Sadly these performances were few and far between during his time at Liverpool. At Aston Villa and Rangers, Mark was known for his step over's and other tricks and an ability to beat defenders with ease. As a Liverpool player Mark was unable to perform like this on a regular basis and he would often fade out of games. It could be argued that he didn't play consistently enough to truly find any real form at Liverpool, but when he was playing poorly it was hard to justify his selection in the team.

During the 1993/94 season, Mark lost his place in midfield to Jamie Redknapp and spent some time on loan at Stoke City. When Roy Evans became manager, Mark played even less and in 1994/95 he was loaned out again, this time to Wolves. Roy played a new system that involved three centre backs and wing backs, so Mark never fit into this. He wasn't involved in the 1995 League Cup final and didn't play a single game in 1995/96, so it was no surprise when he was let go on a free transfer in January 1996.

He joined Southampton, when the team was struggling near the bottom of the league. Mark didn't do much to impress at the club and at the end of the season he was released. Ironically he left just before his old boss, Souness, became manager of The Saints. He joined Swindon Town in July 1996 on a free transfer. He spent three years there where he was occasionally brilliant and at other times awful. In 1999, he joined Bristol Rovers in the third tier of English Football. He stayed for three seasons and his final one was spent in the third division (later renamed the second division) and he announced his retirement in April 2002, a few weeks before he turned 38.

Since retiring from football, Mark has worked extensively in youth football coaching. He works for the Aston Villa academy as head coach of the under 14's and has obtained his UEFA 'A' license. He also still plays in charity and legends games for Villa, Rangers and Liverpool.

Mark Walters was an extremely talented player who unfortunately never showed his abilities on a regular basis at Liverpool. Despite this, he has remained somewhat popular with Liverpool fans who remember the game against Auxerre. Despite working for Aston Villa, Mark still represents Liverpool in legends matches and is a proud member of the former players association, through which he often travels to Liverpool games and appears at Liverpool FC related functions.

Mark Wright

Mark Wright was an excellent defender and the Liverpool club captain when they won the F.A. Cup in 1992. He was already an established England international when he arrived at Anfield, but never made quite as much of an impact as he perhaps could have due to long-term injuries.

Mark was born in 1963 in Dorchester, near Oxford. Despite being born and raised in Southern England Mark has always had strong links to Merseyside through his father who was born and raised in Liverpool. Mark started his football career as a trainee at his local club Oxford United. He signed professional forms as a seventeen year old in 1980 but had to wait until the 1981/82 season to make his first team debut. He only played eleven games during that season but had made enough of a name for himself that First Division side Southampton signed him in March 1982.

Mark was voted the Southampton player of the year at the end of his first season during which he helped The Saints to finish in twelfth place. The following season 1983/84 was an even better one for both Southampton and Mark as he helped Southampton to finish in second place in the First Division behind the champions, Liverpool. Mark's outstanding performances during that season also earned him his first call up to the full England side during a game against Wales in May 1984. In 1985/86 Mark helped Southampton to reach the semi finals of the F.A. Cup where they were beaten 2 – 0 by Liverpool, with Ian Rush scoring both of the goals.

In 1987 Derby County paid £760,000 to take Mark to the Baseball Ground, this was a club record fee for Southampton at that time. This was Derby's first season back in the First Division and they paid big money to bring in proven quality players such as Mark and his Southampton and England colleague Peter Shilton. Mark was made the team captain in his first season and helped them to retain their First Division status with two consecutive mid table finishes. During Mark's third season they improved a lot and went on to finish in fifth spot for 1988/89.

After that good season for The Rams things began to deteriorate with behind the scenes action taking the spotlight. The chairman Robert Maxwell decided to leave and the club owed him millions of pounds. This meant that their best players would need to be sold and in the summer of 1991 Mark and Dean Saunders were both sold to Liverpool for over two million pounds each.

Despite the turmoil behind the scenes at Derby, Mark had continued to put in excellent performances which were rewarded when he was called up to the England squad for the 1990 World Cup in Italy. He was chosen to start at centre back ahead of Tony Adams who was struggling with injury. This definitely made up for Mark missing the previous World Cup in Mexico 1986 when he broke his leg just before the tournament. It was at Italia 90 when Mark scored his only goal for England. It came in a 1 – 0 victory over Egypt with a great header from a Paul Gascoigne free kick. This was a vitally important goal as England had drawn the opening two games against Ireland and Holland and needed to win to progress into the next round of the competition.

Liverpool originally tried to sign Mark after his superb performances at the 1990 World Cup. At the time Alan Hansen was coming to the end of his career and Mark was seen as being the perfect replacement for him. Mark wanted to sign for Kenny Dalglish but was persuaded by Robert Maxwell and Derby manager Arthur Cox to stay one more year with them. At the end of that year Derby were relegated and in debt so when Liverpool, and new boss Graeme Souness, came calling again Mark finally moved to Anfield for £2.2 million.

By the time Mark made his debut for Liverpool, Hansen had retired, Glenn Hysen was on his way out and Gary Gillespie was sold to Celtic. Therefore Liverpool were desperate for a quality player at centre back and Mark was seen as the perfect choice. Most people, including Souness himself, now believe that the players were changed too quickly. Mark Wright was clearly a quality signing but Julian Dicks, Neil Ruddock and Torben Piechnik never lived up to the heights that Hansen, Gillespie and Hysen had reached. Mark was injured in only his second game in a 2 – 1 defeat away to Manchester City, but he soon bounced back and became a commanding presence in the side.

When Ronnie Whelan got injured during Mark's first season, 1991/92, he was handed the captain's armband by Souness. This was one of the starting points for Souness losing the respect of a lot of the older players in the squad. The Liverpool tradition was that the captaincy would go to players who had been there the longest. The captain should have been somebody of the likes of Ian Rush, John Barnes or Steve Nicol. Just because Ronnie Whelan was injured there was no reason to strip him of the captaincy as somebody could have stepped in as vice-captain. Needless to say things were not good behind the scenes during this period.

Despite the team not playing well at this time Mark's first season at Liverpool ended with probably his proudest moment in football when he lifted the F.A. Cup at Wembley. Liverpool defeated Sunderland 2 – 0 in 1992 with goals from Michael Thomas and Ian Rush. Mark got into trouble after the game because he swore clearly and loudly as he lifted the trophy into the air. In an interview with the Liverpool FC website Mark described the moment;

"I remember getting into trouble, though, for something I said. I had to write so many letters of apology for what I said when I lifted the cup in the air! It was the Duchess of Kent who handed me the trophy and she was a lovely lady and she looked fantastic. She actually knew all of the players and all of their backgrounds. As she gave me the trophy I apologised to her for what I was about to say. [Wright swore as he lifted the trophy] She asked me what I was going to say. I got ribbed about it for years and the Duchess said to me: 'Well, you meant it didn't you!'"

Unfortunately after the F.A. Cup Final it was almost all downhill for Mark's playing career. He got a serious injury during the 1992/93 season and lost his place to Piechnik and the captaincy to Rush. When Souness was sacked in 1994 Mark fell out of favour with the new boss Roy Evans. During pre-season in the summer of 1994 Mark & Julian Dicks were both left at home and publicly criticized by Roy Evans for having attitude problems. Evans then paid big money to sign Phil Babb and John Scales and the writing looked to be on the wall for Mark. He was suffering again with a serious Achilles injury problem but as he got fit again Mark worked extremely hard and was eventually rewarded with a return to the side in March 1995 against Manchester United. Mark was awarded the man of the match that day as Liverpool won 2 – 0 and he clearly won over Roy Evans. Unfortunately it wasn't enough for him to make the squad for the 1995 League Cup Final victory over Bolton.

In the summer of 1995 John Scales was sold to Tottenham and Mark's hard work was rewarded with a regular place back in the side. He went on to play forty one games in the 1995/96 season and earned a recall to the England squad for Euro 96. In a stroke of bad

170

luck he was struck down by another injury and had to withdraw from the squad. This season was the last hurrah for Mark as a Liverpool player and he eventually had to retire in 1998 due to injury.

After his playing career ended Mark moved into a management career that has been littered with controversial and colourful moments. He began in 2000 with the Merseyside non-league side Southport. Mark left the club after just one season over a disagreement about whether the club should become professional or not. In 2001 he was back at Oxford Utd where he started his football career but this time it was as the manager. He was sacked after only a few months in December 2001. The official reason given was because the team was performing badly, however there was a far more sordid reason alleged throughout the press suggesting that he was actually sacked for racially abusing a black linesman. This was an offense he had been fined and suspended for by the F.A six months earlier.

Regardless of the dodgy headlines his departure from Oxford Utd had created, Mark soon returned to work as the manager of Chester City for the 2001/02 season. When he took over Chester City was struggling in the Conference Division but Mark did well to help them avoid relegation. The following season was a big improvement as they pushed for promotion before eventually losing a play-off semi final to Doncaster Rovers. Chester City was eventually promoted back into the Football League in 2004 by winning the Conference. Just two days before their first season back in League Two Mark resigned completely out of the blue. This time he was back in the newspapers because it was alleged he was conducting a love affair with the wife of one of his players.

His next managerial post was with Peterborough Utd in 2005 and at first everything went well. Then in January 2006 Mark was sacked and allegedly accused of making racist comments to a member of staff at the club. Mark denies this took place and took the club to court. He then went back at Chester City where he was sacked with just one game remaining of the 2006/07 season. At that point Chester City had won only three of the last twenty games. He rejoined Chester City for a third time in November 2008, unfortunately they were relegated at the end of that season and he left the club again shortly after. He has since spent time working in the media, mostly on LFCTV as well as playing regularly for the Liverpool Legends team. In August 2012 he became manager of Maltese side Floriana.

Despite the scandals that have followed Mark Wright since his departure from Liverpool, he remains a popular figure amongst fans. His terrific performances for the side during a bad period and his captaincy that led to an F.A. Cup victory resulted in him being voted at number 65 in the series '100 Players Who Shook the Kop.'

Michael Thomas

Michael Thomas is a really interesting player to talk about as he went from a villain to a hero for Reds fans within three years. I don't recall any other player who has caused so much despair and misery to Liverpool fans only to then turn it around and cause incredible happiness to the same supporters within such a short period of time.

Michael was born in 1967, in London, and he joined Arsenal as a schoolboy in 1982. He signed professional contract with The Gunners in 1984 and played in the reserves for three years. He played three games on loan at Portsmouth in 1986, before returning to make his full Arsenal debut in a League Cup semi final against their big rivals Spurs, in February 1987. He came on as a substitute in the League Cup final in which they beat Liverpool 2-1. Michael became a regular in the side in 1987/88, playing mostly at right back. Lee Dixon was signed later in the season and Michael was moved into the midfield. Michael was excellent during the 1988/89 season and got two caps for England in 1988. On the 26th May, 1989 at Anfield, he became a true hero to all Arsenal supporters and broke the hearts of Liverpool's players and supporters.

The First Division match between Liverpool and Arsenal at Anfield had been postponed, due to the Hillsborough Disaster and as a result was moved to the final game of the season. Liverpool had already won the FA Cup when the game took place and now had a chance of completing what would have been a historic second double. Arsenal had been top of the league for most of the season, but Liverpool had overtaken them a few games before the end. Coming into the match, Arsenal were on 73 points with 71 goals for and 36 against (a goal difference of +35), while Liverpool had 76 points with 65 goals for and 26 against (a difference of +39). That meant that Arsenal needed to win by at least two goals to take the title on goal difference. Liverpool had not lost by two goals at home for nearly four years, so I definitely thought that there was no way they would blow the title and they would win it for the victims of Hillsborough.

Arsenal's Alan Smith scored early in the second half, heading in a free kick to make it 1-0. Liverpool then held on and as full time approached it looked as if we had done just about enough to secure the title, by the narrowest of margins. The game went into injury time and the TV cameras went to a close-up of Steve McMahon holding up one finger and urging his exhausted teammates to make one final effort to hang on. Then, with literally seconds remaining, Michael Thomas surged forward from midfield, running onto a Smith flick-on, evaded a challenge by Steve Nicol, and chipped the advancing Bruce Grobbelaar to score Arsenal's second, and win the title. It was an unbelievable way to finish a season and heartbreaking for the Reds players and manager Kenny Dalglish, who stood there in disbelief at what had just happened.

What made this game even more memorable was the fact it was played on a Friday night. I will never forget my dad coming home from the pub that night in utter despair. He was absolutely fuming and kicking the furniture. I'm sure our living room was not the only one in Merseyside that played host to such scenes that night. In Peter Beardsley's autobiography, he speculates that part of the reason Liverpool didn't win that night was because they went into the game knowing they could lose and still win the title. The Reds had thrashed West Ham 5-1 a few nights earlier on the Tuesday, and this opened up the goal difference which may have caused the players to go into the game with a different mentality than if they had needed to get a result.

Michael had two more seasons at Arsenal and won his second League title medal in 1990/91. He then fell out with the manager George Graham early in the 1991/92 season. Michael wanted to leave England and move abroad, but George Graham refused to let him leave. Liverpool manager Graeme Souness made repeated enquiries about signing him and eventually Michael moved to Anfield in December 1991.

This caused a lot of fuss at the time due to Michael breaking the hearts of Liverpool fans just two and a half years earlier. However, he was welcomed with open arms by the club and his new teammates who were pleased that we had signed an excellent player. His first few months at Liverpool could not have gone any better. He scored an absolute blinder in front of The Kop, in the FA Cup quarter final against Aston Villa and then went on to make amends for that goal in May 1989.

At the end of Michael's first season at Anfield, we reached the FA Cup final against Sunderland, who were then in the Second Division. The score was 0-0 at half time and I will never forget my dad getting down on his knees and screaming insults at the players, especially Michael who missed a sitter early on in the game. It got to the point where my mum had to step in. It was a bit odd at the time when I was a child, but now I find it highly amusing when I think about how ridiculous it was. I think my dad still held a grudge over the 1989 goal but he was made to eat his words just two minutes into the second half when Michael went from a villain to a hero with one spectacular volley. Steve McManaman provided a cross and Michael turned and hit an incredible volley from outside the area that flew into the net. It was an amazing goal and from that moment, there was only ever going to be one winner. Michael later provided an assist in the build up to the second goal, scored by Ian Rush.

His next two seasons were an absolute nightmare as he suffered terribly with injuries. In January 1993, he snapped an Achilles tendon and was out for an entire year. When Michael returned to the side, during the second half of the 1993/94 season, he was mainly used as a squad player, coming into the side whenever Jamie Redknapp or John Barnes needed a rest.

When Roy Evans took over as manager, he changed the formation of the team for the 1994/95 season, and Michael was excellent as he began to get more games. Sadly for Michael, he was an unused substitute for the 1995 League Cup final victory over Bolton Wanderers. The 1995/96 season was by far his finest at Liverpool as he stayed injury free. Redknapp had long spells out injured and Michael formed a brilliant midfield partnership with Barnes. He was so good that season that there was even calls for him to get called up to the England side. Michael displayed incredible athleticism as a box-to-box midfielder breaking up attacks and allowing Barnes to get forward and join in the attack. Liverpool really should have won the league that season, but sadly they slipped up in crucial games near the end, thanks to David James making big mistakes, especially against Man Utd who went onto win the league. He played an important role in helping Liverpool to reach the 1996 FA Cup final against Man Utd. However, he was disappointed to find himself on the bench for the game and only getting into the action near the end when it was too late to have any influence as the Reds slumped to a 1-0 defeat.

Michael remained a regular in the side during 1996/97 but he was unable to play as well as he had done in the previous season. Jamie Redknapp returned from injury for the 1997/98 season and Michael lost his place in the side. Liverpool accepted a bid for him from Coventry City in December 1997, but the transfer fell through. In February 1998, he went out on loan to Middlesbrough. When he returned to Liverpool, Roy Evans was now playing Leonhardsen and

Danny Murphy and there was no place for Michael to get back into the team.

He rejoined Souness at Benfica in August 1998, but his time in Portugal was an unhappy one. While he enjoyed the lifestyle, living by the sea, he was miserable at the club. At the end of Michaels first season at the club, Souness was sacked and replaced by Jupp Heynckes. Michael was then banished to the reserves for his entire second season, but the club refused to allow him to break his contract and leave.

In July 2000, Michael returned to England and signed for Wimbledon. Injuries curtailed his time there and after just one season and nine games, Michael retired in May 2001. Since his retirement, Michael has continued to live in Merseyside and attends every Liverpool home game. He set up his own personal security service that guards important individuals, including presidents. He plays quite often for the Liverpool Masters team in tournaments and charity games.

Despite what happened in 1989 when he played for Arsenal, Michael Thomas was able to make amends and become popular with the Liverpool supporters. This was reflected when he was voted in at number 83 in the series '100 Players Who Shook the Kop'.

Patrik Berger

Czech midfielder Patrik 'Paddy' Berger spent seven years at Liverpool, during which he had mixed fortunes. He scored a number of goals in important games, many from long distance, and he was involved in the treble winning season of 2000/01. He was a talented player with a great left foot and it is a shame that recurring injuries often stopped him just as he was beginning to show good form.

Patrik Berger was born in November 1973, in Prague in the Czech Republic (formerly Czechoslovakia). He started his football career as a youth player with AC Sparta Praha in 1989. Two years later when he was eighteen, Patrik signed a professional contract with SK Slavia Prague. He was a regular in the side as they began to build a great young side after many years of failure in the Czech league. Patrik's performances started to earn him acclaim and he was to become a regular in the national side. One of his teammates with Slavia Prague was future Liverpool player Vladimir Smicer.

In 1995 he was signed by German Bundesliga side, Borussia Dortmund for £500,000. Patrik played just one season for them in 1995/96. It was a very successful one for the team as they won the Bundesliga Championship and the German Super Cup. Patrik hardly got to play a part however as he was used mostly as a substitute and scored four goals in twenty five appearances. The manager Ottmar Hitzfeld failed to take advantage of Patrik's attacking qualities and deployed him as a defensive midfielder. Ironically for Patrik, his previous club won the Czech First Division that same season for the first time in forty eight years and he missed out on those celebrations.

In 1996 Patrik was part of the excellent Czech Republic side at the European Championships in England, during which they were the losing finalists. I remember watching him play during this tournament in a group game between the Czech's and Italy which was played at Anfield. The Czech Republic won the game 2-1 with goals from Bejbel and the outstanding Pavel Nedved. The Czech Republic were not regarded as genuine contenders before the tournament, but this victory put them on the map. Their final game in the group was also at Anfield. It was a pulsating 3-3 draw with Russia in which Vladimir Smicer scored a last minute equaliser at his future home ground. This result meant that they finished second in the group to Germany and Italy was eliminated in what was a huge shock. In the quarter finals they defeated Portugal 1-0 with a phenomenal goal by Karel Poborsky who was making a name for himself as one of the stars of the tournament. The Czech's then defeated France in the semi finals via penalty shoot out, with Patrik scoring one of the penalties. They then faced Germany in the final who had won their own semi final over England in one of the most heartbreaking games of my life. In fact for me, the heartbreak of that loss was only truly healed in 2005 when Liverpool won a huge penalty shoot out in Istanbul. In the Euro 96 final Patrik scored another penalty but unfortunately for the Czech Republic they lost the game 2-1 with Bierhoff scoring a golden goal for the Germans in extra time.

After the tournament ended a number of the Czech Republic players were suddenly in demand from many of the top clubs in Europe. After witnessing them first hand during the group games at Anfield, Liverpool made serious approaches to both Karel Poborsky and Patrik Berger. Poborsky decided to join Man Utd instead but Patrik was signed by Roy Evans in August 1996 for £3.25 million. Patrik has since described signing for Liverpool as "the greatest day in my football life". In a 2004 interview with the Sunday Times, he talked about how when he was young, a friend's father had been to see a Liverpool game and gave him the match ticket, programme and a

Liverpool scarf. He said he still kept those items that were part of some of his proudest possessions.

Patrik made an explosive start to his Liverpool career by scoring five goals in four games. He made his debut as a substitute in a 2-1 win at home to Southampton. He was a substitute again in his second game against Leicester City. This time Patrik came off the bench to score two great goals in a 3-0 victory for The Reds. In one of the most predictable football headlines ever, the following days tabloid newspapers all carried various versions of the phrase 'Berger King' after this performance. Patrik certainly seemed to live up to this billing the following weekend when he bagged another two goals as we thrashed Chelsea. He then grabbed another goal in a European Cup Winners Cup victory over Finnish side MyPa. These performances earned Patrik the player of the month award for September.

Roy Evans then began using Patrik as a striker alongside Robbie Fowler. However this was never his best position and he struggled to maintain the scoring ratio from his first month at the club. This also unsettled Stan Collymore who had previously been in a successful partnership with Fowler, and was one of the factors in Stan eventually departing. Patrik then got injured and never regained his starting place for the remainder of the season.

He started the 1997/98 season well and scored a hat-trick in a 5-1 win against Chelsea. These were to be his only goals of the season as he had a poor second season at Anfield. He played mostly as a substitute which eventually led to a public falling out with Roy Evans. Roy accused Patrik of having the wrong attitude not being a team player. Patrik countered by saying there was no discipline at the club and training was awful because he knew no matter how hard he worked he wouldn't be picked. He said in an interview with the Sunday Mirror that when he asked Roy why he wasn't being picked, he was told "you don't play very well".

It looked certain that he would be leaving the club in the summer of 1998 and his agent had a contract from Italian side Roma waiting for Patrik to sign. Liverpool's chief executive Peter Robinson convinced Patrik to hold on and wait. Then Gerard Houllier arrived as joint manager and everything changed for Patrik. Houllier immediately convinced Patrik that he had a future at Anfield and backed this up by putting him in the starting eleven in a role just behind the strikers. He flourished in this role and after two quiet games he then went on a run of scoring four goals in the next five games. After Roy Evans departed when the partnership with Houllier collapsed, Patrik finally felt settled at Liverpool.

He had a slow start to the 1999/2000 season but he showed probably his best form during the second half of the season. He scored some of the most spectacular Liverpool goals of that period against Wimbledon, Leeds Utd, Man Utd and Tottenham Hotspur. Patrik has since described the goal against Leeds Utd as his best ever for Liverpool. I clearly remember the spectacular free kick against Man Utd because I watched that game in a pub in St Helens that was frequented by mostly Man Utd fans. I'll never forget me and my mate Pat falling backwards off our chairs in celebration as threats of violence lingered all around us.

Patrik missed the majority of the amazing treble winning season of 2000/01 through a serious knee injury. In November 2000 he badly twisted his knee in a 4-3 defeat away at Leeds Utd. This was the beginning of the end for Patrik's Liverpool career as he remained dogged by injuries from that moment on. He received surgery in Colorado, America and was out for the next five months, returning to the team in March 2001. Patrik was able to play a part in both the

F.A Cup and UEFA Cup finals at the end of that incredible season. No Liverpool fan will ever forget his pass to Michael Owen that led to that incredible winner in the F.A Cup final against Arsenal. The celebrations for that goal remain the wildest I've ever been a part of and the only time I've ever become temporarily insane in my life! This proved to be the last great moment for Patrik as a Liverpool player despite remaining at the club for a further two seasons.

The next two seasons, 2001/02 and 2002/03 were pretty much disasters for Patrik as he missed most of them through a series of recurring injuries. Patrik didn't start a single game during the 2002/03 season and only appeared on the bench four times. At the end of that season his contract expired and although he was offered a new one, he decided to leave the club as his chances in the first team were limited. In the summer of 2003 he joined Premiership new boys Portsmouth on a free transfer.

He had a great start with Pompey, scoring the winning goal on his debut in a 2-1 victory over Aston Villa. He went on to score the winner against Liverpool in October 2003. Fortunately Liverpool got revenge at Anfield when Didi Hamman scored the goal of the season. In February 2004 Patrik re-injured his knee which required surgery and he missed the remainder of the season. During the following season 2004/05 he showed signs of a return to form and scored one of the Premierships greatest goals in a 2-1 defeat to Charlton Athletic. Despite playing well in his second season for Portsmouth, Patrik was released on a free transfer in the summer of 2005.

Patrik then joined Aston Villa on a two year contract. These two years were hampered by injury with Patrik only making nine league appearances. After a rumoured falling out with manager Martin O'Neill, he was loaned out to Stoke City after complaining about playing in the reserves to regain fitness. This seemed to revitalise him and he came back to score goals again at the tail end of the 2006/07 season. Thanks to his performances in the last two months of the season Patrik was offered a one year contract extension. At the end of the 2007/08 season the Villa manager Martin O'Neill stated that Patrik will never play for the club again after newspaper reports claimed that he had urged the club captain, Gareth Barry, to join Liverpool in order to further his career.

Patrik joined his boyhood club Sparta Prague in May 2008 where he spent two seasons before retiring in 2010 due to knee ligament damage.

Despite his last few years at Liverpool being tainted by injuries, Patrik Berger remains a popular figure amongst Liverpool fans. His commitment on the field and spectacular goals in important games will always leave fond memories in the hearts and minds of Reds supporters. Patrik is one of those players that gets the YouTube highlight treatment due to the fact that he never scored tap-ins, only spectacular goals. He was voted in at number 79 in the series '100 Players Who Shook the Kop'.

Robbie Fowler

Robbie Fowler is the finest and most natural striker I have ever seen play the game. I'm not just talking about the finest striker I have seen for Liverpool, I mean for any team. In his first four seasons at Anfield, his 'Golden Period', he was simply breathtaking. Had he not suffered with injuries and an unfortunate falling out with Gerard Houllier, it is probable that he would have been the player to come closest to Ian Rush's incredible record as Liverpool's greatest goal-scorer. Apart from being such an explosive goal-scorer, Robbie is also a local lad and a proper down to earth 'scally' type of character. With all of these attributes going for him, it is no wonder that he is in the top five most popular players ever to wear the famous red shirt.

I still vividly remember the buzz and excitement when he exploded onto the scene back in September 1993. He scored on his debut against Fulham in the League Cup and then followed it up two weeks later with five goals in the second leg. In only his fifth first team game he smashed his first league hat-trick against Southampton and went on to score twelve goals in his first thirteen games. He finished his first season at Liverpool as the clubs top scorer with eighteen goals. Amazing fairytale stuff when you consider that Ian Rush was still a presence and Robbie was still a teenager.

There have been a number of young players in recent years who have had plenty of hype and had high profiles; Wayne Rooney and Michael Owen are probably the two most notable. However nobody has even come close to matching what Robbie Fowler achieved in his first four seasons at Liverpool.

After a terrific first season he went on to score over thirty goals in each of his next three seasons. Within three years he had scored his first one hundred goals, with the hundredth coming in a game against Middlesbrough when he scored four. During these seasons he scored some very memorable goals that really stand out in my memory as I'm sure they do for you as well.

There was the famous four minute hat-trick against Arsenal at Anfield in 1994. I remember another great game against Aston Villa in March 1996. This was another one where he scored pretty quickly at the start of the game. We were 3-0 up after just eight minutes thanks to two goals from Robbie and one from Steve McManaman. One of the goals is pretty famous, it's the one where he nutmegged Steve Staunton with a back heel before smashing it in the top corner in front of the Kop. That game was on Sky on a Sunday afternoon and I had stupidly booked a driving lesson at the same time as the game. Fortunately my instructor was fifteen minutes late so I didn't miss the Fowler blitz! When I told my driving instructor, who was an Evertonian, what had just happened, he had to come into the house and see the score with his own eyes!

I think my favourite Fowler goals during his early days, are the two stunners he scored against Man Utd at Old Trafford in 1995. It was early in the season so Robbie still had the blonde hair from a summer holiday prank. Both goals were absolutely awesome and he beat Peter Schmeichel (the best goalie in the world at that time) from ridiculous angles. Unfortunately for Robbie this game was Eric Cantona's comeback game after his eight month suspension for the scissor kick into the crowd. Cantona scored with a late penalty to make it 2 - 2 and it was the Frenchman who dominated the headlines afterwards so the two pearlers from Fowler never got the attention they deserved.

It's not just amazing goals that made Robbie Fowler so popular with the fans. It was also his propensity to be involved in controversial and often hilarious incidents. Probably the most famous of these would be the goal-line sniffing incident against Everton in 1999 after he'd scored his second goal of the game. This was in reference to the cocaine rumours that were extremely prevalent on Merseyside for many years, mostly spread by Everton fans. I wish I had a pound for every person in the late nineties I met who claimed to know somebody, usually a taxi driver or a relative, who had sworn they'd seen Fowler sneaking into the cubicles in nightclub bathrooms with mysterious white powder. I never really believed it was true (despite convincing arguments thrown at me) but the talk was so strong it really did cause a lot of hurt for Robbie and his family.

Houllier said after the Everton game that Robbie did it as a tribute to Rigobert Song who brought a grass eating celebration from Cameroon. Houllier was laughed out of the press conference (while he himself was deadly serious) and in the papers the next day he was made into a joke. Houllier never forgave Fowler and in Robbie's autobiography he says he's been told that this was the moment Houllier considered him to be finished at Liverpool.

Other notable incidents include the moment he showed his backside to Graeme Le Saux of Chelsea just one week after the goal-line moment. There was history with Le Saux and Liverpool stemming from the previous season when he had a punch up in the Anfield tunnel with Paul Ince. Le Saux had given Robbie a few nasty elbows and as retaliation he began making suggestive comments about Le Saux's sexuality. After Le Saux had complained, Fowler then bent over in a suggestive manner towards him as he went for a throw in and he was booked. Afterwards Robbie was charged by the F.A for the Everton and Chelsea incidents at the same time and received a six game ban and a £32,000 fine.

In 1997 after he had scored a goal in front of the Kop against S.K Brann in the Cup Winners Cup, Robbie celebrated by lifting his shirt to reveal a T-shirt showing support for the striking Liverpool dockers. It's since been revealed the Fowler and Steve McManaman both contributed funds to the families of the dockers. Many of those dockers and their families were regulars at Anfield and it was this type of support from Robbie that made him an idol to the supporters. Amazingly he actually received a fine from UEFA for his actions in revealing the Dockers T-shirt.

Ironically that year, he also won a UEFA Fair Play award for admitting that he had not been fouled by David Seaman against Arsenal after a penalty had been given. After unsuccessfully trying to convince the referee to change his decision about the penalty Fowler took it tamely and Seaman saved, the ball rebounded however and Jason McAteer tucked it home.

Robbie made his England debut under Terry Venables in 1996. He went on to play twenty six times for England scoring seven goals. One of his finest performances at international level came in 2001 during a World Cup qualifier in Greece. He played superbly and scored in a fine victory. I remember being in Greece at the time of this game, which gave it an added level of enjoyment as I watched it in a Greek bar. His final appearance for England came as a second half substitute in the victory over Denmark during the 2002 World Cup finals.

After Gerard Houllier took charge of Liverpool, Robbie's career went downhill. He had a knee ligament injury in 1998 that kept him out for the majority of the year. While he was out injured Michael Owen came to prominence and was showing signs of being the 'new

Fowler' after a memorable World cup and a hatful of goals for The Reds. Houllier liked to play a counter attacking style that involved playing a lone striker with bags of pace. Sadly after he came back from his serious injury, Robbie had lost some of his pace and Houllier preferred to go with Owen and later Emile Heskey who were both a lot faster than him. In both Fowler's and Owen's autobiographies they reveal that Houllier told them they were both competing to partner Heskey who was the main man in Houllier's opinion. Can you believe that? Houllier made some farcical decisions at times (substituting Hamman against Leverkusen) and regularly preferring the hard working but limited Heskey over two of our greatest ever strikers is just absurd.

Despite not getting along with Houllier, he was the team captain during the 2000/01 season while the club captain Jamie Redknapp was out injured for the entire season. This was the year we won the treble and it was definitely Fowler's most successful under Houllier. Robbie scored in two of the finals. He scored a belter in the League Cup Final against Birmingham City. The commentary is memorable for that one by Clive Tyldesley: "Fowler's hit, Fowlers goal". We won the game on penalties and Robbie became the first Liverpool captain to lift a trophy since 1995. He was a substitute during the 2001 F.A Cup Final against Arsenal. This was the Owen show however with his two late goals to steal the cup from Arsenal who had dominated the first eighty minutes. Robbie almost added a third right the end when he went one on one with Seaman.

He was also a substitute for the UEFA Cup Final against Deportivo Alaves in Dortmund but this time he came on and scored a cracker to make it 4 – 3. That was one of my favourite moments ever in football. I stood in the pub screaming "Fowler, Fowler, Fowler" for about thirty seconds, as my dad and other fellas came bursting out of the gents with pee on their pants after hearing the roars from the rest of the pub. Liverpool went on to win the trophy with a 5-4 scoreline after a golden goal in extra time. It was great to see Robbie lift another trophy that season, along with vice captain Sami Hyypia.

The start of the 2001/02 season was littered with controversy and fights between Robbie and Houllier and Phil Thompson. It started badly at the Charity Shield when we beat Man Utd. The week before the game the players were practising penalties at Melwood. Phil Thompson was retrieving balls from the goal net when Robbie blasted one that just missed Thommo's nose by inches. Thompson went berserk and laid into Robbie with his trademark foul language and temper. Houllier informed Robbie that he was dropped for the Charity Shield and wouldn't play again until he apologised for the penalty incident. Robbie travelled to Cardiff with the rest of the team but ended up leaving before the end and making his own way home.

There was still time however for one more magic moment from The Growler when he scored a hat-trick away at Leicester City in his final full game for Liverpool. Just one month later he was sold to Leeds Utd for £11 million in November 2002. He stayed there for one and a half seasons. Injuries blighted his time at Leeds but he still managed to score fifteen goals in thirty one appearances. After Leeds Utd started selling off their big names due to debt, Robbie moved on to Man City where he once again struggled with injury and never really regained the form he showed at Anfield. Notable moments during his time at Man City included scoring against Liverpool and celebrating a goal at Goodison Park by smacking his head in celebration as a taunt to Everton fans over the old 'smackhead' rumours. He also scored in a victory over Man Utd in one of his final games for the club. He celebrated the goal by flashing the five finger wave at the Man Utd fans, in reference to Liverpool's five European Cups. His worst moment with Man City came at the end of the 2004/05 season when he missed a last minute penalty that prevented them from qualifying for the UEFA Cup.

In January 2006 I had moved to Vancouver, Canada. I was at work one day when a text message came from my dad. That was the best text message I have ever received and I still have it on my phone today. The message reads: "Fowler has signed 4 Reds on a free till end of season! How gr8 is that finally a proven goal scorer!" I had no idea at the time that he was even rumoured to be coming back so this text took me completely by surprise. As soon as I read it, I rubbed my eyes and looked at it again. I then jumped out of my chair and began doing a weird form of Irish jig through my workplace in jubilation. When I got home and was able to check on the internet for confirmation, I don't think I stopped smiling for weeks!

He scored an overhead kick in front of the Kop on his first game back but unfortunately it was offside. He had another goal against Charlton ruled out for offside a few weeks later, although that one was a bad decision. He finally got his return goal, ironically against Fulham, and then he was flying for the rest of the season. He scored goals against, Blackburn, Bolton and Portsmouth, showing that his eye for goal was still there. The goal against Bolton on his birthday took him past Kenny Dalglish in the all time goal records at Liverpool. During his second coming, Robbie seemed to be playing with a passion and fitness not displayed in years and all of this was enough for Rafa to offer him a one year contract for 2006/07.

With the purchase of Craig Bellamy and Dirk Kuyt in what was to be Robbie's final season at Anfield, he didn't play very often. When he did play, he certainly made a terrific contribution to the team by scoring seven goals in a handful of appearances. That's only two less than Bellamy who played a considerable amount more games than Robbie. At the end of the season we reached the Champions League final for a rematch with AC Milan. I truly hoped that he would come off the bench to score the winning goal in his final game.

Unfortunately it wasn't to be and Robbie was left out of the squad for the game. He had to be content with a finale at Anfield the week before when he was named as team captain for the final league game against Charlton. In a cruel twist of fate he was denied a final goal in front of the Kop. He was substituted with minutes remaining and almost as soon as he sat down Liverpool was awarded a penalty, which was duly scored by Harry Kewell.

When his contract wasn't renewed at the end of the season, there was lots of speculation as to where he would go next. Talk of an offer to play in Dubai was really strong as well as rumours about offers from teams in Australia and America. In the end Robbie chose to play on a pay as you play basis with Cardiff City in The Championship. Unfortunately the majority of his season there was disrupted by injury and he missed a number of months after having hip surgery in America. Cardiff made the F.A Cup Final that season but unluckily Robbie wasn't fit in time to play in the game and was denied a final hurrah at Wembley.

He spent the latter part of 2008 at Ewood Park with Blackburn Rovers after Paul Ince brought him in to help out the squad at the start of the 2008/09 season. Ince has since been sacked and in December Robbie was released by the club. Robbie then spent two happy years in Australia playing for North Queensland Fury and then Perth Glory. In 2011 he signed a one year contract with Muangthong Utd in Thailand. During the season he also became player manager. During this time he scored his 250th club goal before leaving in February 2012. He spent some time training with Blackpool and almost signed a short term contract with them, but declined their offer of £100 per week, with £5000 for every appearance in the first team. Robbie announced his retirement from playing in September 2012 and has since been taking his coaching badges. He also appears regularly as an ambassador for Liverpool FC.

I have so many great memories of Robbie Fowler and watching Liverpool games have never been quite the same for me since he left the club. In his final season at Anfield, 2006/07, we didn't see as much of The Growler as I'd have liked but even when he was on the bench it was still exciting because it was still possible for him to come on and score. Robbie is one of Liverpool's all time great goal-scorers with 171 goals in his Liverpool career. Robbie was voted in at number four in the series '100 Players Who Shook the Kop'.

Whatever you like to call him, The Toxteth Terror, The Growler or simply God, I prefer to use two words to describe Robbie Fowler – My Hero.

Stan Collymore

Stan Collymore divides opinion among Liverpool supporters, but he gets no complaints from me. He scored thirty five goals in eighty one appearances over two years and he also set up a massive amount of goals for others too. In the two full seasons he was with us his strike partnership with Robbie Fowler was incredibly prolific. They scored over one hundred goals between the two of them during the 1995/96 and 1996/97 seasons.

Stan was born in 1971, in Staffordshire. He started his football career as an apprentice at Walsall and Wolverhampton Wanderers. After being released by Wolves in 1990, Stan signed for Stafford Rangers in the Conference. He gained a reputation for scoring spectacular goals and was signed by Crystal Palace. He didn't play very often for Palace who had Mark Bright and Ian Wright up front, so in 1992 he dropped down a division to join Southend Utd. He scored eighteen goals in 1992/93, which helped them to avoid relegation. In 1993 he joined Nottingham Forest.

Stan became a hot property in the mid nineties thanks to a stunning goal scoring record for Forest of fifty goals in seventy one appearances. His goals were a massive reason why they gained promotion to the Premier League in 1994. He then he scored twenty two league goals in the 94/95 season, helping Forest to finish third in the league.

He was signed by Roy Evans in the summer of 1995 for what was then a British record of 8.5 million pounds. I remember vividly when we signed Stan, we had actually been in a battle with Everton for his signature, and in the end Roy had to pay what seemed a ridiculous amount at the time. I was on a family day out to a theme park the day he signed and I will never forget the moment I heard the news while driving out of the car park. It was the lead story on the radio in the car journey home back to Liverpool and I still recall me and my dad whooping with joy. We were both convinced that this would be the signing that would take the club back at the top of the league. This feeling was only heightened after Stan's debut at Anfield, when he scored an absolute screamer against Sheffield Wednesday. Frustratingly, he got injured in the next game, but when he came back a few games later he scored an even better long range goal against Blackburn Rovers, who were the previous season's league champions

Annoyingly around the same time, we found out about his character as a person too. After he was dropped for Ian Rush, Stan gave an interview to a football magazine in which he criticized Roy Evans, the club and the Liverpool backroom staff. This was a massive story at the time and dominated the back pages of the newspapers for about a week. To be honest, at the time I was so angry, I really thought we should have gotten rid of him there and then.

Fortunately, he was able to move forward from then on after settling his differences with Roy, and ended up scoring quite prolifically for the rest of the season. Between January and May 1996, he banged in fifteen goals and over the course of the season, Stan and Robbie Fowler scored fifty five goals as a partnership. His best moment, as a Liverpool player, came in the 4-3 win against Newcastle, when he scored two goals, including the injury time winner in front of the Kop. I'll never forget watching that game in the spare room of my mum and dad's house on a Monday night. It was an amazing game and fully deserved its title of 'match of the decade'. He played in the 1996 FA Cup final defeat to Man Utd, but had a poor game before being substituted for Ian Rush.

Unfortunately, Stan's second season at Liverpool wasn't quite as successful as his first, although his partnership with Fowler still yielded forty seven goals. It was obvious he wasn't settling in, the fact that he continued to live in Cannock in the Midlands was a major reason for this. Stan refused to move closer to Liverpool, despite pleas to do so from Roy Evans. He chose to commute every day, leaving straight after training instead of forging a bond with his team-mates. He was also known for being quite moody too, especially if things weren't going his way. We now know that he was suffering with depression, but back then this wasn't public information and he just had a reputation for being difficult. He would sometimes go missing in away games and I know a lot of players found it difficult to get along with him. Robbie Fowler and Jamie Carragher talk more about this in their autobiographies. Carragher described witnessing Stan disrespecting Ronnie Moran, which was bang out of order.

Once Michael Owen was ready for the first team, Stan was sold to the club he supported as a child, Aston Villa, for seven million pounds. Despite his reputation off the pitch, he was actually quite a popular player on the Kop. At the end of what turned out to be his final game for Liverpool he went over to salute the fans in the Kop and he threw his boots into the crowd. My Uncle Marty caught one of the boots, which he still cherishes as a fantastic souvenir.

The story of how Marty caught the boot is one I always enjoy hearing. After the last game of the season, the team did its usual lap of honour and Stan came down to the Kop still wearing his boots. Marty was standing on one of the safety bars shouting to him to throw his boots to him. Stan then took one off and threw it directly to him, and as Marty was standing on the safety bar no one else could get it. He shoved it under his top and then shouted to Stan to throw him the other one but he threw that further down the line into another part of the crowd.

After leaving Liverpool, Stan's career went slowly downhill. After three years and only fifteen goals for Aston Villa, he ended up having short stints at Leicester, Bradford and finally Real Oviedo in Spain. His spells at these final three clubs all followed a very similar pattern. He would start explosively (a goal from an overhead kick in his debut for Bradford stands out) and then would get involved in some sort of fight with management, before leaving in controversial circumstances. He left Oviedo after playing just three games and announced his retirement from football in 2001, at the age of just thirty.

At one point it looked like Stan seemed destined to be remembered for his off the field tabloid antics, rather than for anything he did on the pitch. He gained a terrible reputation for things such as assaulting Ulrika Jonsson and admitting to dogging. This was a shame, because Stan was a very gifted player who had a natural instinct for scoring goals. If he could have just curbed his temperament he could have been one of the greats. Fortunately in recent years, Stan has really turned things around and gained a lot of respect for his work in all aspects of the media. He also raises money and awareness for charities related to clinical depression. He hosts a popular phone in show, on the radio for talkSPORT, where he is never short of an opinion.

Stan Collymore is still well regarded by many Liverpool fans, who voted him in at number 77 in the series '100 Players Who Shook the Kop'.

Steve McManaman

Steve McManaman was one of the best and most exciting wingers ever to wear the red shirt. There are so many fond memories of him bursting down the wings and beating players and scoring great goals. He was an exceptional dribbler of the ball. A great example of this can be found in the classic goal he scored against Celtic in the UEFA Cup when he carried the ball almost seventy five yards before unleashing a great shot which flew past the keeper. In my opinion, we haven't had a player of his quality or consistency on the wings ever since he left the club in 1999.

Steve was born in February 1972 and raised in my own neck of the woods, Kirkdale, a small area of Merseyside that borders Bootle and Walton. Like many famous Liverpool players, Steve grew up as a boyhood Evertonian. However, despite his loyalty to the Blue half of Merseyside, Steve joined the Reds as an apprentice when he left school in 1988. As an apprentice he was responsible for cleaning John Barnes boots. Digger's magic must have rubbed off somehow on young Steve and he rose rapidly through the ranks at Anfield. Kenny Dalglish signed him to a professional contract in February 1990 and by the end of the year he had made his first team debut (on my 13th birthday) as a substitute against Sheffield United in December 1990.

Steve made his full debut under new manager Graeme Souness in the opening game of the 1991/92 season against Oldham Athletic. Just four days later he scored his first goal for Liverpool, which was a great diving header in 2-1 defeat to Man City. Despite the team having a poor season in the league, Steve had a great one personally. He was one of the standout players in his first full season playing fifty one games and scoring ten goals. Steve played an important role in the run to the 1992 FA Cup Final, especially with his extra time winner in the fifth round against Ipswich Town. He crowned his season with a man of the match performance in the FA Cup final. He set up a great goal for Michael Thomas as the Reds beat Sunderland 2-0 to lift the famous trophy.

He scored seven goals during the 1992/93 season and was once again a star player in the side. Along with Robbie Fowler he started to get a lot of publicity as one of the young superstars in the newly named Premier League. Despite Steve's performances gaining rave reviews, Liverpool had an awful season domestically and finished in a lowly sixth position, below teams like QPR and Norwich City and twenty five points behind champions Man Utd.

The following season, 1993/94, was even worse for Liverpool as they finished in eighth position behind such giants of the game as Wimbledon. After starting the season well with two goals against Swindon Town, Steve's form went downhill and he didn't score any more goals. He had a well publicized fight with Bruce Grobbelaar in September 1993 during the Merseyside derby. After Steve had made a poor clearance leading to an Everton goal, the two players actually came to blows with Bruce grabbing Steve by the throat. Liverpool's poor form that season eventually led to Graeme Souness departing the club in January 1994, after a defeat to Bristol City in the FA Cup.

New Liverpool manager Roy Evans stated that Macca needed to start scoring more goals and offered him a freer role in the side. Steve responded well to this and now that he was no longer tied to the wings he was able to hurt teams much easier. In the opening game of the 1994/95 season and after almost one full year (363 days to be exact) without a goal he notched two in a 6-1 win over Crystal Palace. In October he made his one hundredth league appearance in a 4-1 win over Sheffield Wednesday. He celebrated reaching this milestone by scoring his first hat-trick, unfortunately one of his goals was later credited as an own goal. He was rewarded for this great form with a four year contract worth one million pounds from Liverpool. He also received his first England cap as a substitute in a friendly with Nigeria in November 1994. In a repeat from his debut season the highlight of 1994/95 for Steve' and the club, came with a man of the match performance at Wembley. This time it came in the League Cup final in which Steve scored two outstanding solo goals in a 2-1 victory over Bolton Wanderers.

The 1995/96 season was probably Steve's finest for Liverpool as they continued to improve under Roy Evans. The side played with a great attacking flair spearheaded by talented young players like Steve, Robbie Fowler and Jamie Redknapp, along with older veterans like John Barnes playing solidly. We finished the season clearly in third place and qualified for the UEFA Cup. The season ended badly for the Reds with a defeat to Man Utd in the FA Cup Final in an atrocious game. What made the defeat especially sickening at the time was that in the process our rivals down the East Lancs became the first English side to win a second League and Cup double.

During this season Steve also made his first start for England against Columbia in September 1995. This game is most memorable for the scorpion kick save from the outrageous Rene Higuita, after a cross from Jamie Redknapp. Steve then became a regular in Terry Venables England team and took his form from the previous season into the 1996 European Championships in England. He was one of the best players in a great side that reached the semi-finals of the tournament before the routine penalty shoot-out defeat to Germany. After this tournament Steve was never able to carry his Liverpool form onto the international stage on a regular basis which drew parallels with the man whose boots he once cleaned, John Barnes.

In the mid nineties a group of Liverpool players became dubbed as the Spice Boys by the Daily Mail. This was referring to the fact that Liverpool had a group of good looking young players who enjoyed a night out and hung out with celebrities. It is a derogatory term that was picked up by a large section of the media and unfortunately the team of the 1995 to 1997 era is often referred to with the name. However what the nickname does not refer to is the fact that Liverpool played some of the best and most exciting football I have ever seen. The players linked with the nickname included Jamie, Robbie Fowler and Steve who were three of the finest players to grace English football in the Premier League era. One of the things that still gets brought up in jest is the cream Armani suits that the team wore before the 1996 FA Cup final against Man Utd. While nobody is denying the suits looked a bit silly, it is a shame that this image has been used to define a team criticized as having more style than substance. While it is true that Liverpool possibly under achieved during the Roy Evans era, we did come close to winning the Premier League and reached two cup finals, winning one.

Liverpool were fantastic for most of the 1996/97 season and came close to winning the league. The Reds led the table for most of the season until they were overtaken by Man Utd in February. We were unable to knock them off the top after that and collapsed completely in the last few games. We lost to Man Utd after mistakes by David James and after that game it looked like the title challenge was over. Steve was the man of the match in the 4-3 victory over Newcastle Utd who were also challenging. The classic match was later voted as the 'game of the decade'. This game was quite typical of Liverpool's form during this period as we were amazing going forward but often quite suspect at the back. We conceded way too many goals and this was a major reason why we didn't win the league title. Just days after the victory over Newcastle we lost to Coventry City and then won only two of the last seven games. We finished the season in fourth spot, level on points with Newcastle and Arsenal but trailing them in goal difference.

Steve was excellent again in that season, although he started to find life a bit more difficult as teams tried to stifle him by man marking him for entire games. He was often criticized during this period for not scoring enough goals. However, his lack of goals were never a big problem for Steve as he regularly led the assists charts. It is doubtful that his best mate Robbie Fowler, or later on Michael Owen, would have been so prolific had Steve not been in the side to create so many chances. Steve currently holds the record at Liverpool for most ever assists, although Steven Gerrard is getting close to breaking that record. He is also ranked second in the all time league records for the most assists based on a goals to games ratio.

For the 1997/98 season, Steve was named as vice-captain to Paul Ince, brought in to replace the outgoing captain John Barnes who moved to Newcastle. Steve scored some spectacular goals during the season including the one against Celtic and a stunning volley against Arsenal in December 1997. Liverpool finished the season in third place behind Man Utd and the champions Arsenal.

The back-story to the 1997/98 season was that Liverpool tried to sell Steve to Barcelona for twelve million pounds. He had been the subject of bids from most of the top clubs in Europe and eventually the Liverpool chairman David Moores decided to accept a bid from Barcelona. Negotiations with Steve over a new contract at Liverpool were not going well and because he only had two years left to run on his contract, Liverpool decided that they needed to get as much money as possible for him before his value would drop. Steve flew over to Spain to enter into negotiations but the deal collapsed under circumstances that have never been fully explained. Barcelona claimed that the deal collapsed due to Steve's excessive wage demands, but it was claimed by Steve that Barcelona were using the situation as a decoy while they finalized a deal to sign Rivaldo. Apparently Steve had never wanted to leave Liverpool at that time but the fact that we were prepared to sell him without any prior warning set the seeds for him to think about a career elsewhere.

In the summer of 1998, Steve agreed a deal with David Moores on a new contract and was then told that the board needed to sanction it first. The board turned it down as they were concerned that it could lead to other players demanding high wages in their future contract negotiations. After what was deemed to be a slap in the face by the board taking away a deal that he had already agreed, Steve felt that he had no other option than to leave the club. Steve wanted to test himself at the top level and at the time this meant playing in the Champions League. With his relationship with the Liverpool board as good as finished, Steve flew over to Spain in January 1999 and signed a pre-contract with Real Madrid. This was a highly publicized situation and many Liverpool fans were angered at the sight of Steve posing in a Real Madrid scarf while he still had five months left as a Liverpool player. What made the situation even harder to handle was that Steve would be leaving on a Bosman style free transfer. Due to the fact there was no transfer fee, Steve was able to negotiate a large wage from Real Madrid and was described by the BBC as the highest paid English footballer of all time. This incensed the Liverpool supporters further and Steve was then labelled as a Judas only interested in how much money he could get. It appeared at the time that he had turned down Barcelona only to run down his contract to get himself a position to make more money from another club. To be fair to him though, he was messed about by Liverpool, especially when he agreed a contract and then had it taken away from him, and it would be hard for anybody to turn down the chance to play for Real Madrid and be paid ridiculous amounts of money.

When Steve turned in mixed performances for the team in his final few months at Liverpool the fans began to turn against him. This appeared even worse when the team was doing badly and he was an easy scapegoat for the lack of focus at times. Liverpool eventually finished the 1998/99 season in seventh place, which was their worst finish for five years. I don't believe however that he simply stopped trying but his form was affected by niggling injuries, tiredness and constantly being used as a substitute by the new manager Gerard Houllier. What was also not widely known at the time was that Steve's mother was extremely ill and she actually passed away just thirty six hours after his final game for Liverpool. The form of Liverpool as a whole cannot be blamed on Steve signing with Real Madrid and a lot of the blame has to fall on the ridiculous idea to start the season with Roy Evans and Gerard Houllier as co-managers. This was a situation that couldn't possibly have worked and clearly derailed the team from the very beginning of the season.

In one of his last games for Liverpool he scored the winning goal against Tottenham after we had trailed 2-0. Despite the bad feelings towards him in Liverpool, Steve managed to end his Anfield career on a high. In the final game of the season he played a blinder against Wimbledon in a 3-0 victory. In his final act in a Liverpool shirt, Steve made one of his trademark runs down the wing and set up Karl-Heinze Riedle to score in front of the Kop. All the bad feelings were temporarily forgotten as Steve left the pitch for the last time to a standing ovation.

Steve did well at first with Real Madrid. He set up Morientes for an injury time winner on his debut against Mallorca. In his second game he scored his first goal in a 4-1 victory over Numancia. He was in and out of the side during his first season with Real Madrid but was popular with the supporters as he played really well whenever he got the chance. His debut season ended in his finest moment as a player when he was (for the third time in a major final) the man of the match in the Champions League Final. He capped off the performance by scoring a spectacular volley in the 3-0 victory over fellow Spanish side Valencia.

In the summer of 2000 there was a new president at the club, Florentino Perez, and in a controversial move he bought Luis Figo from Barcelona in a then world record transfer. Fernando Redondo, who had been Real Madrid's best player in the previous season, was sold and Steve was offered to other clubs for twelve million pounds. Liverpool manager Gerard Houllier turned them down and Steve rejected moves to Middlesbrough and Chelsea. Steve didn't feature in the side for the early part of the 2000/01 season and there were rumours that he hadn't even been given a squad number. However, he was eventually able to win over the manager Del Bosque and from October onwards he featured in almost every game. He was one of the best players in the side as Real Madrid won the La Liga title.

In his third season at Real Madrid, Steve began to see his playing time reduced as he became a victim of the Galactico system. This was where Perez started bringing in superstars like Zidane and Ronaldo and Steve found himself getting lower and lower in the pecking order. He turned down the chance to join Inter Milan as part of the Ronaldo deal and was determined to stay at Real Madrid and fight for his place in the team. This attitude won him the respect of the rest of the squad and he was regularly backed up publicly by Figo, Zidane, Raul and Ronaldo. Steve was popular with the fans in Madrid and was twice voted as their player of the year. His determination to fight for his place was rewarded in April 2002 in the first leg of the Champions League semi final against Barcelona at the Nou Camp. He came off the bench to score an incredible goal lobbing the keeper in injury time to secure a 2-0 victory and a second away goal. This victory helped Real Madrid to reach the Champions League Final against German side Bayer Leverkusen, who had knocked out Liverpool and Man Utd in the quarters and semi final respectively. Steve came off the bench to earn his second Champions League winners medal after the 2-1 victory.

Steve made only 15 appearances in La Liga during the 2002/03 season. He has described this period as the 'Disneyfication' of Real Madrid as the club seemed more focused on marketing the images of their superstar players than actually playing football. This meant that players were often picked because of their marketing value rather than their form. When David Beckham was signed in the summer of 2003 enough was enough and Steve decided that as he was now even lower in the pecking order it was time to leave.

He was linked with Arsenal and Everton before joining his mate Robbie Fowler at Man City. His time at Man City was a disappointment as he was often injured and his preferred position was taken by Shaun Wright-Phillips. Steve was unable to show the pace and form of previous years and whenever he played he just appeared to hang around in central midfield playing simple passes. The most exciting moment for him in his time at Man City came off the field. This was when Steve and Robbie Fowler were caught up in a sleazy sex scandal where they were accused of having a threesome with a woman after a night out in late 2003. The story that broke was that they tried to take the newspaper 'News of the World' to court to stop them publishing the story but allegedly dropped the case after seeing the evidence, leaving them both fifty thousand pounds out of pocket.

When he returned to Anfield with Man City, Steve received a terrible reception and he was booed every time he touched the ball. A banner was also revealed on the Kop which said; 'Sub at Real. Sub at City. Judas'. After the manager Kevin Keegan left Man City in March 2005, Steve never played for them again and at the end of the season he was released by the new manager Stuart Pearce. He then announced his retirement from playing.

Since announcing his retirement Steve has carved out a successful career for himself in the media. During the 2007/08 season he had his own weekly show called 'Macca's Monday Night' on Setanta Sports. In North America he is well known for his entertaining commentary double act with Ian Darke during Premier League games on ESPN. He also still plays occasionally in charity games, sometimes with the Liverpool legends team.

Despite leaving under a cloud Steve is still very fondly remembered for what he did for Liverpool as a player. He was voted in at number 22 in the series '100 players who shook the Kop'.

Stig Inge Bjornebye

Norwegian left back Stig Inge Bjornebye was one of the best crossers of the ball I have ever seen at Liverpool. A cross from his left boot was often a thing of pure aesthetic beauty, as the ball would seem to float before curving away from the goalkeeper, beyond the reach of defenders, before landing on the head of an attacker to bury in the back of the net. A perfect example would be the incredible delivery for Neil Ruddock to score the equaliser in the amazing 3-3 draw with Manchester United, in January 1994.

Stig was born in December 1969 in Elverum, Norway. His father was professional skier, Jo Inge, who competed in the 1972 winter Olympics. Stig showed an interest in becoming a ski jumper when he was a child but found his real talent lay as a footballer. He played in the youth team for his local side Elverum IL, before starting a professional career at Strommen IF in 1987. After two seasons in which he was on the fringes of the first team he moved to Konsvinger in 1989. He became a regular in the first team and received great plaudits, which gained him his first caps at international level. His performances at Konsvinger earned Stig a transfer to the biggest side in Norway, Rosenborg in 1992. In Stig's first season Rosenborg won the domestic double of Norwegian Premier League and the Norwegian Cup. Stig scored the winning goal in the Norwegian Cup Final against Lillestrom SK.

In the summer of 1992, Liverpool under Graeme Souness was on one of their regular pre-season trips to Scandinavia. It was during this trip that Souness first spotted Stig playing in person as the Norwegian season runs from April to November, due to the freezing climate during winter. In December 1992 he was signed by Liverpool for £600,000 after David Burrows suffered a serious long term injury. Stig had five years international experience and as a

Scandinavian he was used to playing during cold weather, so it seemed a great piece of business. Unfortunately Stig took time to adjust to the pace of the Premier League and he was unable to make the left back position his own. He had a poor debut as Liverpool was thrashed 5-1 by Coventry City. He came in for some criticism from the fans as his inconsistency made him a scapegoat for the entire team's poor performances.

In the summer of 1993, David Burrows was sold to West Ham United and the deal involved bringing Julian Dicks to Anfield. Dicks made the left back spot his and Stig barely played during the 1993/94 season. In the few games that Stig did play he failed to impress enough to push his way into a regular place in the side. In 1994 he went back to Rosenborg on loan, where he played eight games.

When Roy Evans took over as manager in February 1994, the upturn in Stig's fortunes at Anfield could not have been more dramatic. After playing for Norway in the 1994 World Cup in the USA, Stig was given a second chance at Liverpool when Julian Dicks was sold after just one poor season. Roy changed the team formation to 5-3-2, which would enable the full backs to bomb up and down the wings without worrying about leaving gaps at the back. Stig's experience as a wing back with Rosenborg was vital for this new formation and he began to thrive as a Liverpool player. He began to show great composure and his balance and strong tackling made him an important member of the side. He understood when to overlap with the forward players and was now free to go forward more often. He showed great creativity with his passing and began to regularly demonstrate his irreproachable crossing abilities. He had a terrific game in the 1995 League Cup final victory over Bolton Wanderers. He almost capped a fine performance with a goal but saw his shot rebound of the post. Sadly his incredible new lease of life at Anfield came to a premature end a few days after the League

Cup final when he broke his leg against Southampton. It was a freak accident as his studs got stuck in the turf when straining to reach the ball.

Stig missed almost the entire 1995/96 season through injury and his place was filled mainly by Steve Harkness and Rob Jones. At the start of the 1996/97 season, injuries to Harkness and Jones gave Stig the chance to reclaim his place at left back. He took this opportunity with relish and was an ever present during an outstanding campaign for Liverpool. Stig was one of the most important players as Liverpool mounted their most serious title challenge since 1991. His pinpoint crosses helped Robbie Fowler and Stan Collymore to score many goals and he finally broke his own duck by scoring against Middlesbrough. At the end of the season his outstanding performances earned him a place in the PFA Team of the Year.

In July 1998 Gerard Houllier arrived at Anfield to join Roy Evans in a short lived stint as joint managers. One of Houllier's first pieces of business was the surprise decision to bring Steve Staunton back from Aston Villa. This was to mark the end for Stig at the club, as Staunton and Dominic Matteo took over the regular left back spot. Seemingly marginalised by Houllier, Stig decided to fight for his place and, after playing in the 1998 World Cup, he retired from international football to concentrate on his club career. He managed another thirty one appearances over the next two seasons but his previous poor form from his early Liverpool career began to return more regularly and his once perfect crossing abilities had also begun decreasing. Houllier's tenure brought an influx of new players that meant that Stig's time at Anfield had come to an end.

In 2000 he joined the Danish champions Brondby IF on loan and, after a brief international comeback in the European

Championship's, his old boss Souness signed him for Blackburn Rovers for £300,000. In his first season at Ewood Park he showed that he was far from finished as he helped Blackburn to gain promotion back to the Premier League. He went on to win his final trophy in football when Blackburn defeated Tottenham Hotspur in the 2002 League Cup final.

Soon after the League Cup final, Stig was the victim of a freak training ground accident and fractured his eye socket. Suffering with double vision he needed corrective surgery and was unable to play for the next seven months. In December 2002 he made a brief return but suffered an injury in a game against Wigan Athletic that required foot surgery. In February 2003, while recovering in Norway, he suffered numbness in his foot and doctors found two failing arteries. After five hours of surgery, Stig was told he was lucky not to have his foot amputated. He never played again and in March 2003 he announced his retirement.

After his retirement from playing, Stig was the assistant manager for the Norway international side from 2003 to 2006. He vacated the position to become manager at Norwegian club IK Start. After a promising first season, in which they competed in the UEFA Cup, he was sacked in September 2007, after a poor run of results leaving the club in a dangerous position in the Norwegian Premier League. The club was eventually relegated two months later at the end of the season.

Stig Inge Bjornebye was a left back who was lucky to get two lives at Liverpool. His poor early career at Anfield was almost forgotten as he rose to new heights and almost helped the side to win the Premier League in 1997. He is still remembered fondly by Liverpool fans who watched his performances between 1994 and 1998 and he is guaranteed a warm welcome anytime at Anfield.

The 2000s

Despite not winning any league titles between 2000 and 2010, it was still a pretty good decade for Liverpool. There was two second place finishes in the league and the club won four European trophies, two FA Cups and to League Cups. There was also numerous European semi final appearances and defeats in other cup finals.

The Champions League final victory in Istanbul, is one of the greatest moments in the history of the club. The 25th of May, 2005, is a date that no Liverpool fan will ever forget and all you have to is say the word Istanbul to any Red, anywhere in the world and they will smile at you. There is a good chance they will even wave five fingers at you and begin to sing '"In Istanbul, we won it five times".

For me personally, the best time in that decade, and possibly my favourite period of supporting Liverpool, was the week when Liverpool completed the historic treble of trophies, it started with the 'Owen Final' and ended with the clinching of a Champions League spot at Charlton.

I watched the FA Cup Final against Arsenal at a barbecue being held at the house of some family friends of my best mate Pat. It was gloriously sunny outside on that Saturday and it was the first Cup final to be held outside of England, at Cardiff's Millennium Stadium. The two teams were only separated by one point in the final League table, Arsenal finishing second with seventy points and Liverpool finishing third with sixty-nine points.

Unfortunately these family friends were quite a reserved lot, unlike me and Pat, so it was difficult getting any atmosphere from them during the game. I don't recall a great deal about the first eighty two minutes except for the Henchoz handball, the Ljunberg goal and the fact we got absolutely pasted beyond belief, including us clearing off the line a couple of times.

The game looked dead and buried, we were creating absolutely nothing and heads were going down fast. Then we got a free kick and when Gary McAllister stepped up to take it we sensed something magic about to happen. McAllister was in the middle of an unbelievable spell of goals and man of the match performances at the end of that season.

The free kick was knocked in an Arsenal defender headed the ball into the air it bounced off Babbel and fell in an amazing position to the one man you would bet your house on to score. Pat and I went absolutely berserk, our hosts were clearly happy and excited but managed to maintain their dignity as Pat and I jumped all over the furniture almost landing on people's heads!

We managed to compose ourselves and sit back down for the restart just hoping we wouldn't blow it and hang on for extra time. We barely had time to discuss the goal when Berger hit a long ball over Arsenal's midfield. We saw Owen sprinting onto it but clearly Adams and Dixon easily had him covered. How wrong we were as the entire season flashed before our eyes when the ball crept past Seaman and into the corner of the net.

The atmosphere in the house went insane as Pat and I burst out the patio doors and into the garden, our shirts flying into the air in our dance of jubilation.

There was a lovely moment as Fowler and Hyypia invited club captain Jamie Redknapp, out injured long term, down onto the pitch to help lift the trophy. I remember his dad Harry, was commentating on BBC at the time and he had tears in his eyes at the moment, as did we. Incredible scenes that never seemed to end as the music was blasted, the cans of ale were cracked open and the party just went on and on.

The next few days went really fast and in a blur as the anticipation built for the UEFA Cup final in Dortmund, against unfancied Spanish side Deportivo Alaves. It had been sixteen years since our last European final and the hype building up to the game was massive. I don't think I've ever felt as excited before a game as I was feeling before this one.

In the month before the game I had spent two weeks doing a temporary job booking travel packages and tickets for the big game. I was really jealous of the customers I dealt with over those two weeks, but it all added to my excitement for the match.

The venue for my viewing of this one was quite different to one on the previous Saturday as my dad and I watched this game in The Sefton Arms pub in West Derby Village, Liverpool. Frustratingly, I was in Vancouver watching Istanbul 2005, but how I imagine the atmosphere back home on that amazing night was probably a more extreme version of my experiences during the UEFA Cup final 2001.

Obviously the pub was unbelievably crowded when we got there, fortunately my dad's mates had saved us a tasty speck near the big screen and with pints in hand we were ready for kick off. We were never too nervous before the start as none of us had ever heard of Alaves so didn't think we had much to worry about, surely we weren't going to blow the treble now, especially after all we went through to win the previous two finals that season.

We didn't have to wait long for the breakthrough, which came from a trademark Markus Babbel header which was then followed shortly by a terrific Gerrard shot.

We were two nil up and absolutely flying, even when they got one back we weren't bothered especially when Owen went clear through with the goalie and there is usually only one outcome in that situation. This time however the Alaves goalie came bursting out of his area and dragged Owen down, fortunately Michael was clever enough to go down inside the area. It was a penalty and surely a straight red card for the goalie. It seemed to take forever while the referee made up his mind before brandishing a yellow to the sound of loud expletives in the boozer. I had a flashback to this during the Gattuso incident during the Champions League Final. Up stepped

Gary Mac to coolly dispense with the penalty and restore our two goal advantage.

Half time arrived and people were already ordering the champagne there and then, I couldn't recall ever seeing such a one sided European final before. We were so far on top we were even starting to take gentleman's bets on how many we'd end up scoring, five, six and even seven was mentioned as it was very possible that Alaves would completely collapse if we scored early in the second half. So a quick trip to the bog and another pint ordered and we were ready for the restart. Jubilation was soon turned to complete shock and silence as our defence collapsed and Javi Moreno fired two quick goals to level the score at three all. We had gone from absolutely flying to basically hanging on for our lives as Alaves began to pile on the pressure with wave after wave of attack dealt with brilliantly by McAllister, who was having the game of his life.

Twenty minutes to go and onto the pitch to replace the hapless Heskey comes Robbie Fowler. Loud cheers and God chants mixed with adults only insults directed at Heskey go up round the pub. The arrival of The Growler combined with Alaves taking off their most dangerous player Moreno, seemed to give us a second wind as we began to create more opportunities. Then the ball fell to McAllister who played a tremendous ball through the Alaves defence. Fowler picked up the ball on the edge of the box and we all shouted for him to pass to Owen who was free in the area, instead Fowler decided to shoot and absolutely buried it in the corner. The pub descended into absolute mayhem, my dad was in the bathroom at that moment and came running out the bathroom in time for the replay describing scenes of men peeing on their trousers in a rush to see what all the screaming was about. My own reaction was to stand still on the spot, arms in the air screaming 'Fowler, Fowler, Fowler' over and over again for about a minute as fellow fans shook me out of it.

Surely that had to be it now, we couldn't take any more drama, clearly Houllier was thinking the same way as he took Michael Owen off. Nobody said anything but I had a horrible thought of what the hell is he doing, what if it goes to extra time? My fears were well founded as Alaves equalized again in the ninetieth minute from a header by Jordi Cruyff, an ex Man Utd player, bloody typical.

Final whistle blows and everyone just collapses onto each other, I don't know how I managed to not throw up or have a heart attack on the spot. The first half of extra time went without incident as it looks like it's heading for penalties as both sides look knackered. Then in the second half things go crazy as Alaves got two players sent off. The second red card led to a free kick on the left edge of the box. Up steps that man (of the match) McAllister again to take it. The TV camera got a close up of his face, as he was about to take it and he had that same look in his eyes as before the derby winner just weeks earlier.

We sensed that something was on and next thing you know the ball is in the net and it's a golden goal. What a way to end such a dramatic game, in the pub we all went absolutely berserk and the noise was so loud that the commentary on the TV was drowned out. None of us knew who had actually scored the winning goal and speculation was rampant as to who got the final touch, it took a while till we realized it was actually an own goal.

'You'll Never Walk Alone' was played loudly and repeatedly as we watched Robbie and Sami lift the trophy and then the disco music came on and we danced into the night and everybody got absolutely bladdered.

Danny Murphy

Boyhood Reds fan Danny Murphy was a popular member of the Liverpool side under Gerrard Houllier. He was a player who blew hot and cold at times but could often be relied upon in the big games, especially against Man Utd.

Danny was born in 1977, in Chester. He started his career as a trainee at Crewe Alexandra and was nurtured into a decent player by the legendary manager Dario Gradi. Over the years, Gradi has turned many youngsters into great players. Some of these players include, David Platt, Dean Ashton and ex Red Rob Jones. Bruce Grobbelaar was spotted playing for Crewe by Liverpool scouts when he was playing there on loan from the Vancouver Whitecaps.

At the same time as he was impressing with Crewe, Danny was also gaining positive notices for his performances in the England youth team. He played superbly during the 1997 Fifa World Youth Championships (now known as the Under 20 World Cup). Also in the England squad for that tournament were Jamie Carragher and Michael Owen.

After the tournament was over Danny was regarded as one of the most impressive young talents in the game. A number of Premier League clubs began to take notice of him but there was only ever going to be one club he would sign for. In 1997 Roy Evans paid £1.5 million to bring him to Anfield and make his dreams come true. Danny had a hard time breaking into the first team at first and near the end of his second season in 1998/99 he was loaned back to Crewe. After playing really well during this loan spell, Liverpool's new boss Gerard Houllier brought him back and this was when his career for the Reds really took off.

During the following season 1999/2000, Danny began to establish himself a regular place in midfield. He was a talented player who could tackle and pass well, with a big strength being his delivery from dead ball situations. During this season however, the fans would often be left totally frustrated with him. When he was on form he would be absolutely amazing and tear opponents apart. He would also go long periods where his form had gone missing and just when we would be about to give up on him he would do something brilliant and win us back. This was pretty much the pattern for a lot of his Liverpool career.

During the 2000/01 season, Danny was an integral part of the treble winning side. He was injured for the 2001 League Cup final against Birmingham City but he started and played well in the following two Cup finals against Arsenal and Deportivo Alaves. It was during this season that Danny started a fantastic run of winning goals against Man Utd at Old Trafford in 1–0 victories for Liverpool.

The first of his winners at Old Trafford came in December 2000. It was a cracking free kick scored after Darren Fletcher had been sent off for bringing down Michael Owen who was clean through on goal. This game was played on my birthday and was a lunchtime kick-off on TV. On this day I had agreed to go on a Christmas shopping trip to Birkenhead with my parents, under the agreement that my dad and I would get to watch the match in a pub. Unfortunately we got stuck in traffic at the Mersey Tunnel and ended up missing the game. We listened to it on the radio in the car and then saw the goal on a TV in an electronics shop.

His next winner at Old Trafford came in early 2002 as Liverpool was chasing Man Utd and Arsenal for the league title. The game was a bit of an anti-climax and neither team had many chances. It was looking like it would finish 0–0 when Steven Gerrard made an absolutely incredible pass that opened up the Man Utd defence. Up popped Danny to delicately lob Barthez and win us the game. It was a midweek evening game and I remember having a feeling that day it would be our night. Under Gerard Houllier Liverpool seemed to have a knack for not losing to Man Utd and I was nearly always confident we could beat them. The only time I was ever in doubt during the later Houllier years was before the 2003 League Cup Final. I stupidly turned down a ticket for that game as we were in terrible form in the weeks before it. I was excited when we won 2–0 but gutted I wasn't there.

In 2002 Danny was chosen for the England World Cup squad in Japan and Korea, ironically as a replacement for Steven Gerrard who had pulled out due to injury. In a cruel twist of fate Danny then broke his metatarsal in training and he too was out before the tournament had even started. The following season 2002/03 was Danny's best individual season for Liverpool as he was voted the fans player of the season. He had a competition with Steven Gerrard that season to see who could score the most goals. This seemed to spur on both players to perform superbly and Danny eventually won the competition with twelve goals to Stevie's ten.

Amazingly he did it again and scored the winner at Old Trafford in April 2004, this time it came from the penalty spot. At the time Houllier was under immense pressure and this victory calmed down the vultures beginning to circle closer in the media. That season had seen Steven Gerrard and Michael Owen miss a number of penalties and it was a big relief to see Danny step up to take it. This victory set us on the path to qualification for the Champions League, which we hadn't been involved in that season. Unfortunately for Houllier it wasn't enough to keep him his job and he was gone just one month later.

Sadly for Danny, the winner against Man Utd wasn't enough for him to stay with the club either as new manager Rafa Benitez decided to sell him. In August 2004 he was sold to Charlton Athletic for £2.5 million. A lot of people at the time considered this a huge mistake and I was one of them. In his autobiography Steven Gerrard talks about his shock at the departure of Danny Murphy. He mentions how during pre-season Rafa was talking Danny up and saying what an intelligent player he was to have in the squad. When Rafa started bringing in unknown Spanish players I was very concerned that we would lose some of the good English players with Danny leaving along with Michael Owen who went to Real Madrid. What made my concern even stronger back then was when Steven Gerrard almost signed for Chelsea, but fortunately he saw sense and decided to remain at Liverpool. With hindsight one has to wonder if we would have gone on to win the Champions League the following year had Danny Murphy stayed. The reason I say this is because it was his replacement Luis Garcia who would score the vital goals to launch us to glory in Europe. Funnily enough Garcia was quite similar to Danny Murphy in that he could also be frustratingly brilliant and awful in consecutive games, whilst also having a knack for scoring in the big games.

Danny had one and a half seasons with Charlton Athletic and he had mixed fortunes. His first season was poor by his previous standards but he improved during his second season that led to his recall to the England squad. In the January transfer window in 2006 he was signed by Tottenham Hotspur for £2 million. He had an unhappy time at Spurs and only played in 22 games over one and a half seasons and on the final day of the transfer window in August 2007 he moved to Fulham for an undisclosed fee.

He was one of Fulham's best players and at the end of his first season, he scored a header against Portsmouth that kept them in the Premier League. Danny was given the captain's armband for the 2008/09 season. In 2010 he led them on an incredible run to the Europa League final defeating Juventus along the way. Sadly for Fulham they lost in the final to Atletico Madrid, who had defeated Liverpool in the semi final. Danny's last season at Fulham was in 2011/12 when he created more goalscoring chances in Premier League than any other player. At the end of the season he moved to Blackburn Rovers after failing to agree a new contract.

Danny Murphy will always remain in the hearts of Reds fans everywhere thanks to his commitment and his goals against Man Utd. Even if he had done nothing else in his career but score against Man Utd he would still be fondly remembered, but he added to his legend by also scoring an incredible winner against Everton. He was voted number 62 in the '100 Players Who Shook the Kop'.

Dietmar Hamann

Nicknamed 'The Kaiser', Dietmar 'Didi' Hamann was a model of German efficiency. He spent seven seasons at Anfield during which he was incredible in the holding midfield role. Possessing a rocket shot, he rarely gave the ball away and never shirked out of a tackle. These attributes as well his cod Scouse accent and his English mentality are just a few of the reasons why he remains so beloved by Liverpool fans everywhere.

Didi was born in September 1973 in Waldsassen, Bavaria. He started his football career with the youth team Wacker Munchen based in Munich, where his father was a coach. It wasn't long before Didi's footballing talents were noticed by bigger sides and he was soon on his way to joining the youth set-up at Bayern Munich. He progressed through the ranks at Bayern Munich and made his debut for the first team in 1991 when he had just turned eighteen. He spent nine years with the Bavarian giants and during that period they won two Bundesliga titles as well as a UEFA Cup and German Cup. In 1998 Didi played for Germany in the World Cup in France. After impressing with his displays during the tournament he was signed by Kenny Dalglish for Newcastle United at a cost of £5.5 million.

Didi had a fine season 1998/99 with Newcastle and was voted by their fans as the player of the season. This great form attracted the attention of a number of top teams, including Barcelona and Arsenal, who began bidding for Didi's services. Didi had fallen out with the Newcastle manager Ruud Gullit which is why he chose to depart St James Park after just one season. Liverpool manager Gerard Houllier had just offloaded the talented but controversial Paul Ince at the end of the previous season and needed a big strong character in the centre of the team. After a failed bid to sign the late Marc-Vivien Foe from West Ham United, Houllier soon realised that

Didi Hamann was a perfect choice to fulfil this role and in July 1999 Didi opted to sign for the Reds for £8 million.

Didi made his league debut for Liverpool against Sheffield Wednesday but it was to end in disaster. He only lasted twenty five minutes before he was off the field with damaged ankle ligaments. After an aborted comeback attempt in September, Didi ended up on the injured list until November 1999. When he eventually started to play regularly in the midfield, Liverpool fans soon realised what a quality player he was. In the holding role he never really did anything spectacular or flashy but what he did do was done with substance. There were some critics in the media around that time who failed to grasp just how good he was, accusing him of being too static and anonymous in midfield. What Didi did do, throughout his career, was protect the defence while quietly organising the midfield and intercepting the ball with some ferocious but perfectly timed tackling. He distributed the ball smoothly, rarely losing possession. He didn't score very often but when he did it was usually spectacular. Memorable goals include one against Newcastle in September 2002 where he beat two players before unleashing an unstoppable shot. Other memorable strikes include a belter from thirty yards against Fulham and one against Portsmouth that was voted Liverpool's goal of the season for 2003/04.

In October 2000 Didi wrote himself into the record books when he scored the last goal ever scored at the legendary Wembley Stadium. This came from a long range free kick in a World Cup qualifier as Germany defeated England 1-0. This was also the final game for Kevin Keegan as England manager who resigned in the dressing room after the team were booed off the pitch.

Didi then went on to have a spectacular season for Liverpool helping them to an incredible treble of League Cup, FA Cup and UEFA Cup during 2000/01. He had a fine game in the League Cup Final against Birmingham City, almost scoring with a spectacular effort in extra time that rebounded off the post. He missed a penalty during the shoot-out but after Sander Westerveld saved from Andrew Johnson the trophy was Liverpool's. Didi had a more subdued game during the FA Cup Final against Arsenal but thanks to Michael Owen the second part of the treble was completed. Another good performance alongside Gary McAllister in Dortmund assisted the Reds to the UEFA Cup in the spectacular 5-4 victory over Deportivo Alaves.

Victories in the Community Shield (over Man Utd) and the European Super Cup against Bayern Munich meant that during the 2001/02 season Liverpool held five trophies at once. Liverpool had a marvellous season in the Premiership and finished in second place. This was a mixed season for Liverpool with Gerard Houllier being struck down with a heart defect during a game against Leeds United. He returned five months later to inspire a 2-0 victory over Roma that meant Liverpool reached the quarter final stage of the Champions League to face German side Bayer Leverkusen. It was during the second leg of this tie that we started to realise that Houllier was possibly losing his managerial abilities. It was also the game when we realised, to painful effect, how vulnerable Liverpool were when Didi wasn't on the pitch. In a game balanced 1-1 with Bayer requiring 2 goals to win, Houllier took off Didi replacing him with Vladmir Smicer and exposing the defence to endless attacks. Leverkusen was lifted by the German's exit as Smicer did little to help the defence. Once Didi was no longer on the field Bayer and particularly Michael Ballack ran riot and scored two goals in quick succession. Jari Litmanen managed to score another goal for Liverpool and at that stage the score was 3-2 to Bayer but Liverpool was leading on away goals. Unfortunately it was not to be for Liverpool and we were deprived the chance to play in Champions League semi final in which our opponents would have been Manchester United. I'll always remember the phone in on Radio City afterwards as I was stuck in traffic leaving the pub. Up to this point the reaction to Houllier was mostly always positive after he had restored the club to winning silverware and he had plenty of goodwill after his comeback from illness. This was the night when I began to hear some serious anger and criticism towards Houllier and this was the moment I personally began to wonder if he knew what he was doing. Had we beaten Bayer Leverkusen I believe that we'd have reached the final that season as we always had the knack of beating Man Utd during this period.

In the summer of 2002, Didi helped Germany to reach the World Cup Final were they lost to a Ronaldo inspired Brazil. This made Didi the first Liverpool player since Roger Hunt in 1966 to play in a World Cup Final.

The following season 2002/03 was a mixed bag for Liverpool as they won a trophy but performed poorly in the league. The Reds won the League Cup beating Man Utd in the final with goals from Steven Gerrard and Michael Owen. I had refused a ticket for this game for a mixture of reasons including Liverpool's poor form at the time and needing any spare cash for my moving to New Zealand two weeks later. This is a decision I have bitterly regretted ever since. This was a particularly bad season for the club because they had invested heavily on players the previous summer trying to build on the promising 2001/02 Premiership finish. Unfortunately the money was wasted on some very mediocre players and this only served to hasten the fans turning on Gerard Houllier.

Houllier was sacked in the summer of 2004 when the Liverpool board finally lost patience. He was replaced by Rafa Benitez and Liverpool went on to have one of their most exciting seasons in recent times during 2004/05. Didi was one of the standout performers during a very stop-start season. Poor results in the league and FA Cup were countered by a run to the League Cup Final and the exciting run in the Champions League. Liverpool lost the League Cup Final in extra time to Chelsea but this pain was soon soothed during the European games. Liverpool got their revenge over Bayer Leverkusen in the first knockout round with Didi scoring a free kick in the first leg at Anfield. Victories over Juventus and Chelsea led us to the final in Istanbul and possibly Didi's defining moment as a Liverpool player.

When the starting line-up was announced before the 2005 Champions League Final against AC Milan I was one of many thousands of Reds around the world yelling at expletives at the inclusion of Harry Kewell in the starting line-up and no place for Didi Hamann. I didn't actually realise at the time that Didi was suffering with a broken toe. As we all know AC Milan ran riot in the first half with Kaka destroying our midfield. With the score at 3-0 at half time I was just praying that it wouldn't become embarrassing with barely any hope we could come back. Didi came on as a second half substitute and most people would agree that his introduction changed the game in our favour. He was responsible for neutralizing Kaka and his solidity in midfield gave Steven Gerrard the freedom to go forward and attack. As we now know Liverpool made the most amazing comeback ever and went on to win the trophy in a penalty shoot out. Despite breaking his foot in extra time, Didi held his nerve to score the opening penalty in the shoot-out. This alone is enough to make him a Liverpool legend in my opinion.

During the summer of 2005 Didi's contract expired and German side Hamburg and Bolton Wanderers both expressed interest in signing him. He was offered a new one year deal by Rafa Benitez and as Didi told the Liverpool Echo;

"Once Liverpool made me an offer, there was only one place I wanted to play my football."

226

In December that year he was offered an additional twelve month extension to the contract signed in the summer. This was a clause triggered after he had made twenty two appearances in the season. However his appearances were fleeting in the starting team during the second half of the 2005/06 season. This was partly due to injuries and the form of new signing Momo Sissoko who was absolutely outstanding that season. Didi was once again a substitute for a final as Liverpool played West Ham United in the FA Cup Final. Didi came on during the second half when Liverpool were 3-2 down and looking like losing the trophy. For the second season in a row, Didi's introduction to a major final was crucial to the eventual comeback with Gerrard scoring the greatest goal ever seen in an FA Cup Final. Just like in Istanbul, Didi stepped up during the penalty shoot-out to coolly blast the ball into the net. For the second successive season Liverpool had won a major trophy and both times Didi Hamann was a major reason.

Didi wasn't included in the Germany squad for the 2006 World Cup and he chose to announce his retirement from international football. He also decided that his chances of playing regularly for Liverpool would be severely limited in the following season and chose, with a heavy heart, to leave the club. Stiff competition from Gerrard, Sissoko and Xabi Alonso meant that Didi was fourth in the pecking order and he was given permission to leave the club. The only club to make him an offer was Bolton Wanderers so Didi signed a pre-contract with them. However Manchester City then made a bid for him after the announcement was made that Didi would join Bolton. Didi said at the time;

"I had agreed to join Bolton, but I quickly realised that going to them would not be the right move for me. I told Bolton my feelings immediately and they understood my decision"

Man City allegedly paid £400,000 compensation to Bolton and Didi signed a two year contract. His first season with Man City was quite poor as Didi wasn't playing anywhere near his previous standards and didn't play very often due to injuries for the most part. His second season under new manager Sven-Goran Eriksson was much better as Didi was a huge influence on Man City's performances and he was playing regularly. The highlight of his 2007/08 season was when Didi inspired Man City to beating their rivals Man Utd 2-1 at Old Trafford. His form during the season led to the offer of a new one year contract taking him up to the end of 2008/09.

In the summer of 2009, Didi was released by Man City at the end of his contract. He received several offers from clubs in the lower divisions, including Notts County, managed at the time by Sven Goran Eriksson. Didi declined these offers feeling he could still play at a higher level, however he ended up spending a year out of the game. In 2010 he joined MK Don's as player coach on a one year contract. He left the club in February 2011 to become a coach at Leicester City. In the summer of 2011 he became the manager of Stockport County. Unfortunately results didn't go too well on the pitch and there was turmoil off it too when a proposed takeover of the club fell through. He resigned in November 2011.

Since leaving Stockport County, Didi has forged a new career as a pundit in Ireland on RTE and also in England on the BBC, Sky Sports and LFCTV where he often does the post match analysis after Liverpool games. He is also well known for his outspoken and often hilarious commentary on Twitter usually discussing cricket or football, as well as engaging in banter with the likes of Robbie Fowler and Joey Barton.

Didi Hamann will forever be one of Liverpool's most beloved players. His fearlessness and calmness on the pitch were just two reasons for Liverpool's resurgence as a trophy winning team again. Even if he had done nothing else in his Liverpool career his performances in Istanbul 2005 and Cardiff 2006 will secure his place in Anfield folklore. He was voted in at number 44 in the series '100 Players Who Shook the Kop'.

Emile Heskey

Emile Heskey was an enigma when playing for Liverpool. Sometimes he was amazing and at other times he could be incredibly frustrating. When he was on top form, he was almost unstoppable, running at defenders with tremendous pace and power, like a tank. Unfortunately he often appeared to be low on confidence, and at these times he would play in a static style and hardly get involved in the action.

Emile Heskey was born in January 1978 in Leicester. He started his career at home-town club Leicester City, where he made his first team debut against Queens Park Rangers in 1995 at the age of seventeen. He went on to spend five seasons there, during which time he helped Leicester win two League Cups in 1997 and 2000. He scored in the 1997 League Cup final victory over Middlesbrough.

During the 1999/2000 season Emile was being regularly linked with a big money move to Liverpool. Liverpool's pursuit of Gareth Barry in 2008 was not the first time that the club has had a struggle with Martin O'Neill over signing one of his most important players. Back in 2000 the then Leicester City manager did everything in his power to try and keep Emile at the club, describing him as "irreplaceable". In a very interesting parallel with events during the summer of 2008, Martin O'Neill said the following back in March 2000.

"We as a club did everything we could to persuade Emile to stay with us for as long as possible. But it was his insistence that the deal had to go through before this weekend.

The club had been negotiating terms that we felt would keep him here, really pushing the boat out to show how much we valued him as a player with us. But apparently it was not enough.

I believe our players will be as bitterly disappointed as I am at Emile's decision, coming as it does when we have just won a trophy, are looking towards Europe and had put together the strongest squad in the club's history."

It is incredible how closely these words echo the comments Martin O'Neill has made over the Gareth Barry saga. It's almost as though, had Liverpool signed Barry, you could literally take this quote and replace the name Emile with Gareth. However unlike in 2008, back in 2000 Liverpool did get their man. In March 2000, Liverpool manager Gerard Houllier paid a club record fee of £11 million to bring Emile Heskey to Anfield. It seemed a strange decision at the time to pay so much for a player who wasn't a prolific goal-scorer. Houllier answered this criticism by saying;

"You take players not for the number of goals they score but for the role they can play for the team. He is English and an international player. A lot of people should be happy that I am not signing a foreign player. I know the way he plays and fights on the field and he will do that for the red shirts."

Despite the obvious faults in Heskey's time at Anfield it cannot be denied that indeed he did give his all in the red shirt. It's certain that Michael Owen wouldn't have scored so many goals without him and he was popular with his team-mates.

Emile made his debut for Liverpool in a home game against Sunderland. It didn't take long for him to make an impact as he won a penalty in only the third minute of the game. He played well during the final two months of the 1999/2000 season but there remained doubts about his goal-scoring prowess. He scored three goals in twelve games.

These doubts were answered in some style during the following season. Emile was to score twenty two goals as Liverpool won the treble of League Cup, FA Cup and UEFA Cup. While he didn't score in any of the finals his contributions during the previous rounds cannot be criticised. A particular highlight during this season was an excellent hat-trick in a 4-0 win away at Derby County in the Premier League. Not only did he score goals regularly but he was involved in many others too. Some of his crossing for Michael Owen to score stands out as memorable as was the way he could take defenders out of the game. In my opinion it is certain that without Emile's contributions Michael Owen may not have went on to become European Player of the Year for 2001.

The only problem I really had with Emile during the treble season was that he regularly kept Robbie Fowler out of the team and I never felt he was good enough to lace Fowler's boots. In both of their autobiographies, Michael Owen and Robbie Fowler described how Houllier indicated to them both that they were competing to partner Heskey, who was his first choice up front. I guess that Houllier had to justify the huge amount of money he had spent on Emile, but still I think most of us would agree that there were occasions for Fowler and Owen to play together rather than fighting for the role of second striker. To be honest I find it quite disgraceful that two of our greatest strikers were kept apart in this way. Houllier often liked to play with a strong target man and unfortunately for Fowler both Owen and Heskey were quicker than him and so they got the nod to start together more often than not.

The 2000/01 season was by far the best of Emile's football career in terms of goals scored. He was unable to match the feats the following season and he scored just thirteen goals in fifty four games. During the 2001/02 season Heskey was a regular target for criticism from many Liverpool supporters, including myself. It was during this season that Emile started to show regular signs of a lack in confidence. This was something that would plague the remainder of his Anfield career and even Houllier would bring it up from time to time.

Despite a disappointing second full season with Liverpool, Emile had successfully transferred his partnership with Michael Owen into the international arena with England. Emile was one of four Liverpool players in the England side for incredible 5–1 victory over Germany in October 2001. Emile scored the fifth goal and the other goal scorers, Michael Owen and Steven Gerrard. Also in the side was another Liverpool player, Nick Barmby. This prompted many Liverpool fans to dub the result afterwards, Liverpool 5 Germany 1. Emile was part of the England squad for the 2002 World Cup in Japan and Korea. He scored his only World Cup Finals goal during the 3-0 victory over Denmark in the second round.

After he returned from the World Cup, Emile was rumoured to be a target for Tottenham Hotspur and a figure of £12 million was quoted by the press. However Emile remained at Liverpool and then had another poor season in 2002/03. He finished the campaign with a paltry nine goals in fifty one games, including a mere six in the league. I feel as though I'm being a little harsh on Emile during this article. I am trying not to be so negative but I am genuinely struggling to justify such awful goals to game ratios. The one positive I can offer for this period was that although Emile wasn't scoring many goals he was assisting in many others for his team-mates. Despite missing out on a Champions League place, Liverpool did have one thing to smile about during this season. We defeated Manchester United in the League Cup final with goals from Michael Owen and Steven Gerrard.

It was during the 2002/03 season that I walked out of Anfield early for the one and only time ever before or since. It was during a defeat to Crystal Palace in the FA Cup. In this game Emile made one of the most infuriating misses I've ever seen. With the score at 1-0 to Crystal Palace late in the game, he was put through one on one with the keeper. He had almost a third of the opposing half of the pitch to himself and loads of time to beat the keeper. However he seemed to panic and put a tame shot in and gave the keeper an easy save. Minutes later we went 2-0 down with just five minutes to go and I could take no more. I usually cannot justify leaving before the final whistle but this performance was so hurtful I simply couldn't take any more punishment and had to call it quits for the evening.

The 2003/04 season was to be the last for both Emile and Gerard Houllier. Emile finished his Liverpool career by scoring twelve goals and helping Liverpool to qualify for the Champions League. At the end of the season Gerard Houllier was dismissed and replaced by Rafa Benitez. However a full month before Benitez came along, Emile was sold to Birmingham City for a fee of £3.5 million, potentially rising to £6.25 million. The signing of Djibril Cisse had already been agreed for £14 million before Houllier's departure. With the club needing funds and Emile unlikely to play many games, he could no longer remain at Anfield.

Emile did fairly well in his debut season, 2004/05, with Birmingham City. He scored eleven goals and was voted as Birmingham's Player of the Season by both the fans and players. He didn't follow this up in the 2005/06 season as he scored just five goals in 40 games and Birmingham City was relegated to The Championship.

Despite a poor return of goals in the 2005/06 season, Emile was snapped up in July 2006 by Wigan Athletic for a fee of £5.5 million. In his first season he scored eight goals and endeared himself to the Wigan supporters with some very heartfelt performances as Wigan battled relegation. The season culminated in Wigan staying in the Premier League on the final day of the season when they defeated Sheffield United, who themselves were relegated.

In September 2007 Emile was recalled to the England squad after a long absence. This was regarded as a huge shock at the time but Emile played superbly in the two World Cup qualifiers against Israel and Russia. Sadly he then broke his metatarsal bone and was out for three months. The highlight of his second season with Wigan Athletic, 2007/08 came in April 2008 when he scored a ninetieth minute equaliser against Chelsea, derailing their title hopes.

Emile joined Aston Villa in January 2009 for £3.5 million. He scored a screamer against Portsmouth on his debut, but only scored one more goal before the end of the season. In 2010 he was in the England squad for the World Cup in South Africa. He started the opening game and set up a goal for Steven Gerrard. Unluckily for Emile, his biggest contribution to England's World Cup campaign was when he injured Rio Ferdinand in training and ruled him out of the tournament.

He spent three full seasons at Villa Park before moving to Australia in September 2012, to play for Newcastle Jets.

Emile Heskey was a noble competitor for Liverpool. He was never doubted by his team-mates or his manager, despite the often savage criticism from Liverpool supporters and football writers. While I feel that he didn't score enough goals to justify his large transfer fee, he did play a huge part in Liverpool winning four major trophies during his time at Anfield. For this reason alone I am able to remember his time in a red shirt with some fondness.

Gary McAllister

Legendary Scottish midfielder Gary McAllister was described by former Liverpool manager Gerrard Houllier as; "my most inspirational signing". Nobody can argue with this statement and none of us will ever forget Gary's incredible contributions to the treble winning season of 2000/01.

Gary was born in Motherwell, Scotland on Christmas Day 1964. He started his football career for his hometown club Motherwell at just sixteen years old in 1981. He played for Motherwell for four seasons making seventy appearances. In 1985 he had an impressive game in the semi final of the Scottish Cup against Celtic and was snapped up by English side Leicester City for £250,000. This fee also included the purchase of another Motherwell player, Ally Mauchlen.

Gary spent five seasons with Leicester and was consistently one of their best players. His performances earned him a call up to the Scotland squad for the 1990 World Cup in Italy. After the World Cup ended, Gary moved on to Leeds Utd who had just been promoted to the First Division under manager Howard Wilkinson. It was at Leeds that Gary really began to make a serious name for himself as a top quality player. In Gary's second season at Elland Road, 1991/92, he was part of an incredible midfield alongside Gordon Strachan, Gary Speed and David Batty. Gary's influence from dead ball situations was to prove deadly to their opponents, as Leeds were to finish the season as the last First Division champions, before the name was changed to The Premier League.

Unfortunately for Leeds, they followed up their title victory by finishing a dreadful seventeenth in the league in 1992/93. In 1995 Gary was rewarded with the club captaincy when Gordon Strachan moved to Coventry City to become player coach. Gary's first season as captain proved to be his last one for Leeds and in 1996 he was to achieve his boyhood dream of captaining a team at Wembley in the League Cup final against Aston Villa. Sadly for Gary, he didn't get to lift the trophy as Villa won the game comfortably 3–0.

More disappointment was to follow in the summer of 1996, during the European Championships in England. Scotland had been drawn in the same group as England and the game against each other was the most anticipated for both sets of supporters. Gary was the captain of the Scotland side and was a proud man as he led his country into battle against the auld enemy at Wembley. Unfortunately the game was to be a complete disaster for Scotland and for Gary personally. England was leading 1–0 after a goal from Alan Shearer in the first half. Scotland was awarded a second half penalty after a foul by Tony Adams. Gary stepped up to take it, looking as cool as a cucumber. With his great reputation from dead ball situations there seemed no way he would miss. Unfortunately he hit the ball straight down the middle of the goal and England keeper David Seaman was able to save with his legs. Gary claims now that he was put off by the ball moving slightly and subsequent replays have proven this. Sadly for Scotland, England got a second wind after this penalty save and minutes later Paul Gascoigne was to score one of the most famous England goals of all time. Scotland fans never really forgave him for missing that penalty and despite remaining as captain until 1998, he was often disgracefully booed by his own so-called supporters.

After Euro 96 ended, Gary joined his former colleague Strachan at Coventry City for three million pounds. He spent four seasons at Highfield Road, and became a huge fan favourite thanks to his long range goals and his great efforts in helping the Sky Blues maintain their top flight status.

In the summer of 2000, Gary was allowed to leave Coventry City free of charge, and it was a major shock when Liverpool manager Gerard Houllier decided to bring him to Anfield. By this stage Gary was almost thirty six years old and was thought to be many years past his best. He was to prove many people wrong, including me.

Gary's Liverpool career started badly when he was sent off in his debut at Arsenal. This was an ill-tempered game in which Patrick Vieira for Arsenal and Didi Hamman for Liverpool were also sent off. After that poor beginning, Gary went on to prove all his doubters wrong by establishing himself as a regular in the midfield alongside Hamman. Despite his age, he remained extremely fit and went on to make twenty one starts during that fantastic season. His fitness was certainly proven as the season was approaching a breathtaking climax, with Liverpool going for three trophies and a top three finish in the league. He came on as a substitute in the League Cup final victory over Birmingham City and scored in the penalty shoot out.

The defining moment in Gary's Liverpool career came in the 3–2 victory over Everton in April 2001. It was an entertaining game and it looked to be heading for a 2–2 draw when we got a free kick in the dying seconds. Surely this was to be our last chance to snatch the victory. My dad and I watched this game at a neighbour's house on Easter Monday. Our neighbours and their family were all Evertonian's. We expected Gary to float the ball in to the box because it was so far away from the goal. However I saw the look in his eye as he put the ball down and said; "he's gonna hit this". My prediction was correct as it sailed straight into the bottom corner of the Everton goal. The Liverpool fans, the bench and the players went absolutely berserk. So did me and my dad as we jumped all over the Evertonian's furniture! This was an extremely crucial win, as we needed every point we could get in our chase for that crucial third

Champions League place. This victory, and that goal, gave us that extra bit of confidence we needed for the exciting climax to the treble season. In my opinion this was the defining moment that led to us winning the treble.

After the derby victory, Gary went on to score the winning goal in Liverpool's next four games and all of them were from dead ball situations. Just a few days after the Everton game, we played Barcelona at Anfield in the semi final second leg of the UEFA Cup. We had drawn 0–0 in the first leg and the match at Anfield proved to be a tense affair. Liverpool defended superbly against the likes of Kluivert and Rivaldo. The game was settled with a penalty at the Anfield Road end after Kluivert had handballed. Gary was the coolest man on Merseyside as he expertly slotted home the penalty to send the Reds into yet another European final. An interesting fact about this match was that the Barcelona goalkeeper that night was a young Pepe Reina.

Gary followed this up with another penalty against Tottenham Hotspur and free kicks against Coventry City and Bradford City. His reaction to the goal against Coventry City, which basically caused them to be relegated, showed how classy Gary is as a man and player. Rather than celebrating with his team-mates he walked away calmly with a sad look on his face, rather than rubbing it in the faces of his former supporters.

Gary was a substitute in the FA Cup final victory over Arsenal and it was his floating free kick that led to the equaliser from Michael Owen. After coming on as a substitute in the previous two finals, Gary was named in the starting line-up for the 2001 UEFA Cup final against Deportivo Alaves in Dortmund. Gary turned back the clock with a breathtaking man of the match performance, as he led Liverpool to victory in one of the most exciting finals of all time. He had a hand in four of Liverpool's goals that night in a 5–4 victory. He took the free kick for the first goal by Markus Babbel and he played the through balls for goals by Steven Gerrard and Robbie Fowler. In extra time, Gary then put the icing on the cake of a truly historic performance by taking the free kick that led to the golden own goal that won Liverpool the trophy.

Gary played one more season for the Reds but he was more of a squad player as Steven Gerrard began to become one of the best players in Europe in the centre of midfield. Despite not starting as many games in his second season Gary still managed some memorable moments, including scoring a penalty in the 2001 Charity Shield victory over Man Utd. He was still a great player even at the age of thirty seven, as he helped Liverpool to a second place finish in the Premiership. At the end of the 2001/02 season Gary departed Anfield after the 5–0 victory over Ipswich, and he was given a standing ovation by everybody at Anfield.

In the summer of 2002 Gary moved back to Coventry City as player manager. He proved himself to be a very capable manager but sadly his time there was cut short by tragedy. After just one season Gary resigned in 2003 to look after his wife Denise who was diagnosed with breast cancer. She passed away in 2006.

He took a number of years away from the game and worked regularly as a television pundit for Sky and Setanta, usually in the studio for most Liverpool games. In 2006 he was rumoured to have been offered a coaching position at Liverpool but declined as it was still too soon after his wife's passing. During this time he maintained a link with the club by writing a column in the match programme.

Gary returned to management in January 2008, at his old club Leeds Utd, playing in the third tier of English football. He took them to the playoff final in his first season, but they lost to Doncaster Rovers. He was then sacked in December 2008, after some poor results and an FA Cup defeat to part timer's Histon.

After leaving Leeds, Gary was linked with the manager's job at Motherwell and a coaching role with Scotland. He eventually joined Aston Villa as assistant manager alongside his old boss Gerard Houllier, in September 2010. When Gerard was hospitalized midway through the season, Gary took over the management of the first team. At the end of the season Gerard was let go by Villa and so was Gary.

It wasn't just his performances on the pitch that make Gary such an Anfield legend, it is also the positive influence he had on the younger players at the time. Steven Gerrard has talked about what a positive influence Gary was on himself and describes him as a "class act" in his autobiography. Despite only playing for Liverpool for two seasons, Gary did more for the club than many others who played for the club for far more time. His efforts during the climax to the 2000/01 season mean that Gary McAllister deserves his place alongside any of the Anfield Legends. These efforts have not been forgotten by the Liverpool supporters, as proven by his placing of number 32 in the series '100 Players Who Shook the Kop'.

Gerard Houllier

In September 1969 a twenty-two year old Frenchman was standing on the Kop watching Liverpool thrash Irish side Dundalk 10-0. This was the start of a lifelong admiration and support for the club from a young trainee teacher named Gerard Houllier. Whilst studying at Lille University in France he elected to spend one year in Liverpool at Alsop Comprehensive in 1969/70. It was during this time that a great love for everything Liverpool red was ingrained in him. So when he returned to Anfield as manager twenty eight years later it was the culmination of a dream.

Gerard was a handy player in his youth in France and he played part-time, combining this with his career as a school headmaster. In 1973 when he was just twenty six, he became the player manager at Le Touquet Athletic Club and commenced his full time career in football. After three years Gerard moved on to become manager of Noex Les-Mines, a small provincial club in the Calais region of France. He had great success there and led the club through two consecutive promotions up to Ligue Two. This gained him a great reputation and in 1982 he moved to a bigger club RC Lens. In three seasons he led the side to promotion to the top division and then into qualification for the UEFA Cup. This led Gerard into even bigger things and in 1985 he became the manager of one France's biggest clubs Paris Saint-Germain. He led them to the Ligue One title in 1985/86 and his reputation as one of French football's best managers was confirmed.

In 1988, Michel Platini who was managing the French national team, invited Gerard to become a technical director and his assistant. In 1992 he graduated to become the boss of the national side during the qualifying campaign for the 1994 World Cup. He lasted just over a year in the role and resigned after France failed to qualify for USA

94. Gerard's reign ended in controversy when he publicly blamed David Ginola for a mistake he made in the crucial final qualifying game against Bulgaria. France needed only a draw at home to qualify, but with the game locked at 1-1, Ginola over-hit a pass, which was intercepted and led to the winning goal for Bulgaria. Ginola was subsequently branded as an 'assassin of French Football' and he later threatened to take legal action against Gerard for as good as ending his international career and his subsequent barracking by French football fans. Gerard remained as technical director for the national side and was credited as a key person behind the scenes as France won the World Cup at home in 1998.

After the 1998 World Cup in France, Gerard was invited by the Liverpool board to form a joint managerial partnership with Roy Evans. Roy now says that at the time when he was asked about it, he'd just returned from a holiday and wasn't thinking straight. He says that if he had been thinking straight, he would never have agreed. The joint manager role didn't go well and it seemed like Roy's nose was being pushed out. Whenever the team did badly Roy would be blamed and when we won Gerard would get the credit. The image being portrayed in the media at the time was that Roy's ideas and boot room methods were outdated while Gerard was bringing fresh new ideas from the continent. One of the big problems with the joint managers was that the players never knew who the actual boss was. Gerard is well known for avoiding confrontation so Roy (as was Phil Thompson later on) was often made to look the bad guy delivering bad news to players on his own. Both managers would agree to give players being dropped the bad news together, but apparently when the time came Gerard was often nowhere to be found.

Things came to a head after an away game at Valencia in the UEFA Cup. Steve McManaman, Paul Ince and Valencia's Carboni were all sent off after a brawl on the touchline. Roy was furious with his players and the officials and was steaming mad at full time after we'd managed to scrape through on away goals. Roy later revealed that Gerard refused to close ranks in the dressing room and instead seemed more interested in handing out shirts to the officials. On the flight home Roy decided that the partnership would never work and one of them had to go. Gerard wasn't going anywhere so Roy made the ultimate sacrifice for the club he loves so much and resigned a week later in November 1998 after a 3-1 defeat at home to Spurs.

Gerard was now free to stamp his own authority on the club and he brought in Liverpool legend Phil Thompson as his assistant. This was a very sensible decision as not only is Thommo very well respected he is also an intelligent man with a great knowledge of the game. He was also a great person to have as a buffer between Gerard and the players. With all the problems during the 1998/99 season, Liverpool finished in a lowly seventh place and didn't qualify for Europe the following season.

In the summer of 1999 Gerard began what he described as a five year program to rebuild the team. Paul Ince was sold as he was considered a disruptive influence and Gerard wanted to establish a stronger discipline within the squad. Also sold were, Jason McAteer, Rob Jones, David James and Steve Harkness. Steve McManaman joined Real Madrid on a free transfer that had been agreed months earlier. Joining Liverpool that summer were, Vladmir Smicer, Sander Westerweld, Titi Camara and Djimi Traore. They were followed by possibly Gerard's three finest signings, Sami Hyypia, Stephane Henchoz and Dietmar Hamman. The signing of Hyypia in particular (for just 2.5 million pounds) was a moment of genius as he went on to become one of the club's greatest ever defenders.

Also that summer Gerard started the huge overhaul of the training facility Melwood to help bring the club into the future. He also continued with his plans to change the dietary habits of the players and curb any indiscipline. After the 1998 Christmas party got out of hand and embarrassing photos appeared in the tabloids of players frolicking with strippers, Gerard began to make inspirational speeches to the players about how to look after themselves properly and behave away from the pitch. He instigated a ban on alcohol, which had been a staple diet of many Liverpool legends of the past, and encouraged the younger players to settle down and become family men. It cannot be underestimated just how much Gerard did to drag the club into the modern age of football at that time.

1999/2000 was a big improvement on the previous season and thanks to Hyypia and Henchoz the defence conceded nineteen less goals than in 1998/99. At one stage it looked like we were going to make the Champions League spots as we went on a run of one defeat in eighteen games. Unfortunately there were no wins or goals in the final five games and the team had to contend with a UEFA Cup place instead. The final game of the season was quite dramatic as Liverpool could still have qualified for the Champions league with a victory away to Bradford City. However the Yorkshiremen were playing for Premiership survival and sunk Liverpool to defeat.

In the summer of 2000 there was another overhaul of the playing staff as Gerard sought to continue the good work and improvements of the previous season. Emile Heskey had been bought in March for a club record of 11 million pounds. Joining him that summer were Igor Biscan, Markus Babbel, Christian Ziege and Nick Barmby who caused controversy by crossing Stanley Park to join from Everton. In my opinion though, the most inspired signing of that summer was Gary McAllister on a free transfer. McAllister famously inspired the team to the amazing treble with his important goals and sublime performances in the middle of the park. Departing the club that summer were, David Thompson, Phil Babb, Brad Friedel, Dominic Matteo and Stig Inge Bjornebye.

There isn't a great deal I can say about the amazing 2000/01 season that hasn't been said a thousand times already. Istanbul in 2005 has tended to overshadow the achievements of 2000/01 but they really cannot be underestimated. Apart from the three trophies we won that season there were also a number of memorable games in the final months. The greatest (apart from the finals) was possibly the derby with the last minute goal by McAllister at Goodison Park that inspired us to go on and clinch third place and a Champions League spot. Who can forget the excited look on Gerard Houllier's face at the end of the game? There was also the UEFA Cup semi final victory over Barcelona at Anfield and the win at Roma earlier in the competition. Michael Owen was inspired that season and he was later awarded the European Player of the Year. Emile Heskey also had the most productive season of his career by scoring twenty three goals. The season is best remembered for us winning the fantastic treble of League Cup, FA Cup and UEFA Cup as well as clinching that third league place to enter the Champions league for the first time. At the end of the season, Gerard was robbed of the manager of the year award, when it was given to George Burley for guiding Ipswich to fourth in the league.

Unlike the previous two summers there were no major changes to the side in the 2001 pre-season, though in another inspired signing, Jari Litmanen had joined the previous January. Sander Westerweld was ruthlessly sold in August after making two high profile errors in a defeat to Bolton Wanderers. Jerzy Dudek and Chris Kirkland arrived pretty much the next day and Westerweld was sold to Real Sociedad in Spain. John Arne Riise also joined in August and he proved to be a really tremendous signing, scoring on his debut in the Super Cup Final. He also went on to score some brilliant goals that season against Everton and Arsenal and a rocket of a free kick against Man Utd.

The 2001/02 season started in style with a victory over Man Utd in the Charity Shield. We then made it five trophies held at the same time by beating the Champions League winners Bayern Munich in the Super Cup Final. Unfortunately these two fabulous victories and the start of the season were disrupted with fights between Robbie Fowler, Gerard Houllier and Phil Thompson. The week before the Charity Shield, the players were practising penalties at Melwood. Phil Thompson was retrieving balls from the net when Robbie blasted one that just missed Thommo's nose by inches. Thompson went berserk and laid into Robbie and demanded an apology as Robbie and some other players were laughing. Gerard informed Robbie that he was dropped for the Charity Shield and wouldn't play again until he apologised for the incident. Robbie travelled to Cardiff with the rest of the team but ended up leaving before the end and making his own way home. Robbie was later sold to Leeds Utd in November 2001.

However all of these incidents were massively overshadowed in October 2001 during a home game against Leeds. Gerard didn't come back out for the second half and speculation was rife that something bad had happened, the game was televised and I remember being really worried about what was going on. I hadn't noticed Gerard looking ill during the first half but after the game had ended the news broke that he had been rushed to hospital with heart problems. He had to have an emergency life-saving operation on a dissected aorta and almost died. While he recuperated, Phil Thompson took over the reins and did a magnificent job steering the side through the Champions League group stages and the Premier League. Gerard returned after five months on one of the most emotional nights in Anfield history as we needed to beat Roma by two goals to advance to the quarter finals of the Champions League. Gerard's presence on the bench inspired the team and the crowd as we won the game 2-0 with goals from Litmanen and Heskey.

Unfortunately Gerard's magic touch with tactics deserted him in the second leg of the quarter final against Bayer Leverkusen. We won the first leg at home 1-0 and went into the second leg full of optimism. With the tie looking firmly in the bag, Gerard controversially substituted Hamman and brought on Smicer. With a huge hole now in our defensive unit, Leverkusen and Michael Ballack in particular, ran riot and we were knocked out of the competition. This moment was probably the start of Gerard being seriously questioned after he had previously appeared to have a touch of genius.

The season did end on a high note though as we played brilliantly in the league, and inspired by Nicolas Anelka on loan, we went on to finish in second place behind Arsenal, and more crucially ahead of Man Utd for the first time ever in the Premier League era. Gerard had guided the team to five trophies and a third then second place finish in two seasons, it appeared that the next logical step was to finally win the league title again. Unfortunately, what happened next is still one of the most incredible turnarounds in Liverpool's recent history.

Jari Litmanen and Gary McAllister were both released in the summer of 2002, both were in the tail end of their careers and had been excellent servants during the previous two seasons. Unfortunately they were both vital to the creativity of the side and needed to be replaced with younger players of similar or better ability. Gerard decided to replace them with Salif Diao and Bruno Cheyrou, surely two of the worst signings in the clubs history. However worse was yet to come when the option to sign Anelka permanently was not taken up and instead Senegalese striker El Hadji Diouf was signed for 11 million pounds. As I write this all these years later I still cannot fathom what on earth was going through Gerard's mind at the time. I have heard that these players had been recommended by Michel Platini, but surely Gerard and

Phil Thompson must have scouted them in advance. What they saw in them is a mystery to me, especially to equal the club's transfer record on Diouf.

The 2002/03 season began well with nine wins and three draws in the opening twelve games. It really did appear that our prophecy of taking the next step in the league was going to come true. Diouf had scored two goals on his debut and hadn't yet shown just how awful he was to become. Unfortunately in the next game we lost 1-0 to Middlesbrough and Gerard was heavily criticised for his cautious tactics in that game when we should have been over-confident going into it. After that defeat we then went on what was at the time our worst run for almost fifty years and didn't win another game until January 2003.

As the season just seemed to get worse and worse, Gerard started coming out with a never ending stream of poor excuses, blaming everything except himself and his tactics. He was replacing strikers with defenders in games we were losing and it really did appear that he had lost the plot. It's been said many times that he was never the same after his illness and it appeared to be true. I wish I could explain why it all went so pear shaped so quickly with some unbelievable decisions throughout that season. I went to quite a few matches that season and was almost always disgusted with what I was watching. This was never worse than during the FA Cup defeat at home to Crystal Palace, the one and only time I walked out of Anfield before the final whistle. We also failed to get out of the group in the Champions League. Making things worse we were then knocked out of the UEFA Cup by Celtic, after Diouf had disgraced himself and the club by spitting at a fan on live television in the away leg. We failed to qualify for the Champions League again with our place going to Chelsea who took it by beating us on the last day of the season.

The 2002/03 season wasn't all doom and gloom though, as we did win a trophy by beating Man Utd in the League Cup Final. It was a fantastic and quite frankly unexpected victory, thanks to goals from Steven Gerrard and Michael Owen and an inspired performance from Jerzy Dudek. This victory probably saved Gerard from the sack and he was given another season to turn things around again and hopefully complete his five year plan.

Harry Kewell arrived in the summer of 2003 and this seemed to be a really exciting signing at the time. Also joining the club were French youngsters Le Tallec and Sinama-Pongolle. Unfortunately the following season wasn't much of an improvement on the previous one, although we weren't helped by serious injuries to many of the key players including Carragher breaking his leg and Owen missing a fair bit too. As the season progressed it appeared that Gerard was now living on borrowed time and the noose around his neck seemed to get tighter and tighter with every poor result. The local radio phone in shows and the letters pages of The Echo were inundated with demands to sack him, which I'm sure put a lot of pressure on the Liverpool board. Fortunately for Liverpool, England now had four Champions League spots and Gerard was able to guide the team into fourth place at the end of the season. Unfortunately for him this wasn't enough to save his job and at the end of the season Gerard and Thompson were both dismissed. In probably his final transfer act as Liverpool manager Gerard agreed the deal to bring Djibril Cisse to the club for the following season.

After leaving Liverpool, Gerard returned to France and walked straight into the manager's chair at Lyon. The team had just won four successive league titles and Gerard was hired to help take their domestic success into Europe. Lyon won two Ligue One titles in a row under Gerard but were unable to win anything in Europe with arguably their best result being an unlucky defeat to AC Milan in the Champions League quarter final in 2006. After rumours of unrest behind the scenes Gerard stepped down from his role at the end of the 2006/07 season.

After leaving Lyon, Gerard went back into his old role as a technical director with the French FA. In September 2010 he returned to club management by taking over as full time manager at Aston Villa. Unfortunately he was not too successful at the club and after suffering ill health in April, 2011 he left the club by mutual consent at the end of the 2010/11 season.

It is my sincere hope that Gerard Houllier is not just remembered by Liverpool fans for what happened during his final two seasons at the club. What he achieved in his first three seasons should never be underestimated. Not only did we win five major trophies (six if you include the Charity Shield) under his stewardship, he did so much more on top of that. He arranged a major overhaul of the training facilities and the academy, as well as changing the culture of the dressing room to improve fitness and overall attitudes. Gerard is massively responsible for Liverpool remaining amongst the elite clubs in Europe, when it really looked like we were going backwards before he arrived, without meaning any disrespect to Roy Evans. I am able to look back on his early years as manager with a lot of fondness. The treble can never be forgotten and the fact that he was so devoted that he risked his health and possibly his life for the club means that the man should be regarded as a hero at Anfield. He also brought Steven Gerrard through the ranks, gave him the captaincy and helped make him the legend he has since become. Whenever Gerard Houllier returns to Anfield as either a fan or an opposition manager I for one will stand and applaud him for what he did for our club.

Igor Biscan

Croatian defensive midfielder Igor Biscan was a cult favourite amongst Liverpool supporters. He was sarcastically nicknamed Zinedine Biscan by the Reds fans, partly because he drew comparisons to the former France captain Zidane earlier in his career. He was actually a more talented player than he is often given credit for and part of his problem at Liverpool stemmed from being played out of position most of the time, especially by Gerard Houllier.

Igor Biscan was born in May 1978 in Zagreb, Croatia (then part of Yugoslavia). He was a talented player as a youngster and represented Croatia at youth level. In 1997 he began his professional career with local side Dinamo Zagreb. Igor spent part of his first season, 1997/98, on loan at NK Samobor but only managed to make five appearances for the Dinamo Zagreb first team. Afterwards, he then became one of the most important players in the side helping them to win the Croatian Championship for the fourth consecutive season in 1998/99. They also competed in the Champions League for the first time, where they finished second in their first group stage with wins over Porto and Ajax. For the 1999/2000 season Igor was made the club captain and began to make a name for himself around Europe. He captained the side to a fifth league title as well as during the clubs second campaign in the Champions League. Although they finished bottom of their group in the Champions League they had a famous 0-0 draw away at Man Utd, with Igor playing a blinder.

During the European Under-21 Championships in the summer of 2000, Igor played superbly and started attracting the attentions of some major clubs. Juventus, AC Milan, Ajax and Barcelona were all heavily linked with him in late 2000. So when Liverpool manager

Gerard Houllier signed him for £5.5 million in December 2000 it was seen as a real coup for the Reds. There were a few rumours at the time that Houllier was losing faith with Didi Hamman, and the signing of Igor seemed to add fuel to these stories.

Igor made his Liverpool debut two days after signing, as a substitute in a 1-0 defeat to Ipswich. Despite the loss, Igor impressed in his cameo showing some nice touches and neat passing. He played a bit part during the remainder of the season as Liverpool went on to win the treble of League Cup, FA Cup and UEFA Cup. He didn't play regularly because Hamman was playing brilliantly, Steven Gerrard was in form and Gary McAllister was turning back the clock in every game he played. Igor did have a few standout performances during the season. He dominated the midfield in victories over Man Utd and Arsenal, during which he won huge battles with Roy Keane and Patrick Vieira. He also scored his first Liverpool goal in the 5-0 victory over Crystal Palace in the League Cup semi final.

Igor became a cult hero on the terraces at Anfield, especially after the two performances against Man Utd and Arsenal. Cries of 'Eeeeeeegor' would regularly be heard whenever he was playing. Stories also started emerging around Merseyside of Igor being a bit of a character off the field, including rumours of him being a ladies man. I regularly used to hear various tales about him being spotted in different locations with stunning dolly birds on his arm. Igor was actually a really quiet fella and therefore it was easy for this type of image to be attached to him without it being questioned. Whether these stories were true or not, it all added to the cult status he was starting to achieve with the supporters.

After showing plenty of promise during his first season and an ageing Gary McAllister now playing less games, it looked obvious that Igor was ready to take on a more important role in central midfield for the 2001/02 season. Well obvious to everybody except Gerard Houllier who insisted that Igor's best position was at centre back. Stephane Henchoz had spells out injured during the season and Igor was chosen to play alongside Sami Hyypia. They never looked good as a partnership and it was thanks to Sami that we didn't concede more goals. I was always frustrated whenever Igor was playing in central defence because I knew that Jamie Carragher was the natural choice to play there. We now had Christian Ziege to play at full back so Jamie could have easily slotted in there. However despite the cries for Jamie to play there from the supporters, local media and even Phil Thompson, Houllier insisted that Carra was too short for the position and Igor was the man to play there when Hyypia or Henchoz were injured.

In late 2002 there was a seven week spell when Henchoz was out and Igor stepped in again. During this period we played quite poorly and despite Sami's best efforts we shipped a load of goals, which eventually contributed to Liverpool's failure to qualify for a Champions League place for the 2003/04 season.

The 2003/04 season was more of the same for Igor whose performances for Liverpool were now becoming a bit of a joke. From being compared to Zidane earlier in his career he was now looking more like Torben Piechnik (the man whose signing caused many a Red to consider giving away their season tickets). He was being played all over the park from defence to the wings but never in his strongest position, central midfield. Things went from bad to worse for his Liverpool career when he was sent off away to Marseille in the UEFA Cup quarter final. With Liverpool down to ten men, Drogba ran riot and the Reds were knocked out of the tournament. When discussing this game in his autobiography, Steven Gerrard refers to Igor as "that tit". This defeat signalled that the axe was drawing closer for Houllier and his insistence at playing Igor in defence was often touted in the media as proof that he was clueless.

This is a very harsh judgement considering what Houllier did for the club in his early seasons but it was certainly clear that he was making decisions that were not beneficial to Liverpool at all.

A perfect example of Houllier losing his touch is the fact that he insisted on playing Igor in defence or on the wings, while at the same time the likes of Bruno Cheyrou and Salif Diao where getting games in midfield. Both players lacked athleticism, ability to pass a ball and any of the qualities required to succeed at the top level. Igor had proven at Dinamo Zagreb, and during his first season at Liverpool, that he had something to offer in midfield but three seasons played out of position undoubtedly contributed to a decline in his abilities and possibly his confidence.

In the summer of 2004, Houllier left the club and Rafa Benitez took over as Liverpool manager. When Xabi Alonso was signed to play in midfield it appeared that Igor's Liverpool career would be over. However, thanks in part to injuries and suspensions, the 2004/05 season would end up being his finest in a Liverpool shirt and etched him into the hearts of Reds supporters everywhere.

When Steven Gerrard suffered a broken metatarsal against Man Utd in September 2004, Igor got his chance to finally start playing in central midfield. Three years removed from the position meant that he was rusty and his performances were inconsistent. He was able to turn it on from time to time though and played a few absolute blinders, especially in the Champions League. In late 2004 he came off the bench and scored a belter with his second touch in the 4-2 victory over Fulham. He also played really well in the Champions League game against Deportivo La Coruna. When Steven Gerrard came back into the side it looked like Igor would be back playing in the reserves and the League Cup, where he played well helping the Reds to reach the final. Xabi Alonso then suffered a broken ankle against Chelsea in December, and Igor was back in the first team. He had a few bad performances, particularly in the FA Cup defeat to Burnley, but he also had some outstanding performances too.

His finest game for Liverpool came in the Champions League against Bayer Leverkusen at Anfield, where he deputised for the suspended Gerrard. He set up Luis Garcia for the opening goal and played superbly alongside Didi Hamman as he looked graceful on the ball and made lots of great passes. He also played well against Juventus in the quarter finals. I was present inside Anfield to witness Igor's final goal for Liverpool when he headed a late winner in a 1-0 victory over Bolton in April 2005. His last big game came against Chelsea in the Champions League semi final where he was one of the heroes that battled to reach the final in Istanbul. Igor's final appearance in the Liverpool squad came when he was an unused substitute in the Champions League final. After the heroic victory, Igor received a winner's medal that was fully deserved after his efforts to help Liverpool reach the final.

In July 2005, Igor was released by Liverpool and he moved on to join Greek side Panathinaikos for two seasons. This coincided in a poor period for the club and the highlight of his two seasons there was when they reached the 2007 Greek Cup Final, losing to Larissa. In December 2007, he moved back to Croatia to join Dinamo Zagreb. In his first season back at the club he helped them to win the Croatian league and cup double in 2007/08. His efforts were rewarded when he was named the club captain for the 2008/09 season after Luka Modric moved to Tottenham Hotspur. They won another league and cup double the following season. In 2012, Igor terminated his contract with the club and retired from playing.

Igor Biscan is never going to be regarded as one of Liverpool's greatest players, but no matter how we may have rated him as a player, his name rarely fails to make us smile. Despite three horrendous seasons at the club, his revival in his final season and the performances on the road to Istanbul, have given him a place in the hearts of Reds supporters everywhere.

Jari Litmanen

Jari Litmanen is widely regarded Finland's greatest ever footballer. He is the most capped player for the Finnish national team as well as being their leading goal scorer. A fantastic player who was often too quick in his thinking even for his team-mates, Jari was consistently one of the best players in Europe during the 1990's. He is also the only footballer to play for his national side in four different decades.

Jari was born in 1971 in Lahti, Finland. He was raised in a footballing family, as both of his parents played for Finnish club Reipas Lahti at the highest level. His father was also an international player. It was only fitting that Jari should begin his career at Reipas Lahti, with his parents having played for the club. He made his first team debut in 1987, when he was just sixteen years old. In 1990 he was voted as the Finnish player of the year for the first time. This was an award he went on to win nine times over the next decade. In 1991 he moved to the biggest club in Finland, HJK Helsinki, where he stayed for just one year. In 1992 he joined rival team MyPa for half a season and helped them to win the Finnish Cup during the 1991/92 season.

After an eye catching performance in the 1992 Finnish Cup final, Jari was chased by a host of top European clubs. He signed for the great Dutch side Ajax that summer and thus began a golden period of his career. In his first season in Holland, Jari had to play second fiddle to Dennis Bergkamp. When Bergkamp moved to Inter Milan in 1993, Jari became the main man up front. He did not disappoint during the 1993/94 season as he scored twenty six goals. He was the league's leading scorer and Ajax was crowned league champions.

Ajax had an incredible team during the mid nineties that contained such amazing talents as Rijkaard, Kluivert, Overmars and Davids. Incredibly Jari stood out above these great players to become the star player as they reached two Champions League finals in a row in 1994/95 and 1995/96. They won the trophy in 1995 after beating AC Milan 1-0 with a goal from Kluivert. Jari scored nine goals during the 1995/96 Champions League campaign including the equalising goal in the final against Juventus, which Ajax lost on penalties. After an outstanding season, Jari came third in the voting for the 1996 European Player of the Year.

Jari spent seven seasons at Ajax, during which time he helped them win four Dutch Championships, three Dutch Cups, one Champions League Final and the Intercontinental Cup. He was nicknamed Merlin by the Ajax supporters because of his magical football abilities and he remains their third most popular player of all time behind Johan Cruyff and Marco Van Basten.

In 1997/98 Liverpool manager Roy Evans wanted to sign Jari but was refused the funds to make the purchase. This was a terrible shame as I genuinely feel that had Liverpool signed him at that time he would have turned the club from decent to outstanding, that's how good he was in his prime. In 1999 Jari's former Ajax boss Louis Van Gaal signed him for Spanish giants Barcelona. After two poor seasons, largely interrupted by injury, Jari eventually moved to Anfield.

In January 2001, Liverpool manager Gerard Houllier described the free purchase of Jari as; "one of the most exciting signings Liverpool have ever made". Jari was a lifelong Liverpool fan from childhood, so this was a pretty huge transfer for both parties.

260

For the one and a half seasons that he spent as a Liverpool player I always felt he wasn't played enough. I was a huge fan of Jari and I remember being really angry whenever he wasn't in the team for a game. I often wondered, what was the point in having one of the best players in Europe, if he wasn't going to play very often. What I didn't realise until a long time later, was that Jari could hardly train due to problems with his ankles and he was barely able to play for ninety minutes week in and week out.

Jari missed the three finals during the 2000/01 treble winning season due to injuries, but he did play an important part in some other big games for Liverpool. He was an important player during the 2001/02 Champions League campaign. With injuries to Michael Owen during the season, Jari stepped up to score some important goals. Just days after an incredible goal from thirty yards against Tottenham Hotspur, he scored a cheeky goal against Dynamo Kiev in a Champions League group game. He then scored an important penalty against Roma in the crucial final group game at Anfield. This was the game where Houllier made his return after his heart operation and inspired the Reds to the 2-0 victory they required to reach the quarter finals. Jari then scored an outstanding individual goal in the quarter final second leg against Bayer Leverkusen. At this stage the goal was enough to send Liverpool through to the semi finals, but the teams collapse after Didi Hamman was taken off, led to an eventful 4-2 defeat.

Jari was a really popular player during his time at Anfield, his incredible skills could light up a dull game and he was always quiet and humble, despite his stature as one of the games greatest players. His work ethic was outstanding as he would chase lost causes and poor passes from team mates. Unfortunately due to injuries and lack of match fitness, he was mostly utilised from the bench. It is tantalising to wonder just how important he could have been to the team had he been able to play a more central role in the side.

At the end of the 2001/02 season Jari was given a free transfer and left Liverpool with nothing but best wishes from all the supporters. He decided to return to Ajax where he was given a heroes welcome by their supporters. In his first season back in Amsterdam, Jari turned back the clock as he was an inspirational figure leading the side to the Champions League quarter finals. Sadly, during the following season he was plagued by niggling injuries and in the summer of 2004 he was released by the club.

He then made a heroes welcome to Finland and joined FC Lahti where his signing was billed as 'The Return of the King'. However he didn't stay very long and in January 2005 he moved to Hansa Rostock, who was struggling in the German Bundesliga. Despite a prolonged run in the first team, Jari was unable to help them avoid relegation and he left the club at the end of the season.

Jari then spent two seasons in Sweden playing for Malmo. His two years there were the usual mix of long spells injured and flashes of pure genius whenever he was fit. After an ankle operation in June 2007 he decided not to enter into a third season with Malmo. Jari then spent the next six months without a club as he recovered from his ankle operation. However, he did play for Finland in their qualifying games for Euro 2008.

In January 2008 his former Finland coach Roy Hodgson invited Jari for a ten day trial at Fulham. He was offered a first team contract but then returned to Finland after a heart concern. He played for the reserves at Fulham but never made a single appearance in the first team before his release at the end of the 2007/08 season. In August 2008 he rejoined FC Lahti in Finland where he scored goals and played an important role helping the side to finish third in the league and qualify for Europe for the first time in the clubs history. He stayed for three seasons and continued to play an important role at the club. In September 2010, he scored an overhead kick when he was thirty nine.

Jari played his final game for Finland in an 8-0 victory over San Marino in November 2010. He became the oldest player ever to score in the Qualifiers for the European Championships when he netted a penalty. In April 2011, he signed a one year contract at the age of forty, with reigning Finnish champions HJK. This was Jari's final season as a player and he helped HJK to win the league and cup double.

Jari Litmanen was one of the most naturally gifted players ever to represent Liverpool. It is just a terrible shame that he wasn't given the opportunity to light up Anfield during his prime, before injuries restricted him to a part time role in the team. Despite his limited time as a Liverpool player he will never be forgotten by Reds fans who appreciated his outstanding skills and vital goals. This was proven with his placing of number 69 in the series '100 Players Who Shook the Kop'.

Jerzy Dudek

Whenever I think about Polish goalkeeper Jerzy Dudek, I am always torn between thinking he wasn't as good as he appeared in his first season at Liverpool and remembering his heroics in Istanbul. Regardless of what happened in his Liverpool career before or after Istanbul he will forever be regarded as a hero to Reds fans for what he did on that special night in May 2005.

Jerzy was born in March 1973 in Rybnik, Poland. He began his career at youth level with Gornik II Knurow where he played for six years, until he was eighteen. He began his professional career in 1991 with Polish third division side Concordia Knurow. He was an immediate success in the Polish third division and went on to set the record in the division of going 416 minutes without conceding a goal. In 1995 he moved to another Polish lower division side Sokol Tychy. He only made fifteen appearances for the club during the 1995/96 season before he moved to Holland in 1996 and joined Feyenoord.

It was during his time in Holland that Jerzy really began to make a name for himself in the football world. However before this would happen he had to spend a year on the sidelines before he made his first team debut in the 1997/98 season. He then made the goalkeepers position his own as he went on to make 140 consecutive appearances. The highlight of his first season with Feyenoord was a 2-0 victory over Juventus in the Champions League group stages. After impressing during this season he was picked to make his full debut for the Polish national side in February 1998. Poland failed to qualify for the 1998 World Cup but Jerzy got over this disappointment by having his finest season so far in 1998/99.

Feyenoord had an outstanding season in 1998/99 as they won the Dutch League Championship and the Dutch Super Cup. In the Cup final they beat Ajax at their own stadium 3-2. This was also a great season for Jerzy personally as he was voted the Dutch Goalkeeper of the Year. He went on to retain the award the following season and was described by legendary Dutch coach Leo Beenhakker as "the best goalkeeper I've seen in thirty years".

In August 2001 Liverpool manager Gerard Houllier bombed out the goalkeeper Sander Westerveld after one howler too many in a defeat to Bolton Wanderers. Despite playing a part in the clubs treble success the season before, Westerveld was never rated that highly by many people and the day after the Bolton game Houllier brought in two new goalkeepers, Chris Kirkland and Jerzy Dudek. Jerzy was very highly rated at the time and in fact had been courted by Arsenal during the summer of 2001. He immediately became the first choice keeper at Anfield and quickly became a fan favourite with some outstanding displays.

During his first season on Merseyside, 2001/02, Jerzy kept twenty six clean sheets and began to garner comparisons to the great Ray Clemence. He was absolutely brilliant as he helped the Reds to win the UEFA Super Cup and finish second in the Premiership behind Arsenal and ahead of Man Utd. He was nominated for UEFA Goalkeeper of the Year and then capped of a great year by helping Poland reach the 2002 World Cup Finals.

Jerzy's second season at Liverpool was not as successful as his first one was. Unfortunately he seemed to have problems with his confidence and suffered a terrible loss of form. A series of errors in games eventually culminated in a serious mistake in a 2-1 defeat to Man Utd in the league in December 2002. In one of the biggest howlers ever seen at Anfield, Jerzy allowed a tame header from Jamie Carragher slip through his hands and legs and Diego Forlan slipped in to score. After this mistake Jerzy's confidence was lower than ever and he immediately lost his place in the side to Chris Kirkland. However the injury prone keeper got himself hurt after a run of fourteen games (and six clean sheets) and Jerzy was back in the side. This time he seemed to have put his poor form behind him and started to play like he had during the previous season. Jerzy was able to avenge the mistake against Man Utd when he was awarded the man of the match in the 2003 League Cup final victory over our rivals from down the East Lancs. Jerzy rebuilt his reputation in this game by pulling off a string of unbelievable saves and was later described as an octopus in the Guardian newspaper report.

In 2004 Jerzy was invited to meet with Pope John Paul II at The Vatican. The pope had been a goalkeeper in Poland during his youth and revealed that he had closely followed Jerzy's career with Liverpool. Jerzy was honoured to present the pontiff with a replica goalkeeper's jersey.

Jerzy made thirty eight appearances during the 2003/04 season as Liverpool finished in fourth place to qualify for the Champions League. Unfortunately for Gerard Houllier this wasn't enough for the Liverpool board and the Frenchman was sacked at the end of the season. The new manager Rafa Benitez brought Scott Carson into the first team squad and although Jerzy was usually first choice during the season, the goalkeeping duties were occasionally shared between himself, Carson and Kirkland. Despite not always being first choice during the 2004/05 season it was to be the one that made him into Anfield legend.

Jerzy played an important role during the Reds European campaign in 2004/05 and played really well in helping them to reach the 2005 Champions League final against AC Milan in Istanbul. Jerzy had a really good game that night as the Liverpool side wrote themselves into football history. He made an incredible free kick save at full stretch at the very start of the second half. The importance of this save should never be underestimated because if AC Milan had gone 4-0 up, the game would most likely have been all over. However his save just about kept Liverpool in the game and gave the hope that led to the incredible comeback a few minutes later. As good as this save was, the best was still to come.

With three minutes left in extra time Jerzy made a double save that I still find hard to believe. This save certainly fits the bill whenever the phrase miracle of Istanbul is uttered. I remember looking away from the TV screen as the cross came in because surely there was no chance that Shevchenko could miss a header from point blank range. I opened my eyes to see the ball had gone behind for a corner.

266

Somehow Jerzy had blocked Shevchenko's header then somehow diverted his follow up shot over the bar from only a yard out. From that moment on, it appeared to be destiny for Liverpool to win the trophy. After coming back from 3-0 down and then Jerzy making his amazing double save there seemed no way that we wouldn't be taking Old Big Ears back to Anfield for keeps.

The game went to a penalty shoot-out and then Jerzy had another chance to make himself a hero. AC Milan was up first and the Brazilian Serghino was to take the first penalty. Jerzy then started jumping around on the goal line waving his arms and doing a starfish stance. This proved enough to cause a distraction and the penalty was blasted wide. Didi Hamman then stepped up to put the ball in the net. Up next was Pirlo for Milan and once again Jerzy was jumping around like a madman. Once again the tactics worked and he saved the pen. Cisse stepped up to put the Reds 2-0 up in the shoot-out and give us a massive advantage. The next two Milan penalties were scored and after Riise missed, Smicer had knocked his one in to put us just one penalty away from victory. Up stepped Shevchenko and I just knew that he was going to miss. After the save from Jerzy in extra time it was clear from the Ukrainian's eyes that he just felt it wasn't going to be his night. This was proved correct as Jerzy saved the penalty and sent Liverpool fans all over the world into a celebration that has never been rivalled.

After such incredible heroics this was to prove the final highlight of Jerzy's Liverpool career. During the summer of 2005 Pepe Reina was brought in and after Jerzy suffered an arm injury in pre-season he never got his place back. It seemed a cruel blow after he had been a hero just a few months earlier, but unfortunately for him Reina is a better goalkeeper and Jerzy had to be sacrificed for the benefit of the club. Jerzy remained at Liverpool for another two seasons but only made another twelve appearances in the first team, mostly in domestic cup games when Rafa decided to rest first team players. This was to have a major effect on Jerzy's international career as he was left out of the Poland squad for the 2006 World Cup Finals due to his lack of playing time during the 2005/06 season.

Jerzy was released by Liverpool at the end of the 2006/07 season and it was a massive shock to everybody when it was revealed that he would be joining Real Madrid. He had complained previously about being treated like a slave by Rafa and he was clearly unhappy about being the second choice goalkeeper. This made his move to Real Madrid even more of a surprise as it meant he was swopping one bench for another, as there was no chance of displacing the outstanding Iker Casillas at the Bernabeu.

Jerzy spent four seasons at Real Madrid and only played two La Liga games and a few cup games, due to Casillas being possibly the finest goalkeeper in the world at the time. When Real Madrid played Liverpool in the Champions League in 2008, Jerzy was denied a chance to play at Anfield one more time when he was left on the bench. In the few games when he did play, he was actually really good and in a couple of games he was chosen as the man of the match. He has been praised by his team-mates and manager as being a fantastic professional. He left the club in the summer of 2011 and his last game was in the 8-1 win over Almeria. During this game, Jerzy was substituted in the 77th minute and given a standing ovation from the crowd and a guard of honour from his teammates.

Jerzy is a massive hero in Poland and he played a role in securing the countries status as joint hosts for the 2012 European Championships. He was part of the Polish football association's delegation and he is major ambassador for the country all over the world. He is also an honorary citizen of Knurow where he began his football career. Despite not playing for any clubs since leaving Real Madrid, Jerzy still played for Poland in a couple of games. His farewell game was in June 2013 against Liechtenstein. He was the captain for the game and was substituted at half time. He wore number 60 on his shirt as it was his 60th cap.

Jerzy Dudek is still thought of very fondly by Liverpool supporters. His heroics in Istanbul will never be forgotten and neither will his performance to help us beat Man Utd in the 2003 League Cup Final. It was also very much appreciated when he chose to stay one more season at Liverpool despite knowing he would be second choice and potentially lose out on his international career. He was voted in at number 36 in the series '100 Players Who Shook the Kop'.

John Arne Riise

John Arne Riise is one of those players loved by many but disliked by others. Personally I found him to be very frustrating. He could be brilliant at times and awful at others, especially in his last two seasons at Liverpool. He was prone to making some terrible (and occasionally devastating) mistakes in defence while at the same time having an unbelievable left foot with which he scored some of the most spectacular Liverpool goals I have ever seen.

John was born in September 1980, in Molde, Norway. He comes from a sporting family and his younger brother Bjorn is also a professional footballer who has played many times at international level. John began his professional career as a sixteen year old with Norwegian second division side Aalesund. After just two seasons he moved to France and joined AS Monaco in 1998. He became a regular in the side during the 1999/2000 season when Monaco became Ligue 1 champions. Unfortunately, after the manager Jean Tigana left the club, John fell out with the new manager Claude Puel and expressed a desire to leave. He was frozen out of the team and came close to joining Tigana at Fulham. Leeds Utd also made a bid for him but both Leeds and Fulham had bids of 4 million pounds rejected in the summer of 2000. After one more season in France, John signed for Liverpool in August 2001 after the Reds hijacked a deal that had already been agreed with Fulham.

Riise made his debut for Liverpool in the 2001 Super Cup Final against Bayern Munich, which was ironically held at the Stade Louis II, the home of his previous club. It was a fantastic start for him as a Red as we won the game 3-2 to take home the trophy against the previous season's Champions League winners. He had a great debut season with Liverpool in which we reached the quarter final of the Champions League and finished second in the Premier League. John scored ten goals that season, including some really famous ones against Everton, Man Utd and Arsenal. His goal in the derby came in just his third start in the league and he ran half the length of the pitch with the ball before slotting it home to give us a 3-1 victory. He then did his trademark celebration by sliding on his knees with his shirt over his head. A few months later he scored a screamer against Man Utd at the Anfield Road end. It is one of the most powerful shots I have ever seen and almost burst the net. It was later clocked in at 70mph and it was lucky for the fans in the crowd that it went in, because if it had gone wide it could have really hurt somebody.

Around the time of the goal against Man Utd, there was a novelty song that was a massive hit in England called 'Hey Baby' by DJ Otzi. Liverpool fans began to parody it with a tribute to Riise which became one of the more memorable terrace chants in recent years at Anfield. It was sung to the same tune of 'Hey Baby' and the lyrics were changed to;

John Arne Riise

Ooh Ah

I wanna know

How you scored that goal!

In the following two seasons John's form really deserted him. He was still quite decent going forward but all too often his defensive abilities left a lot to be desired. Consequently he played quite a few games in left midfield. Despite his less than stellar form, John was still able to win the League Cup in 2003 and help Liverpool to a Champions League spot in 2003/04.

In 2004/05 under new manager Rafa Benitez, John suddenly became quite brilliant again. He found his scoring boots as well and banged in a few memorable goals that season. He scored an absolute beauty against Charlton at Anfield, a game I watched live in Coogee Beach, Australia. That was a memorable night for me as I was wearing my Liverpool shirt in a pub and this aboriginal bloke came over to me and shook my hand for my choice of attire. I was a bit wary of him and he disappeared for a while before returning wearing his own Reds shirt! The rest of the night was spent arm in arm singing Liverpool songs and enjoying the win over Charlton, which also featured another spectacular goal from Luis Garcia. Whenever I see or think of Riise's long range goal in that game I have a big smile thinking of that bloke in the pub in Australia.

John also scored a beauty in the first minute of the League Cup Final against Chelsea. Unfortunately, we lost that game 3-2 after extra time. He was one of the heroes in Istanbul for the Champions League final victory over AC Milan, providing the assist for Gerrard's goal that started the amazing comeback. Although he missed his penalty in the shoot-out, John was more than deserving of his winners medal after what I, and many other Reds, consider to be the greatest night in the club's history.

He continued his fine form into the 2005/06 season and almost scored what could have been a contender for goal of the decade against Spurs. He caught a volley in mid air that crashed against the crossbar. To this day I don't know how the goal frame didn't collapse because I have never seen a ball kicked so hard before or since. During the season he also claimed his second Super Cup winner's medal when we defeated CSKA Moscow. John was a vital member of the side during the run to the FA Cup final with goals against Portsmouth and Birmingham City. The goal against Birmingham came in a 7-0 win and was from really far out. Had it not been for the equalizer from Gerrard in the final, I have no doubt that this goal against Birmingham would have been a strong contender for our goal of the season. He displayed just how powerful his left foot is during the cup match against Man Utd when he kicked the ball so hard it broke Alan Smith's leg. He scored the opening goal in the semi final victory over Chelsea. In the final against West Ham Utd, John made up for his penalty miss in Istanbul by blasting one down the middle during the shoot out and helped us to another incredible victory.

During the 2006/07 season, John's defensive form began to slip and crucial mistakes started appearing in his game. He was particularly bad at controlling the ball. However he was still able to pop up with spectacular goals such as the screamer against Spurs in front of The Kop. The season started in spectacular fashion for him in the Community Shield victory over Chelsea. He carried the ball out of Liverpool's area and ran up the pitch before unleashing an unstoppable shot that flew past the Chelsea keeper Petr Cech. He also played a vital role in our run to another Champions League final. He scored the winner against Barcelona in the Nou Camp after a pass from Craig Bellamy. There was a back story to this goal in that just days earlier, Bellamy had tried to attack John with a golf club during a drunken rage at a training camp in Portugal. We will never forget Bellamy's golf swing celebration when he scored our first goal at the Nou Camp. John scored another long range beauty in the quarter final away to PSV Eindhoven. Regrettably, he was denied another Champions League winners medal when AC Milan got their revenge for their defeat two years earlier.

John's form seemed to desert him during the 2007/08 season, he was a shadow of the player he had been just two years earlier and became a liability for us. He completely lost the ability to control the ball and pass it to a teammate. Anyone who watched a game in the pub with me that season will remember just how often I would yell at the TV in frustration at one of his mistakes. John lost his place to

Fabio Aurelio who established himself as first choice left back, whenever he was fit. John's poor form resulted in an own goal in the FA Cup match away to Luton Town, however even worse was still to come. We once again reached the Champions League semi final and were drawn against Chelsea for the third time at that stage of the competition in just four seasons. Dirk Kuyt had put us into the lead during the first half and as the clock ticked down we were headed for another famous European victory. In injury time we conceded a throw in near the corner flag at the Kop end. The ball came into the box and fell to Riise, all he had to do was boot it clear and victory would have been as good as confirmed. In a moment that still keeps me awake at night, John chose not to kick the ball but instead stooped down to head it. Time seemed to stand still for a second as the ball went into our own goal, giving Chelsea a draw and a crucial away goal. How he ever played for the club again is beyond me and for the pain this moment continues to cause me to the present day, I just cannot ever forgive him for it.

At the end of the season John left Liverpool and signed for AS Roma in June 2008. He got his form back in Italy and became a real favourite with the Roma fans. He scored his first goal for the club in a massive top of the table clash against Inter Milan. He also played a blinder against AC Milan at the San Siro, scoring a fantastic free kick and setting up Roma's second goal of the game in a 3-2 victory. One of his more memorable games came at Juventus. He got the Juventus keeper Buffon sent off after going on a run and being brought down. Later in the same game John scored the winning goal with a header in the 93rd minute.

After three really good seasons in Italy, John returned to England and finally signed for Fulham, nine years after almost joining them before, where he joined his brother Bjorn. He has been a regular starter for Fulham, but surprisingly considering how good he is at attacking, John was unable to score a single goal in his first two seasons with The Cottagers. During his time at Fulham, John played his 100th game for Norway and has since gone on to become their most capped player of all time.

Despite his own goal in the Champions League semi final, John Arne Riise is fondly remembered by Liverpool fans, who recognise his seven years giving his all in the red shirt. Some of the goals he scored for us are among the finest ever seen at Anfield and his contributions in a number of cup finals will never be forgotten. On 22 December, 2012, John received a standing ovation from the Anfield crowd when he returned with Fulham. The Liverpool fans paid him the ultimate tribute by singing his famous song.

Luis Garcia

Spanish midfielder Luis Garcia belongs to a special club of Liverpool cult heroes. His goals on the road to Istanbul gave him almost legendary status in the minds of many Reds supporters. Despite being prone to errors, particularly losing possession in domestic fixtures, it was impossible not to love him. He could be almost invisible at times but then out of nowhere pop up with a match winner, particularly in some very important games.

Luis Javier Garcia Sanz was born in June 1978, in Badalona, Spain. He started his football career in the youth squad at Barcelona. He made it into the reserve side before being sold to Valladolid in 1999. He spent his first two seasons at the club out on loan at Toledo and Tenerife. At Tenerife he first worked under Rafa Benitez who was in the process of making his name as one of Spanish football's hottest young managers. Luis was one of the key players as Tenerife finished third in the Spanish Segunda Division and gained promotion to La Liga in 2001. He returned to Valladolid for the 2001/02 season and scored ten goals in thirty five games. His performances during this campaign persuaded Barcelona to buy him back, before immediately reselling him to Atletico Madrid. After another fine season in 2003/03, Barcelona exercised a buy back clause to bring him back to the Camp Nou in the summer of 2003. After three false starts at Barcelona, Luis Garcia finally made it into their first team for the 2003/04 season. He did well and went on to score eight times in thirty eight games.

In the summer of 2004, Liverpool's new manager Rafa Benitez found himself with a talented but underperforming squad. Michael Owen and Danny Murphy left the club soon after Rafa's arrival and during his first season several players from La Liga were brought to Anfield to reinforce the squad. The first two that arrived, Josemi and

Antonio Nunez were subsequent failures, but the second two sets of Spanish players to arrive turned out to be popular with the fans and a hit on the pitch. Luis Garcia and Xabi Alonso arrived at the same time in August 2004 and didn't take long to make an impact as Liverpool players.

Luis made his Liverpool debut in an away fixture against Bolton Wanderers. It was a bad debut for him as the Reds lost the game 1-0 and Luis had a late goal wrongly disallowed for offside. Subsequent television replays proved that it was an incorrect decision and Luis was clearly onside when the ball was played through to him. He didn't have to wait very long to score his first goal in a Red shirt however, as he scored in the very next game. He scored the third goal, finishing off a sublime passing move, in a 3-0 home victory over West Bromwich Albion. This gave the crowd at Anfield their first glimpse of Luis' trademark celebration where he sucks his thumb in honour of his son Joel.

He scored his second goal in the next home game which was another 3-0 victory, this time over Norwich City. Just a few weeks later he scored one of his most spectacular goals with a twenty five yard volley against Charlton Athletic. This particular goal holds very special memories for me as I watched the game live at a bar in Sydney, Australia. Luis went on to finish his first Premier League season with eight goals, including the winner in the Merseyside derby at Anfield. This goal was a close range header after a long range strike from Fernando Morientes had struck the crossbar.

His form in the Premier League was patchy and his tendency to go missing for long periods in games, as well as his giving the ball away needlessly, led to a mixed response from supporters. While he was utterly frustrating in league games, his performances and goals in the Champions League made him a hero at Anfield. He scored five goals during the run to the final in Istanbul. Liverpool qualified to the knockout stages of the competition thanks to that famous night where we defeated Olympiakos. Liverpool drew German side Bayer Leverkusen in the first knockout stage, giving them the chance of revenge for the defeat in 2002. Luis' first European goal for Liverpool came when he finished off a sublime Igor Biscan through pass to open the scoring in the first leg. The Reds went on to win 3-1 on the night. The Germans were finished off in the second leg when Luis scored two more goals in Leverkusen. The game finished in another 3-1 victory with Baros adding a late third goal and Luis almost netting a hat-trick with a couple of near misses.

Without doubt Luis' finest goal for Liverpool came in the next round, the first leg of the quarter final against Juventus at Anfield. It was a beautiful finish that was voted his best ever goal in a 2007 poll on the official Liverpool website. This goal capped off an incredible first half that night against the giants of Turin. Sami Hyypia gave us the lead with a lovely volley from a corner, which won my dad £200. Not longer after Sami had put the Reds into the lead came Luis' moment of history. He latched onto the ball thirty yards from the goal and struck an unstoppable volley that flew past Buffon and straight into the top corner. It was a goal that deserved to win any game and it was at that precise moment that I started to believe that we might actually be capable of winning the trophy that year.

After a heroic performance in Turin, the Reds were matched up with Chelsea in the semi-final. After three defeats against Chelsea that season, two in the league and also the League Cup Final, the Liverpool players and supporters were extremely fired up for this tie. Just two games now stood between them and a return to the summit of European football, after a twenty year absence from the final. After a hard fought nil-nil draw at Stamford Bridge the crowd at Anfield for the second leg was electric. Many sides over the years have buckled under the incredible noise from the Kop and this night proved to be no exception. On the pitch, Luis Garcia and the officials turned out to be the difference between the two teams on the night. Just three minutes into the game, Steven Gerrard knocked the ball over the Chelsea defence and Milan Baros raced onto it. He knocked the ball over the advancing Petr Cech before being brought down. While the crowd screamed for a penalty, Luis kept a cool head and knocked the loose ball towards the goal where it was cleared by William Gallas. The referee blew for a goal and the crowd, the players and the fans watching on television went berserk. The Chelsea players were unable to come up with a reply, despite a heart stopping six minutes of injury time, and Liverpool were through to the final. Chelsea manager at the time Jose Mourinho was bitter afterwards claiming the ball never crossed the line for the wining goal. Despite technology not being able to prove anything about the legitimacy of the goal, what is not in doubt is that if the goal had not been given, Cech would have been sent off and Liverpool had a penalty. So in my opinion the argument against the goal is essentially nonsense.

As we all know, Liverpool went on to defeat AC Milan in the final after an incredible comeback and a penalty shoot-out. Luis played well and played a big part in the first half with a clearance of the goal-line. An interesting note about the game is that Luis wanted to take the penalty to conclude the comeback after Gerrard was fouled. Jamie Carragher took the ball out of Luis' hands and insisted that Xabi Alonso take it instead, as was Rafa's pre game instruction.

Overall Luis' second season at Liverpool could not be considered as successful as the previous one but he still played his part and scored some important goals during the campaign. Highlights from Luis during the first half of the 2005/06 season included a goal in the Super Cup Final against CSKA Moscow and a phenomenal flicked headed goal in the 3-0 victory over Anderlecht in the Champions League. During the second half of the season he scored against Everton again with a superb chip over the keeper. For the second season in a row Liverpool were drawn against Chelsea in a major semi-final. This time it was in the FA Cup and once again Luis was to score the winning goal. The game was played at Old Trafford and Liverpool went into the lead from a John Arne Riise thunderbolt into the bottom corner of the goal. In the second half Luis scored a spectacular goal to put the Reds two up. Drogba got one back for Chelsea but Liverpool held on the reach Rafa's third cup final in two seasons. Unfortunately Luis missed the 2006 FA Cup Final against West Ham United. He was suspended after being sent off, ironically against West Ham, in a league game just four days after his winner in the semi final.

Luis scored a hat-trick for Spain in November 2005, in a World Cup qualifying playoff against Slovakia. He was then chosen in the squad for the 2006 World Cup in Germany, where he played three games.

During the 2006/07 season Luis was more of a squad player and didn't start games as regularly as he had previously. Despite this he still made valuable contributions such as a headed goal against Galatasaray in the Champions League, two against Bordeaux and the winner against Tottenham Hotspur in the league. Unfortunately in January 2007, he then suffered a cruciate knee ligament injury in the 6-3 League cup defeat at home to Arsenal. The depressing sight of him being stretchered off the Anfield pitch was to be the last we'd see of him in a red shirt. This was a tragic way to end his Liverpool career.

In the summer of 2007 Fernando Torres joined Liverpool from Atletico Madrid and Luis went in the opposite direction in a separate deal worth around £4 million. After he had left Liverpool he published a letter to the supporters via the official Liverpool FC website. It was a wonderful tribute and a heartfelt thank you from Luis to all the players, the staff and the supporters of Liverpool.

In his second stint at Atletico Madrid, Luis was a valuable squad player during his first season, even if he didn't start every game. He made a brief comeback at Anfield in November 2008 when he came on as a late substitute in a Champions League group game. The ovation he received when entering the field, despite Liverpool losing at that moment, was a tribute to how much he is still loved by the supporters. During the 2008/09 season, Luis found himself out of favour at Atletico and was often not even on the bench. In 2009 he moved to Racing Santander where he played just fifteen games as they narrowly avoided relegation.

Luis then moved to Greece in August 2010 and spent one season playing for Panathinaikos. After Panathinaikos, Luis Garcia signed for Mexican Primera Division (now Liga MX) side Puebla in July of 2011. He went on to make 33 appearances and scored an impressive 13 goals, including an equalizing penalty against Chivas Guadalajara that started a remarkable turnaround with Puebla running out 4-1 winners on the day. Despite his goal scoring efforts Puebla finished both seasons in a disappointing 12th place.

In June of 2012 he signed a deal taking him to the 2011 league champions Pumas UNAM. Although his appearances have been limited he expressed his happiness at the club.

Without a doubt, Luis Garcia proved himself to be a man for the big occasion during his Liverpool career. His goals in massive games won him the hearts of Liverpool supporters around the world. He was even given a popular song by the fans, sung to the tune of 'You Are My Sunshine' the lyrics are;

"Luis García, he drinks Sangria

He came from Barca to bring us joy

He's five foot seven, he's football heaven

So please don't take our Luis away!"

His popularity amongst the Liverpool supporters was reflected in his position at number 24 in the poll "100 Players Who Shook the Kop".

Markus Babbel

European Championship winning defender Markus Babbel was part of what I consider to have been the best Liverpool back four since the millennium. He was also a popular and integral part of Liverpool's treble winning season in 2000/01. He was struck down with a debilitating illness in his second season at the club, which called a halt to his time at Anfield far too soon.

Markus was born in September 1972, in Munich, Germany. He began his football career in the youth team at Bayern Munich. He rose through the ranks, and made his first team debut during the 1991/92 season. After twelve appearances (four as substitute) for Bayern, Markus moved to Hamburg in August 1992. He became a first team regular at Hamburg and also made the first of twelve appearances for the German under 21 side.

After two seasons at Hamburg, Markus was transferred back to Bayern Munich in 1994. At this time they were the Bundesliga champions, after Franz Beckenbauer had returned to coach them for one season in 1993/94. Markus had six fine seasons at Bayern Munich and was an integral part of the team. He also won a number of medals during his time at the club. In 1996 they won the UEFA Cup, beating Bordeaux in the final, after the club president Beckenbauer had stepped back in as caretaker manager. They won the Bundesliga again in 1996/97 and also in 1998/99. In the 1998/99 season they reached the Champions League final, losing in injury time to Manchester Utd at the Camp Nou in Barcelona. In Markus' final season at Bayern Munich, 1999/2000, they won the German league and cup double.

During his time at Bayern Munich, Markus began playing for the German national side. He was an important member of the team that won the 1996 European Championships in England. He also played for Germany during the 1998 World Cup and 2000 European Championships.

During the 2000 European Championships, Liverpool's main right back Vegard Heggem suffered a serious injury. This meant that he lost his place for the following season, which eventually pretty much ended his Anfield career. A slot had opened up at right back and fortunately for Liverpool's manager Gerard Houllier an outstanding player was ready to make the position his own. In June 2000, Markus was snapped up by Liverpool on a Bosman-style free transfer.

He had a few teething troubles when he first arrived at Anfield. He was ordered by Houllier, in front of the squad, to explain remarks to a German newspaper about being played out of position. He apparently felt he would be best deployed as a centre back. Despite this slight setback, Markus took his place for the 2000/01 season in what I consider to be the best Liverpool back four since the 1980's. The regular defence was Markus at right back, the outstanding combination of Hyypia and Henchoz at centre back and Jamie Carragher at left back. With some tremendous defensive performances, Liverpool had the second best goal difference that season, after the eventual Premier League champions Manchester Utd.

Markus made his league debut for Liverpool in August 2000 during a 1-0 victory at home to Bradford City. He established an instant rapport with the Liverpool supporters thanks to his incredible stamina and his never say die attitude. He was like a racehorse with his rampaging runs up and down the right flank. He scored three goals during the season, two of which came in season defining matches. His first goal for the Reds came in an 8-0 victory away at Stoke City in the League Cup. His second goal came in the incredible Merseyside derby in April 2001. This is the game most famous for Gary McAllister's amazing free kick in the dying seconds to win the game 3-2. Markus scored Liverpool's second goal as he latched on to a rebound on the edge of the Everton area before smashing the ball into the back of the net. His third goal of the season came in an even bigger game, the UEFA Cup final against Spanish side Deportivo Alaves. Markus opened the scoring with a fantastic header from a McAllister free kick. Liverpool went on to win the trophy in a 5-4 score-line after a golden goal in extra time. It is a game still regarded as the greatest UEFA Cup final of all time.

Markus played in all three cup finals as Liverpool won the phenomenal treble of League Cup, FA Cup and UEFA Cup. He had an absolutely fantastic game in the UEFA Cup Final and in my opinion he was only just behind McAllister for the man of the match award. He was also a major contributor to Liverpool finishing third in the Premiership and qualifying for the Champions League for the first time. He started every league game and missed just three of Liverpool's sixty three games in that incredible season. It is possible that this may have been a factor in the illness that struck him down soon after.

Markus started the following season and helped Liverpool win two more trophies at the start of 2001/02. The Charity Shield was secured with a great victory over Man Utd and the European Super Cup was won in a victory over Markus' old club Bayern Munich in Monaco. This meant that Markus now had five medals in just over one year at Anfield. This was an amazing start to his Anfield career, but unfortunately tragedy was just around the corner to prevent Markus from playing in the Champions League, after he had done so much to assist in qualification the previous season.

He had looked poor and slow in the Super Cup Final, but at the time I had assumed he was carrying a minor injury. Sadly I was wrong and, after complaining of tiredness, he was substituted at half time in game against Bolton Wanderers in late August 2001. He was diagnosed with Guillan-Barre Syndrome and didn't play again for fifteen months. Guillan-Barre Syndrome is a life threatening, energy wasting illness that affects the peripheral nervous system. The disease is characterized by weakness which affects the lower limbs first, and rapidly progresses in an ascending fashion. Patients generally notice weakness in their legs, before it progresses into the upper parts of the body. Fortunately the illness is treatable and 80% of patients have a complete recovery within six months to a year. Patients usually recover with the aid of hospitalisation, rest and, once the early stages are over, rehabilitation and physical therapy. I will never forget how shocking and upsetting it was when photo's surfaced of Markus in a wheelchair looking weak, gaunt and a shadow of how he had looked striding on the Anfield turf just a few months earlier. He was one of our fittest players during the treble season and now he was too weak to even walk. All of a sudden with the release of these photo's, no Liverpool fan was concerned about when he'd be back in the team, we were now more concerned about his life.

A lot of bad things have been said about Gerard Houllier's time as Liverpool manager, but one thing that has never been doubted is how much he cared about his players. This was never proven more strongly than when he offered Markus a new contract during this dark period. The loyalty that Houllier showed and the support and well wishes he received from Liverpool supporters must have given him a huge boost as he embarked upon his long and slow recovery.

Thanks to Markus' natural fitness he did eventually recover and made his first team comeback in November 2002 against Sunderland. Sadly he never managed to regain his outstanding previous form and didn't play a regular part in the team during the 2002/03 season. After spending the majority of the season playing in the reserves, Markus was justifiably concerned for his Anfield future. When Steve Finnan was signed in the summer of 2003 it was clear that his future lay elsewhere and he spent the 2003/04 season on loan at Blackburn Rovers.

He played twenty five league games for Blackburn and scored three times as he helped them to a sixth place finish in the Premier League and qualification for the UEFA Cup. Despite playing well during the season, Markus wasn't signed permanently by Blackburn and in 2004 he returned to Germany to sign for VfB Stuttgart on a free transfer, where he teamed up with his old Bayern Munich manager Giovanni Trapattoni. He was a semi-regular in the team over the following three seasons and helped them to become the Bundesliga Champions in his final season as a player in 2006/07.

After he retired from playing in May 2007, Markus became the assistant coach at Stuttgart. After finishing sixth in the Bundesliga in 2007/08 and having a bad start to the following season, Stuttgart fired the manager Armin Veh. After impressing as a coach Markus was given his first football management position when he was promoted to first team manager at Stuttgart in November 2008. When he took over as manager, the club were in eleventh place in the league. Markus led them up the table to finish third and qualification for the Champions League. He was sacked in December 2009, after a poor start to the season. He then took over as manager of Hertha BSC in the second tier of German football. They finished second in the league and were promoted to the Bundesliga. He was sacked in December 2011, after announcing he was going to leave at the end of the season. His most recent managerial post was with

Hoffenheim, who he joined in February 2012. December turned out to be an unlucky month once again for Markus, as he was sacked in December 2012.

Markus Babbel is fondly remembered by Liverpool supporters as much for his performances during the treble season, as for his brave recovery from a life threatening illness. He was an outstanding right back and had he not been struck down and lost some of his abilities, I believe he could have played for Liverpool for at least another five years thanks to his incredible fitness. He was voted in at number 53 in the series '100 Players Who Shook the Kop'. This was despite only playing one full season for Liverpool and is a testament to how integral he was to the Reds winning five trophies in his short time at the club.

Michael Owen

Of all the Liverpool players over the last decade there is nobody who divides supporter's opinions as much as Michael Owen. He seems to be a player that fans either love or hate, often passionately. I fall more into the former category and I have had plenty of heated debates with Owen haters over the last few years. Over the course of this article I'm hoping that my reasons for my support of Michael Owen will be clear. I understand why there are plenty of people out there who dislike Owen, especially since he joined Manchester Utd, but I cannot forget what he did for us even though I cannot forgive his decision to go to Old Trafford.

Michael Owen was born in December 1979 (the day before my second birthday!) in Chester, which is on the border of North West England and North Wales. His father, Terry, was a professional footballer who once played for Everton. Therefore like many other future Liverpool players (Carragher, Fowler, McManaman) Michael grew up as an Everton fan. He was a well known player as a kid in North Wales and went on to break a number of local goal-scoring records.

When he was thirteen, Michael became eligible to sign schoolboy forms for a professional club. After being courted by the likes of Chelsea, Arsenal and Man Utd, Michael signed for Liverpool in 1993. When he was fourteen, he was accepted to the prestigious FA School of Excellence in Lilleshall, which he attended for two years. Upon his return from Lilleshall, Michael signed youth forms with Liverpool and graduated to the youth team, coached by Steve Heighway. Michael was the star player of the youth team during the 1995/96 season in which Liverpool won the FA Youth Cup. The side contained other future first team players such as Jamie Carragher.

Michael signed professional forms with Liverpool in December 1996 as soon as he turned seventeen. He made his debut in May 1997 in an away game against Wimbledon, coming off the bench to score a goal in a style that became his trademark. He used his pace to run on to a pass before clinically beating the keeper in a one on one situation. It was a dream start to his first team football career and from that moment on the goals seemed to come naturally for him. Michael went on to be Liverpool's top scorer in every season from 1997/98 until 2003/04. In his first full season with the club he hit eighteen league goals and was voted the PFA Young Player of the Year. Unfortunately this wasn't enough for Liverpool to win any honours during what was Roy Evans final season as sole manager.

In the summer of 1998 Michael became a football superstar thanks to his performances for England at the World Cup in France. He made his World Cup debut as a substitute in the final group game against Romania. He made an immediate impact by scoring the equaliser for England and then hitting the post before Romania went on to win the game 2 – 1. It was in the quarter final game against Argentina that Michael scored the goal that changed his life. It is to this day one of the best goals ever scored by an England player and a superb individual goal. Michael used his pace to beat the Argentine defenders before chipping the keeper. Unfortunately for England, they went on to lose the game on penalties and David Beckham stole all the headlines by getting sent off for childishly kicking Simeone (who made a real meal of rolling around on the ground afterwards).

After the World Cup ended, Michael had become a sporting superstar and at this stage he became a public property. His popularity with the British public was reflected in his award for BBC Sports Personality of the Year for 1998. It is my opinion that it was at this time Michael lost some of the support from Liverpool supporters who began to think of him as more of an England player rather than just a Liverpool player. In the pre Beckham mania era, he was without any doubt the most popular footballer in England and he seemed to lose a lot of rapport with a section of the Liverpool fans. Once he became popular with fans all around the world he somehow seemed, to a lot of Reds fans, to cease to be the sole property of the Kop.

Michael has made no secret of the fact he was hurt that sections of the Liverpool fans never sang a lot of songs for him and didn't take him to their hearts like they did with other players such as Robbie Fowler. I've heard people suggest it's because he wasn't a local lad like Fowler, but I completely disagree with that one. Michael comes from the same area as Ian Rush and Rushie is clearly one of the most popular Liverpool players of all time. I also feel that had Michael remained at Liverpool and stayed injury free he could have been the player to get closest to Rush's goal scoring record. In recent times I've lost count of the number of arguments I've had with people about Michael Owen caring more about England than Liverpool. The amount of goals he scored for Liverpool, especially in major games and the enjoyment in his face every time should be more than enough evidence to support the fact that he loved playing for Liverpool.

During the 1999/2000 season Michael started to have the injury problems that would go on to blight the rest of his career so far. He suffered hamstring problems that season which would hinder him throughout the campaign. In the summer of 2000 he finally got proper medical help and was placed on a weight routine to strengthen his hamstrings. After a disappointing European Championships in the summer of 2000 (during which he scored against Romania again) Michael came back to Merseyside like a man on a mission to improve on the disappointing previous season for Liverpool.

2000/01 was Michael's best so far in his career as he scored 24 goals as Liverpool won the incredible treble of League Cup, F.A. Cup and UEFA Cup. Robbie Fowler spent periods of the season out through injury and Michael formed a prolific partnership with Emile Heskey who scored 23 goals. Michael missed the League Cup final victory over Birmingham City when Robbie Fowler was chosen up front. The 2001 F.A. Cup Final is often called 'The Owen Final' thanks to his two late goals to win the trophy for Liverpool.

Arsenal had battered us for the majority of the game and were deservedly 1 – 0 in the lead with just minutes remaining.

Unfortunately for Arsenal these were the days before Michael Owen became injury prone and was still an incredible match winner, especially in big games. He scored from a corner to level the game and then came the winner with one of my favourite goals ever.

I barely had time to discuss the goal with my mates when Berger hit a long ball over Arsenal's midfield. We saw Owen sprinting onto it but thought that Adams and Dixon had him covered. How wrong we were as the entire season flashed before our eyes when the ball crept past Seaman and into the corner of the net. It is moments like this that will always make me a Michael Owen fan no matter who he plays for (except when he plays against Liverpool).

We barely had time to finish celebrating when just four days later Liverpool faced Deportivo Alaves in the UEFA Cup Final in Dortmund. Liverpool won the game 5 – 4 with an extra time golden goal in what most people agree was the greatest UEFA Cup Final of all time. Michael played well in the game and his most important contribution was winning the penalty for Liverpool's third goal. He was put clean through on goal when the Alaves keeper came rushing out of his area and grabbed at Michael's legs. Owen brilliantly managed to remain on his feet until he got inside the area and then went down to force the penalty. How the goalkeeper managed to stay on the pitch I will never know.

Michael started the following season, 2001/02, the same way he had ended the previous one (domestically) by scoring at the Millennium Stadium as Liverpool defeated Man Utd in the Community Shield. Michael then went on to score just seconds after the second half kicked off in the Super Cup Final against Bayern Munich. Liverpool won that game 3 – 2 to hold an incredible five trophies at the same time. Just a week later Michael tormented the Bayern Munich goalkeeper Oliver Kahn again, by hitting an amazing hat-trick as England beat Germany 5 – 1. There were three other Liverpool players in the England side that night, Steven Gerrard, Emile Heskey and Nick Barmby. Gerrard and Heskey scored the other two England goals and this prompted many Liverpool fans to dub the result afterwards, Liverpool 5 Germany 1.

Michael's incredible year was completed in December 2001 when he was awarded the prestigious Balon D'Or to be the first ever Liverpool player to become European Player of the Year. His year was completed on December 21st when he scored his one hundredth goal for Liverpool in a league game against West Ham Utd. Liverpool went on to finish second in the Premiership in 2001/02 and Michael hit a career best 28 goals in 43 games.

He scored two goals during the 2002 World Cup in Korea and Japan, despite playing through the pain of injury. In his autobiography, Michael talks about receiving pain killing injections before every game.

He repeated his best goal tally the following season, 2002/03 with another 28 goals including his one hundredth Premiership goal against West Brom. He also scored in the League Cup Final when we defeated Man Utd 2 – 0, with Steven Gerrard scoring the first via a David Beckham deflection.

Michael's final season for Liverpool, 2003/04 was interrupted by injuries and speculation was constant about his future as he would only have one more season remaining on his contract. Despite all the distractions he still managed to finish as Liverpool's top goal scorer with 19 goals. During this season Michael also broke Ian Rush's European goal scoring record in September 2003 during a 1 – 1 draw with Slovenian side Olimpija in the UEFA cup. During his final season Michael was linked with a number of other clubs as contract talks seemed to be stalling. Michael stated publicly that he wanted to stay at Liverpool and yet no announcements were coming from within the club regarding a contract extension. At the end of the season Gerard Houllier was fired and Rafael Benitez was appointed as Liverpool manager.

Rafa's first task as manager was to fly to Portugal and meet up with Michael Owen and Steven Gerrard who were there with the England squad for the 2004 European Championships. Gerrard was being heavily linked with a move to Chelsea at the time and Michael's new contract had still not been signed. After a late change of heart

Gerrard chose to stay with Liverpool but unfortunately Michael Owen was to depart in August 2004 when Real Madrid came in with an offer which he chose to accept. A lot of Liverpool fans still feel that Michael had screwed the club by not signing a contract before leaving. As he only had one year left on his contract, Liverpool were in a weaker bargaining position than Real Madrid and they only received £8 million (plus Antonio Nunez) for a player who was worth at least double that amount. In my opinion I don't feel that Liverpool did enough to convince Michael to stay and perhaps they should have been quicker to sort out the contract earlier than they were. Steven Gerrard has since talked about the problems he had with the Liverpool board to sort out his contract in 2005 and I have a feeling that Owen may have had the same problem the year before. I have heard plenty of people describe Michael as being ruthless and this is something I disagree with. He is an ambitious person and opportunities to sign for Real Madrid don't come around too often, and the chance to test himself in a different country must have been too tough to resist.

Despite spending most of his time at Real Madrid on the substitute bench I would consider Michael's one season at The Bernabeu to be a success. This is because he finished the La Liga season with the best ratio for goals scored against minutes on the pitch. He scored 16 goals overall, with 13 in the league.

1. In the summer of 2005 Michael was once again in the news with speculation that he would be leaving Spain after Real Madrid signed the Brazilian strikers Robinho and Julio Baptista. It's an open secret that he wanted to rejoin Liverpool and that Rafa Benitez was keen to bring him back to Anfield. The main stumbling block appeared to be the transfer fee with Real Madrid rumoured to be asking for a fee in excess of £11 million. Liverpool were unwilling to pay that much for a player they let leave for less just twelve months earlier. According to the journalist Guillem Balagué in his book 'A Season on the Brink – A Portrait of Rafa Benitez's Liverpool', Rafa and Michael were in secret negotiations right up until the last day of the summer transfer window. By this time Newcastle Utd had offered £16 million for his services and Real Madrid were putting the pressure on to get him to accept that offer. Realising it was too late to sort out the transfer at

that late stage Rafa asked Michael to wait until January when Liverpool could reopen negotiations. However fearing he would be left on the Real Madrid bench, hindering his chances with Liverpool (and the England World Cup squad) Michael made the decision to join Newcastle Utd instead.

Michael spent three seasons at Newcastle Utd with most of it being spent injured. He broke a metatarsal bone in his foot on New Years Eve 2005 and missed the next four months, only returning for the last two weeks of the season. At the 2006 World Cup in Germany he seriously damaged the cruciate ligament in his right knee in the first minute of England's final group game against Sweden. This injury kept him out for the majority of the 2006/07 season, with his comeback game not until April 2007. In the summer of 2009 he decided not to repay the loyalty of Newcastle's supporters by staying with the side to help them back into the Premier League after they were relegated. Instead he shocked the football world, and angered and disgusted Liverpool supporters by joining Manchester United. Michael had his reasons for joining our bitterest enemies and I understand why he chose to go there. However just because I understand those reasons doesn't mean I have to like them and I may never forgive him for it.

His two seasons at Man Utd were mostly spent on the subs bench with the occasional personal highlight such as a winning goal in the Manchester derby and a hat-trick in the Champions League. He was released from the club at the end of the season in 2012.

He was linked in the press with a few clubs as he was a free agent and eventually joined Stoke City. His time at Stoke City was similar to his time at Man Utd in which he was a squad player only playing occasionally when fit.

During his time as a Stoke player Michael started doing a lot of media work, mostly for the BBC acting as a pundit and commentator on Match of the Day and appearing on Five Live a fair bit as well. Due to his decreased playing time in combination with his work on TV and radio, it came as no surprise when he announced his intention to retire from playing at the end of the 2012/13 season.

It's a shame that a player who came onto the scene as a teenager with so much incredible promise was essentially finished as a world class player when still in his mid twenties. Thirty three is a young age to retire in the modern game but perhaps the sheer number of injuries as well as his outside interests in horse racing and media work have made the decision for him.

Michael Owen scored 158 goals for Liverpool in seven seasons which is a terrific return considering he regularly suffered with injuries. He scored goals that won us trophies and he gave us all plenty to cheer about during periods when there was nothing else to get excited about. These are the reasons why Michael Owen will always remain one of my LFC heroes, even though I no longer love him. Despite many people not appearing to appreciate his services to Liverpool as much as I do, he was still thought enough of to be voted in at number 14 in the series '100 Players Who Shook the Kop.'

Nick Barmby

There have been a number of transfers between Everton and Liverpool over the years but between 1959 and 2000, all of those transfers involved players moving from Anfield to Goodison Park. The most famous player to make this transfer was Peter Beardsley in 1991 but there have been other notable players such as Kevin Sheedy and David Johnson who have made the move from Liverpool to Everton. For some strange reason, players moving from Liverpool to Everton have never been made to suffer by the fans but there has always been a big stigma when a player goes in the opposite direction. A transfer between two teams who are each other's biggest and nearest rival will always be a cause for controversy but Everton's fans seem to take it far more bitterly and personally than Liverpool fans do when the reverse occurs. In 1991 the anger over Peter Beardsley's move was not directed at the player himself but more towards Graeme Souness and the Liverpool board for allowing him to leave. In 2000 when Nick Barmby became the first Everton player to join Liverpool since Dave Hickson in 1959, the anger and hatred he received from the Everton fans was so severe it was incredible. The public chants of 'Judas' were so loud and often that you'd have thought he'd stood in the middle of Goodison Park and set fire to a blue shirt.

Nick Barmby was born in February 1974 in Hull. He was a talented footballer when he was growing up and he played for a number of local sides before gaining a place at the FA's School of Excellence. As a teenager he was courted by a number of clubs including Liverpool, with whom he had a two week trial in 1991. Despite the advances from many clubs to sign him, Nick eventually decided to sign for Tottenham Hotspur as a trainee in 1991.

When Nick signed for them, Spurs had just finished the previous season as FA Cup winners and their manager Terry Venables had built an exciting side that included Paul Gascoigne and Gary Lineker. Nick was popular with Venables and he didn't have to wait too long to make his first team debut as an eighteen year old in 1992. He went on to play alongside quality strikers like Jurgen Klinsmann and Teddy Sheringham and he started to gain notice as a player of tremendous ability. During this period Nick was a regular in the England under 21 and B sides and eventually made his first full England appearance in 1995 under his old manager Terry Venables.

After over one hundred appearances for Spurs, Nick moved to Middlesbrough in 1995 for £5.25 million. Nick played really well under Bryan Robson and after just one and a half seasons at The Riverside he was on the move again when Everton manager Joe Royle paid £5.75 million to take him to Goodison Park. Nicks first three seasons at Everton were dotted with inconsistency, as he struggled to maintain his previous good form for long periods. He did however have an excellent season for Everton under Walter Smith in 1999/2000. His form during that season earned Nick a call up to Kevin Keegan's England Squad for the 2000 European Championships. His performances the previous season had brought him back into the spotlight and he was once again linked to other clubs.

After the European Championships ended, the announcement was made that Nick was to join Liverpool for £6 million. The shock and anger from the Everton fans was so strong that the Liverpool manager Gerard Houllier seemed shocked, saying at the time; "He has not changed his religion". The move was always going to be a controversial one, especially as it was the first such transfer for forty one years, but it seemed to be made worse when it emerged that Nick had been actively seeking the transfer to Liverpool rather than Liverpool having to convince him to move. Nick described the move

298

as a "dream come true" which is a comment that would obviously upset those on the blue half of Merseyside who had put a lot of their hopes in him for the following season, after he had been so good in the previous one. Since the Nick Barmby transfer there has been only one other transfer from Everton to Liverpool. However the player involved on that occasion was Abel Xavier. The Everton fans were happy to see him go and the Liverpool fans were the ones upset that we were signing a player who, with all due respect, was seen as a bit of a joke.

Despite the controversies off the field, Nick began his Liverpool career with some great form and he was a regular starter. He was given an advanced role on the left and right sides of midfield and played really well. Early in the season he started in the first Merseyside derby since his transfer. He seemed to be inspired by the hatred from the Everton fans, who were chanting "Judas" and holding signs against him. Predictably it was in this game that Nick was to score his first goal for Liverpool with a header at the Anfield Road end, inspiring Liverpool to go on to win the game 3-1.

This was just the beginning of a good run for Nick as after the game against Everton he went on to score further seven goals for the Reds. A number of these goals came in the UEFA cup as Liverpool were heading towards the final stages of the competition. Unfortunately for Nick he was struck down with a serious injury ruling him out for the final three months of the season. This would be bad for a player at any time of his career, but in this case it was made far worse for him, as it meant he missed out on playing in three cup finals and playing in the three games that won Liverpool the historic treble. Despite missing out on the finals, Nicks contributions in the previous rounds of each competition, especially the UEFA Cup, meant that he was still regarded a valued member of the 2000/01 squad.

The 2001/02 season was a complete disaster for Nick as he only played nine games for Liverpool, after he suffered a serious ankle injury that required surgery. Before he suffered the injury he did manage one final big performance, which came in his last appearance in an England shirt. Nick was one of four Liverpool players in the incredible 5–1 victory over Germany in October 2001.

After almost an entire season missed through injury, Nick was sold to Leeds Utd for £2.75 million in the summer of 2002. He was reunited at Leeds with manager Terry Venables and his former Liverpool and England team-mate Robbie Fowler. Regrettably for him it came at a terrible time for Leeds, with the club sliding into incredible debts and most of the first team squad being sold to ease the financial situation. He spent a loan spell at Nottingham Forest during the 2003/04 season. In May 2004, Leeds was relegated and Nick moved to his hometown club, Hull City, that summer.

Nick helped Hull City to gain promotion from Division One in his first season at the club. A personal highlight came when he scored the fastest goal in the club's history after just seven seconds against Walsall in November 2004. He was an important player for the club as they were promoted twice, first to The Championship in 2005 and then to the Premier League in 2008. This was the first time in the club's history that they had been in the top division, and meant Nick would now have played for 6 different teams in the Premier League. Hull was relegated in 2010 and Nick became a player coach during the 2010/11 season back in The Championship. He took over as caretaker manager in November 2011, when the manager Nigel Pearson joined Leicester City. In January 2012, Nick retired as a player and became permanent manager of Hull a week later. Sadly for Nick he was sacked in May 2012, after a falling out with the owners over comments he made about transfers and money.

Despite never playing a full season for the Reds, Nick Barmby is recognised by the Liverpool fans for what he did for the team during his short time with the club. The dignity he displayed over his controversial signing as well as his performances and goals that helped us win the treble in 2001 were very much appreciated and this was reflected in his position at number 86 in the series '100 Players Who Shook the Kop'.

Sami Hyypia

Sami Hyypia is one of the best centre backs ever to play for Liverpool and in my opinion, he represents the clubs best value for money since the Premier League era began. His dominance in defence and the outstanding service he gave during his time at Liverpool means that he stands alongside such defensive legends as Ron Yeats, Tommy Smith, and Alan Hansen. He was part of two of Liverpool's all time finest centre back partnerships, alongside Stephane Henchoz and Jamie Carragher.

Sami was born in 1973, in Porvoo, Finland. His parents were both footballers and although he showed early promise playing ice hockey, it was his destiny to follow the family tradition and become a footballer. He started his career with local club Pallo-Peikot as a teenager. Ironically he played in every position except defence during his time at the club. In 1990 he joined Kumu and then after one season he left football for one year to undertake his national service. After twelve months away, Sami signed for one of the biggest clubs in Finland, MyPa, in 1992, and played in the same side as the great Jari Litmanen. During his three years at MyPa, Sami won two Finnish Cups, in 1992 and 1995. In his final game for the club Sami scored the winning goal in the 1995 cup final with a trademark header. During his time at MyPa he also began playing for the Finland national side, making his debut in November 1992. Sami had a two-week trial with Kevin Keegan's Newcastle in 1995, which he later said gave him a good experience of life at a big English club. He didn't join Newcastle and instead moved to Holland to sign for Willem II.

Sami spent four seasons at Willem II and earned a place in the hearts of the supporters as he captained them to a runner's up finish in the Eredivisie in 1998/99 and qualification for the Champions

League. He was awarded the fan's player of the year for this achievement. Sami never got to play in the competition for the side because in May 1999 Liverpool came calling. This was a really big deal for Sami as the Reds were his favourite team as a boy. He later told BBC Sport: "The day I signed my contract with Liverpool, that's one day I will never forget because Liverpool was my favourite team when I was younger and it was a dream come true." Sami had initially been recommended to Liverpool's then chief executive Peter Robinson by a TV cameraman who followed games all over Europe. The guy knew that the club was looking for a strong centre back and recommended that they take a look at Sami. Members of staff went over to Holland to watch him several times, including chief scout Ron Yeats, who then recommended that the manager Gerard Houllier and Phil Thompson go take a look, which is what they did. They were impressed by his passing and his unbelievable ability to read what an opposition player was going to do. Sami travelled to Liverpool and signed for just £2.5 million, which to this day I still cannot believe as he proved over the next ten years to be worth at least ten times that figure. Ron Yeats later admitted: "When I was told how little money Liverpool had spent on Sami, I nearly fell off my chair!"

Sami joined a new look Liverpool defence for the 1999/2000 season with the arrival of his main partner at centre back, Stephane Henchoz and Sander Westerveld replacing David James in goal. Sami's league debut started well with a 2-1 win away to Sheffield Wednesday, unfortunately things took a turn for the worse in the following game with a 1-0 defeat at home to newly promoted Watford. September was a disaster with defeats to Man Utd and Everton plus a 2-2 draw with Leicester, leaving the Reds in twelfth place in the league. Sami scored his first goal for Liverpool in the game against Man Utd, unfortunately two own goals from Jamie Carragher contributed to a 3-2 loss. Things steadily improved and by Christmas Liverpool were in fifth place, six points behind the leaders Man Utd. During the second half of the season the Reds battled with Leeds Utd over the third and fourth places in the league with a third place finish now becoming a Champions league spot for the following season. Liverpool went into the final day with the knowledge that a victory over Bradford City would guarantee that third spot. Unfortunately Bradford also had something to play for as a win would guarantee them survival in the Premier League. Bradford won the game 1-0 to stay up and Liverpool ended up finishing fourth, just two points behind Leeds.

The following season was one of the greatest ever in both Liverpool's history and Sami's career. Sami was made the joint captain alongside Robbie Fowler as the club captain Jamie Redknapp was suffering from a long term injury that would keep him out for the entire season. Sami played an incredible 58 games as Liverpool went on to play the maximum number of games it is possible to play by winning an amazing treble of FA Cup, League Cup and the UEFA Cup. They also captured further glory by finishing third in the league and qualifying for the Champions league for the first time, since the old days when it was the European Cup. Sami got to proudly share the honour of lifting all three trophies along with Fowler and Redknapp. He was so immaculate during this season that he went the entire season without a single yellow card. This was in the middle of a run of 87 games without a booking between January and October 2001. In 2001 he received the first of three consecutive awards as the Finnish player of the year.

The following season started brilliantly as Liverpool added another two trophies to the cabinet by beating Man Utd in the Charity Shield and Bayern Munich in the European Super Cup. Sami finally got to play in the Champions League and showed how he belonged among the elite in European football with some outstanding performances. He was particularly good in the 2-0 win over Roma which secured the Reds a place in the last eight of the tournament. Liverpool had a fine season in the Premier League as they finished in second place behind Arsenal and ahead of Man Utd.

In the summer of 2002 Jamie Redknapp left the club and Sami was handed the armband and became the club captain. Unluckily this coincided with a poor season for the side, thanks in part to some terrible transfers in the summer. Liverpool were expected to push on and mount a title challenge after the previous season but a loss of form meant that defeat to Chelsea on the final day condemned them to a fifth place finish. The only bright spot on the season was a victory over Man Utd in the 2003 League Cup final. Sami's own form took a real nosedive while he was captain, leading many to speculate that the armband put too much pressure on him. In October 2003 the captaincy was taken away and given to Steven Gerrard. They may have been some truth to the speculation about the armband wearing heavy on the big Finn as his form seemed to improve a great deal when he was no longer the captain.

The 2003/04 season was manager Houllier's last as Liverpool finished fourth and qualified for the Champions League. For the following season Liverpool had a new manager in Rafa Benitez and Sami had a new partner in Jamie Carragher who was moved inside. The decision to move Carra to centre back seemed to invigorate Sami and he once again became an absolute colossus and it was during this period that he really proved himself to be a true great as Liverpool reached two cup finals. They lost the first one in the League Cup to Chelsea. Sami was absolutely immense during the road to Istanbul as Liverpool reached the Champions League final. In the quarter final against Juventus he scored an absolutely brilliant volley that any striker would have been proud of. I was watching the game with my dad and when the goal went in we both jumped in the air and when we realized it was Sami who had scored we let out a second even bigger cheer. This was because my dad had bet ten pounds at odds of 20-1 on Sami to score the first goal in the game. In the second leg in Turin, Sami and Carragher put in an absolute master class in how to defend as Liverpool secured a 0-0 draw to advance to the semi final against Chelsea, where revenge was gained for the League Cup final defeat a few months earlier. In the final itself against AC Milan, Sami was a true hero. Liverpool came back from 3-0 down to draw level at 3-3. After this point it was almost backs to the wall for about an hour of normal and extra time and Sami put in an unbelievable performance to keep the Milan players from scoring. The Reds went on to win on penalties and Sami got his hands on the world's greatest club trophy.

The 2005/06 season saw Sami continue his fine form and his partnership with Carragher was proving to be just as good as the one he had enjoyed with Henchoz a few years previously. In December 2005 against Middlesbrough, Sami was involved in one of my favourite moments of any Liverpool game. He went off injured after a really bad clash of heads, only to reappear a few moments later with a heavily bandaged head. He received a nice applause from the Anfield crowd as he came back on with Middlesbrough on the attack. Within seconds of coming back on, Sami launched himself into the air and headed away a cross. This brought about an incredible cheer from the crowd, even louder than the one that greeted the two goals in the same game from Morientes. This particular moment defines perfectly what a player and a person Sami was and is, they called Ron Yeats a colossus in the 1960's; well this proved that Sami was a colossus in the new millennium. The Reds finished the league season in third place and reached the FA Cup final against West Ham Utd. Just like the final in the precious season this was another incredibly dramatic game that required a comeback from Liverpool, this time thanks to Stevie Gerrard with two of the finest cup final goals you will ever see. Once again it went to a penalty shoot out and Sami stepped up to take one, probably because so many players were suffering with cramp. His tame penalty was saved but fortunately it didn't matter as Pepe Reina's heroics meant that Liverpool lifted the trophy.

During the 2006/07 season Daniel Agger came to prominence and for the first time Sami's place in the starting eleven at Liverpool came under threat. When he did play Sami remained a class act but for the majority of the season he was on the bench. Liverpool reached the 2007 Champions League final but Sami didn't play a part in the game as he was an unused substitute. In the summer of 2007 he was linked with a number of clubs but Sami insisted on staying with Liverpool. This was a good decision because Agger got injured and Sami ended up playing 44 games during the 2007/08 season. He scored another vital European goal in the Champions League quarter final victory over Arsenal. This was the third time he had scored at this stage of the tournament having previously done so against Bayer Leverkusen in 2002 and Juventus in 2005.

At the end of the season Sami signed a one year contract extension, until May 2009, which would take him to a full ten years at Liverpool. He didn't play much in his final season as Martin Skrtel had pushed him into fourth choice and Sami wasn't included in the 25 man European squad. He still played his part during the domestic season though and he played 19 games. He scored his final Liverpool goal in a 5-1 win at Newcastle on Boxing Day and then he was involved in one of the greatest league victories in the last twenty years. During the warm up at Old Trafford, Arbeloa got injured. So Carragher moved to right back and Sami came in at the last second to partner Skrtel. He rolled back the years to put in a great performance as the Reds went on to in 4-1 in an absolutely incredible win. It was announced that Sami would leave the club at the end of the season and he made his final appearance coming off the bench in the last game of the season against Spurs. He came on for Steven Gerrard who handed him the armband as he came off. Incredibly he almost scored within seconds of coming on as he had a trademark header from a corner saved. At the final whistle Sami was lifted up and carried on the shoulders of his team-mates and at this point he became very emotional and burst into tears. The ovation he received from the crowd was proof of just how appreciated he was for everything he had done for the club. I myself joined in a rowdy chorus of "Oh Sami Sami" in the pub.

Liverpool offered Sami a coaching role, but he declined as he felt he could still play regularly. He moved to Bayer Leverkusen and proved how good he still was. He helped the side finish fourth in the Bundesliga and at the end of the 2009/10 season he was voted as the best defender in the league and voted into the team of the year. Roy Hodgson tried to bring Sami back to Liverpool after one year away in the summer of 2010 but was unable to get him out of his contract. At the end of the 2010/11 season Sami announced his retirement from playing and joined the coaching staff at Leverkusen. During his time at Leverkusen he became only the fourth player to reach 100 caps for Finland and he eventually reached 105 caps before his retirement.

In May 2012 Sami was confirmed as team manager of Bayer Leverkusen in a partnership with Sacha Lewandowski who is the head coach. Both men share responsibilities for the first team.

Sami Hyypia made 464 appearances for Liverpool and scored an incredible 35 goals during his ten seasons at the club. He has firmly cemented his place as a bona-fide club legend and from my own personal standpoint he is one of my absolute favourite players of all time.

Stephane Henchoz

Swiss defender Stephane Henchoz was part of the best central defensive partnership in the Premier League for a few years. He was described by then Newcastle Utd manager Bobby Robson as; "a bloody oak tree, you just can't get past him". A lot of Liverpool supporters remember him the fondest for publicly stating that he would never ever join Man Utd. He made us even happier a few days later completely marking Van Nistelrooy out of the game against the Mancs.

Stephane was born in September 1974 in Billens, Switzerland. He started his football career in 1989 with the Swiss youth team FC Bulle. He began his professional career in 1992 with Neuchatal Xamax in the Swiss Super league. In 1995 he joined SV Hamburg in the German Bundesliga. Stephane spent two years in Germany and in 1996 he was part of the Switzerland squad for the European Championships in England. In 1997 he signed for Blackburn Rovers and started to make a name for himself as a great player. Blackburn Rovers weren't having a successful time during the next two seasons and at the end of 1998/99 they were relegated from the Premier League. Despite the team under performing, Stephane was regarded as one of the most consistent players in the side and had started to build a reputation as a great defender.

In the summer of 1999, Liverpool manager Gerard Houllier made, in my opinion, his two greatest signings in Stephane Henchoz and Sami Hyypia, who joined from Dutch side Willem II. Stephane was signed for a fee of £3.75 million from Blackburn Rovers. The Hyypia, Henchoz partnership gelled pretty quickly during their debut season at Liverpool in 1999/2000. They did however have to wait until October 1999 for Stephane to make his debut as he arrived at Anfield in need of a hernia operation.

Reds fans were initially frustrated with him as he played for Switzerland in an international game before making his Liverpool debut. However, it did not take very long for him to win the supporters over with his no nonsense defending. He complimented Hyypia perfectly, as he very rarely ventured forward and allowed Sami to go up field for set pieces while he remained as the last line of defence. I have heard people criticise Stephane for not scoring goals but that was never his role. His role was to stop the opposition from scoring and this was something that Stephane did with aplomb on a regular basis.

In the 2000/01 season Stephane really stood out in the team that won the treble. He hardly missed a game and seemed to be getting better with every game he played. There is no doubt that during this season Henchoz and Hyypia were by far the best central defenders in English football, possibly even Europe. Some of the best attacking players in Europe were regularly stopped in their tracks by Stephane during this season. Players of the calibre of Kluivert and Ronaldo at Barcelona and Henry at Arsenal were made to look fairly ordinary. Stephane was arguably the best shot blocker in the Premier League when he would dive into tackles and more often than not come away with the ball. He was also very reliable when it came to dealing with simple balls into the box and getting rid of crosses.

He played a big part in two of Liverpool's three cup finals in 2000/01. He gave away the late penalty in the League Cup final against Birmingham City. This led to an equalising goal but as we all know the Reds went on to win via a penalty shoot-out. In the 2001 FA Cup final against Arsenal, Thierry Henry found out just how much Stephane would do to stop a goal. The path to goal was blocked by every inch of his anatomy including his arm and hand which stopped two goal-bound shots. Though these were both accidental incidents you understand!

Stephane suffered a few injuries in the 2001/02 season which kept him out of the side. However, he still made a huge contribution as the Reds finished second in the Premier League and reached the quarter finals of the Champions League. During the 2002/03 season he suffered more frustrating injuries as Liverpool had a poor season domestically and exited the Champions League at the group stage. It was during a seven week stretch in late 2002, when he was out injured, that the Liverpool supporters realised just how good Stephane was. As awesome as Sami Hyypia was, there was no doubt that he often looked less formidable without Stephane Henchoz alongside him. During the 2002/03 season Liverpool were alarmingly vulnerable whenever Stephane was out injured. Despite the poor results that season, there was one success as Stephane helped the Reds to a 2-0 victory over Man Utd in the 2003 League Cup Final.

Stephane missed a large part of the 2003/04 season with persistent ankle, knee and groin injuries. Even when he was fit however, Igor Biscan was often preferred at centre back and occasionally Jamie Carragher was moved inside from right back. Carragher was sensational alongside Hyypia and once Stephane was fit again he ended up playing at right back. The problem for Stephane was that he often appeared sluggish after his injuries, and Steve Finnan was absolutely brilliant at right back, so he had a hard time getting back into the team.

In the summer of 2004, Gerard Houllier was let go and Rafa Benitez became the new Liverpool manager. This signalled the end of Stephane's time as a regular in the first team. Jamie Carragher was installed as permanent partner to Hyypia and was an absolute sensation. With no place for him in the back four, Stephane was reduced to a bit part role and appearances in the League Cup and reserves. In January 2005, he was loaned out to Celtic on a six month contract and he never played for Liverpool again.

After his contract expired at Celtic, Stephane joined Premier League new boys Wigan Athletic in the summer of 2005. After just one season with Wigan, Stephane rejoined his old club Blackburn Rovers on a one year contract. Stephane didn't play too regularly during the 2006/07 season but he impressed Blackburn manager Mark Hughes enough to earn another one year contract. He didn't play during the 2007/08 season and in the summer of 2008 he was released from the club. He retired from playing soon after being released by Blackburn.

Stephane Henchoz was often overshadowed by Sami Hyypia during his time at Liverpool. However anybody who followed football between 1999 and 2003 knows that he was extremely vital to the success of Liverpool as they won four major trophies in three seasons. It is a shame that Stephane isn't acknowledged more for what he did during his early seasons at Liverpool and hopefully in the future his contributions will be remembered. He was voted in at number 58 in the series '100 Players Who Shook the Kop'.

Steve Finnan

Irish right back Steve Finnan was a bit of an unsung hero at Liverpool. He wasn't unsung by me though, he was one of my favourite players during his time as a Red and I always found him to be solid and reliable. I honestly don't recall him ever having a bad game for us and he's one of the best right backs I have seen for Liverpool, in the three decades I have been following the club. He is the only player to have played in a World Cup, Champions League, UEFA Cup, Intertoto Cup, all four divisions in England and also the Football Conference.

Steve was born in 1976, in Limerick, Ireland. He moved to Chelmsford, Essex in England when he was young and played for the Wimbledon youth team. He was released at the age of sixteen and joined non league-side Welling Utd. After two years there, Steve turned professional when he joined Birmingham City in 1995. He played fifteen games in 1995/96 before going to Notts County on loan in March 1996. Steve played every game for the rest of the season and helped them reach the Second Division playoff final, where they lost to Bradford City. Notts County signed Steve permanently in October 1996 and he spent two seasons at the club.

His first season at Notts County, 1996/97 was a disaster as the club were relegated to the Third Division. This was quite the drop considering they were beaten playoff finalists just the season before. In 1997/98 Steve played all 51 games and helped Notts County to win the Third Division title with a record points haul and get promoted back to Division Two.

He was signed by Fulham, also in the Second Division at the time, in November 1998. Fulham were managed by Kevin Keegan, and he led the club to the Division Two title in the 1998/99 season. They finished ninth in their first season in Division One before winning the league title in 2000/01, under manager Jean Tigana, and were promoted to the Premier League. Steve was fantastic in his first season in the Premier League and at the end of the season he was voted as Fulham Player of the Year and was also voted into the PFA Team of the Year.

While at Fulham, he made his international debut for Ireland in 2000, against Greece. He was excellent during the World Cup qualifiers and supplied the cross for McAteer to score the winner against Holland in a crucial game. His form cemented his place in the starting line-up for all of Ireland's matches at the 2002 World Cup in Japan and Korea.

Steve was excellent at the World Cup and bigger clubs began to take notice. After one more season with Fulham he was linked with a move away and signed for Liverpool for £3.5 million in the summer of 2003. His first season as a Red was interrupted by injury and Jamie Carragher played a lot of games at right back. When Rafa Benitez arrived in the summer of 2004, he moved Carragher to centre back and Steve had his chance to make the right back position his own. He did just that and had an outstanding season in 2004/05.

Steve played fifty two games in the 2004/05 season and was a key member of the team that went to two finals. He played in the League Cup final which we lost to Chelsea, but bigger and better was still to come. Steve was a key member of the team on the road to Istanbul and had an outstanding game in the semi final second leg against Chelsea. He started the Champions League final against AC Milan but unfortunately for him, he had to come off injured at half time. This was the moment that changed the game and without meaning any disrespect to Steve, I've never been happier to see a player get replaced in a game before or since. This is because he was replaced by Didi Hamman and it was the German's introduction that completely changed the game. We were losing 3-0 at half time with Kaka running rampant for AC Milan, when Didi took to the pitch and grabbed hold of the game. As every Liverpool fan knows, we came back to draw 3-3 and win the trophy on penalties. Steve may not have finished the game, but he had more than earned his winners medal, for his contributions in the previous games.

Steve had another outstanding season in 2005/06 and easily held off the challenge from Jan Krompkamp who was signed in the January transfer window. He was so fantastic that Krompkamp was eventually sold without making any impact at the club. Steve was an important part of the side that finished second in the Premier League and then won the FA Cup, beating West Ham in the final.

In 2006/07, Steve was so good and so consistent that he was my choice, and the choice of the majority of Liverpool fans for the player of the season. This was a well deserved reward for the very fact that he never had a bad game. He started the 2007 Champions League final against AC Milan, but was substituted in the 88th minute for new signing Arbeloa. This was a sign of the future and during the following season, Steve lost his guaranteed starting place to Arbeloa.

Steve had signed a new two year contract in the summer of 2007, but he spent a lot of time on the bench during the 2007/08 season. In the summer of 2008, after 217 appearances as a Red, he moved to Espanyol on the final day of the transfer window. Sadly for Steve, he spent the majority of his time in Spain injured and he only played four games in the 2008/09 season. At the end of the season, his contract at Espanyol was terminated and Steve moved back to England to join Portsmouth.

He was a regular for Pompey during the 2009/10 season but regrettably he was unable to save the club from relegation. The club went into administration and had to sell a lot of their best player's, Steve's contract was not renewed at the end of the season. His time at Portsmouth came to an end when he played in the FA Cup final defeat to Chelsea. The FA Cup final turned out to be his last game as a player and he retired shortly afterwards.

Steve Finnan was a very popular player among Liverpool fans during his time at Anfield. He may not have been a household name but Reds knew his qualities and just how important he was to the team. He was voted in at number 55 in the series '100 Players Who Shook the Kop'.

Vladimir Smicer

I have always thought that Vladimir Smicer was a very frustrating player to watch. He had plenty of skill and ability, but never much product at the end. He would go on some terrific runs into the area and then he would often fluff his shot. I remember one game against Olympiakos, during our UEFA Cup campaign in 2000/01, when he missed a number of sitters and then we fell behind. Fortunately we went on to win the tie on aggregate, but I remember watching it on TV and getting really angry. The way he ended his Liverpool career in Istanbul however, has ensured that no matter how annoying he was at times, he will always be remembered fondly by Kopites everywhere.

Smicer first shot to prominence in 1996, helping Slavia Prague reach the semi-finals of the UEFA Cup. That same year he starred for the Czech Republic national side as they had a fantastic European Championship in England. They started the tournament as underdogs but surprised everyone by reaching the final, before losing to Germany with a golden goal. After that tournament Smicer signed for RC Lens in France where he scored 16 goals in 91 appearances. Vladi built himself a decent reputation in France with some terrific performances and leadership in midfield. In the 1997/98 season he was a prominent part of the RC Lens team that won it's first ever French First Division title.

In June 1999 Gerard Houllier brought in Patrick Berger's mate Vladimir Smicer, as the replacement for Steve McManaman, who had joined Real Madrid. Vladi certainly had some big boots to fill and he struggled. He impressed on his debut in a 2-0 victory against Sheffield Wednesday but that was about the last time he was any good for the next couple of years. Sadly, he suffered a succession of injuries keeping him on the sidelines for long periods.

The 2000/01 season was a big improvement for Smicer as he was injury free. He played more games and showed flashes of what he was capable of. Frustratingly, he continued to frustrate with greediness on the ball at times, but he did enough to be considered an important part of the treble winning team.

The next few seasons were pretty much the same as before with moments of brilliance followed by long periods of frustration. Every now and again during this period he would do something to blow your mind and make you instantly forget about the bad moments. He had a blinder against Roma in the Champions League. This was the classic game when Houllier returned from his heart problems and we won 2-0 to reach the quarter finals. I remember him scoring a belter against Borussia Dortmund too. However the moment he will be best remembered for (after Istanbul) will be the last minute winner he scored against Chelsea at Anfield. The game was approaching injury time with the score locked at 0-0 and nobody looked like scoring. All of a sudden we broke down the left flank and a superb cross came in from Emile Heskey. Smicer caught the ball perfectly on the volley and it flew like a rocket into the back of the net. It was an incredible goal and an incredible moment. I was watching the game at my mate Pat's house, with a small group of people, and we all just took off into the air nearly knocking down wall ornaments and pictures with our celebrations.

Sadly just as he was starting to show the form he had displayed in France, Vladi was struck down with a serious knee injury in 2004 which required major surgery. He ended up missing the majority of the 2004/05 season and only returned to play in a few games as a substitute near the end of the season. During early 2005 he was told by Rafa Benitez that he didn't figure in his future plans and would be released at the end of the season. Then in May 2005 came the night that Vladi made himself a hero and became a legend at Liverpool.

Smicer's final game as a Liverpool player came as a substitute during the Champions League final against AC Milan. Mid-way through the first half Harry Kewell, who was also returning from long term injury, injured his hamstring and had to come off to be replaced by Vladi. At this moment you could hear loud audible anger from the Liverpool fans at the substitution. They were probably booing Kewell but possibly also angry at the choice of bringing on Smicer instead of Didi Hamman who most people thought should have started the match.

At this stage nobody could have dreamed just how important Vladi would be to the outcome of the game. About ten minutes into the second half Steven Gerrard scored a terrific header to make the score 3-1 to Milan. At this stage it appeared to be nothing more than a consolation goal but just two minutes later came Vladi's big moment. Hamman passed it to Smicer well outside the area and he decided to shoot. I remember thinking "oh no" and then a second later screaming "OH YES" as the ball crept past Dida into the corner of the net. Vladi had just repaid us for all the anger he'd caused us over the years with one kick of the ball. The scene as he runs away with his arms in the air is one of the defining moments of a night in which there were many. To quote Phil Thompson in the documentary 'One Night in May', "that moment when he runs away with his arms in the air, that was belief, belief that we could do it".

We all know the rest and then we get to the penalty shoot-out. Smicer was our fourth penalty taker and at this stage the score in the shoot-out was 2-2 but we had the advantage due to Milan missing their first two spot kicks. I couldn't recall Smicer ever having taken a penalty before and this was genuinely the only

Liverpool penalty in the shoot-out that I really felt nervous about. Memories of last second Smicer misses ran through my head as I willed him to just put it away and put the pressure back on Milan. Despite suffering with cramp Vladi's penalty was probably the best of the night as he calmly sent Dida the wrong way, before turning to the fans and kissing the Liverpool badge for the last time. Dudek saved from Shevchenko and we were the champions of Europe for the fifth time. Thanks in part to Smicer's goal and fantastic penalty under extreme pressure. In one amazing game, Smicer went from Anfield flop to hero. It was to be his final game for Liverpool, but he left with his head held high, content that his contribution to the club would never be forgotten.

In the summer of 2005 he went back to France and joined Bordeaux. When we drew them in this season's Champions League group stage it looked like Vladi would get the chance for one more game at Anfield. Unfortunately he was denied the chance to say thank you to the fans as he was injured for both legs of the tie. He suffered another serious knee injury that kept him out for a year, and caused him to miss playing in the 2006 World Cup. He considered retiring during this period but eventually decided to carry on playing.

He left Bordeaux in 2007 and rejoined Slavia Prague, on a one year contract, where he was welcomed with a heroes return. His return was triumphant as he played a big part in Slavia Prague winning their first league title in twelve years. In 2008 Vladi won Personality of the League at the Czech football awards. In November 2009, Vladi officially retired from playing football. The next day after his retirement, he was unveiled as the sports manager for the Czech Republic national side.

He was inconsistent and frustrating but his heroics in Istanbul will ensure that Vladimir Smicer is one 'Ex Red' who will never be forgotten.

Acknowledgements

The first person I want to thank is Keith Perkins, for inspiring me to start writing in the first place. Keith has been invaluable to me as a writer with his encouragement and feedback over the years. You will always be my favourite writer on the subject of Liverpool FC.

Thanks to Martin Bullock for double checking this entire book for me for free and offering valuable suggestions just for the love of the subject matter. Without your invaluable help, I am scared at how bad my writing might have been.

Thanks to Matt Ladson and Max Munton, for allowing me to write regularly for their website www.thisisanfield.com and for helping me to fulfil a lifelong dream and write my first book.

Finally, I want to thank my wife Tracy, who has encouraged and supported me with my writing, despite the many hours of our free time that I have sat typing away at the computer. Sorry for making you a football widow!

Printed in Great Britain
by Amazon.co.uk, Ltd.,
Marston Gate.